S. Bredenbeck
7860 Chaffee Rd.
Sagamore Hills, OH 44067

AMERICA'S UPtown PUBLISHERS

"With God's help we will do mighty things"
[Psalms 60:12]

AF722911

Fort Lauderdale Beach and AIA   Photo: Alexander Koyler

SHADOWS *of* IRS

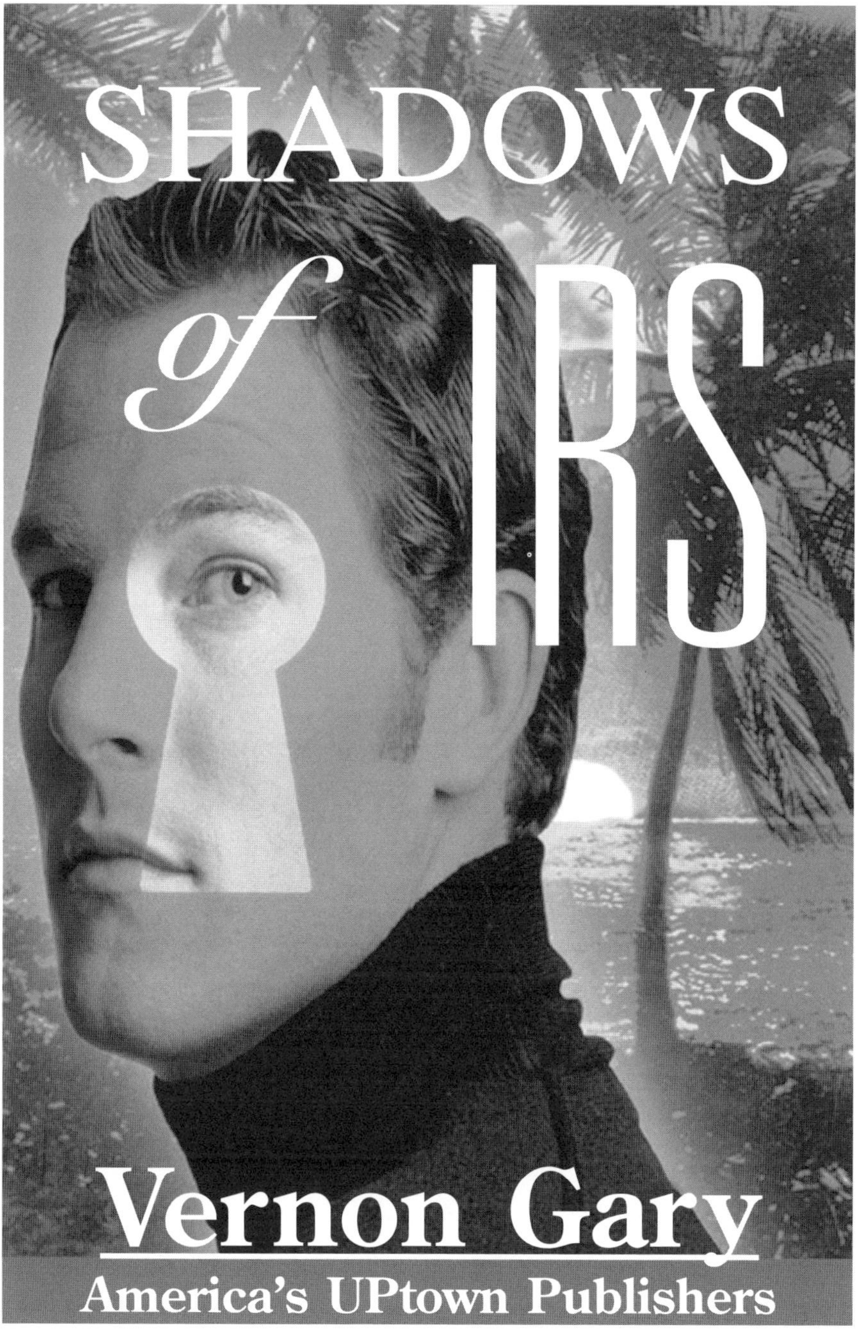
SHADOWS
of
IRS
Vernon Gary
America's UPtown Publishers

Port Royale Financial Center
6550 North Federal Highway
Fort Lauderdale, Florida

Copyright © Vernon Gary, 1998
All rights reserved

PUBLISHER'S NOTE

This is a work of fiction. Names, characters, and incidences either are the product of the author's imagination or are used fictitiously, and any resemblance to actual persons, living or dead, events, or locales is entirely coincidental.

LIBRARY OF CONGRESS CATALOGING-IN-PUBLICATION DATA
Gary,Vernon.
Shadows of IRS/Vernon Gary
p. cm.
ISBN 0-967-1881-3-X (acid free paper)

98-74821

All rights reserved. No part of this publication may be reproduced electronically, stored in or introduced into a retrieval system, or transmitted, in any form or by any means (mechanical photocopying, recording or otherwise), without the prior written permission of both the copyright owner and the above publisher of this book.

Printed in the United States of America
April 2000

1st Edition

Book Design by Gregory Earle Dyer

10 9 8 7 6 5 4 3 2 1

To my loving mother, Evelyn, who first taught me about God's awesome love and that through Him all things are possible.

Acknowledgements

Thank you, Lord Jesus Christ for your faithfulness even when I am not...you are an awesome and loving God!

I want to thank my loving wife, Yolanda, for being patient when I was not and for keeping her eyes on our Lord when I did not. Also, family and friends here...and there, who assisted me in the preparation of this manuscript. You know who you are and I can't thank you enough. Your encouragement and critiques made this novel possible. A special thanks to my brother, Gregory, who simply would not let me give up!

My gratitude goes, as well, to the wonderful people at America's UPtown Publishers, especially my editor, Jenni Andrew. Your sense of humor made this project so much more enjoyable.

And to the many fine, dedicated and ethical employees of the Internal Revenue Service...I pray the very best for you.

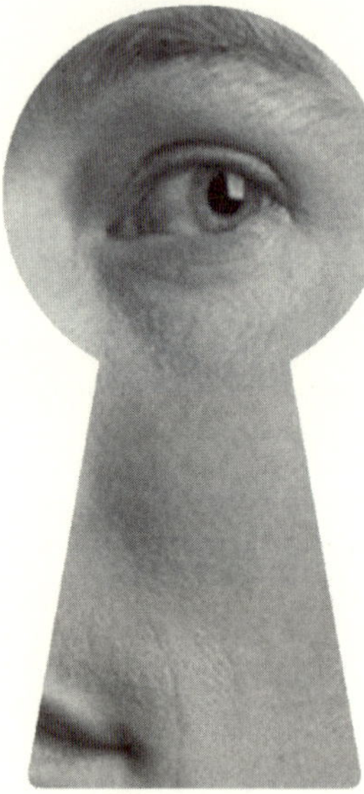

Check us out at: www.americasuptown.com

SHADOWS *of* IRS

Quick Reference

Abbreviations - page 336
List of Recurring Characters - pages 337 - 338

Prologue

Bogota, Colombia
February 1980
2:14 p.m.

Smoke-colored glass walls entombed fourteen men dressed in the finest suits. Some were members of the most prosperous drug cartel in the world. A few were prestigious South Florida entrepreneurs. One was a Federal judge. The view from the penthouse was breathtaking. Drug lord Carlos Rosario only called a meeting here when he was unhappy about something and, today, he was very unhappy. The first deadly sin of the Rosario Drug Cartel had been committed. The only remedy for easing his pain would be to hold someone accountable for what had taken place. Everyone sitting at the circular marble table knew that accountability would fall on one of them...and that person would not be leaving.

A few incessantly checked their watches as if that offered some form of relief...perhaps Rosario would not show. He was already late. Others around the table smoked, but no one uttered a word. Moments later an ominous swooshing noise outside the room made several heads snap in the direction of the sound. Others found swallowing difficult. Rosario's helicopter had arrived.

A medium-sized man known only to the group as Miguel donned a bone-white jacket, which concealed his excess weight very well as he exited the helicopter. His tan bald head reflected the surprisingly harsh mid-afternoon sun. The sparse black hair he did have was neatly trimmed and matched his pencil-thin mustache. Bodyguards, more like linebackers, flanked each side of him. While it wasn't Rosario, the tension increased a few notches as Miguel entered the glass cage. He was Rosario's right-hand and his executioner.

"Please, begin," he stated motioning with his hand. The linebackers took their position by the doors. No one was leaving. Their motionlessness transformed them into statues. Phillip Ward, the financial advisor, a handsome American in his late thirties, began what should have been a twenty-minute financial report on the Cartel. Six minutes later the man in the bone-white suit slowly rose, motioned Ward to stop, and turned his back to the meeting. He had heard enough. The report was clear. Someone was skimming from the Rosario Drug Cartel and an example would have to be set, once again. A lesson, he thought, they should have already learned.

"The Cartel has been good to everyone in this room," he announced in a thick accent, still gazing out. Subconsciously, one of the Colombians tugged at his shrinking shirt collar. "We have more capital...more lucrative investments than any..." He paused a moment, "...than any bank in the world!" It wasn't the Colombian's choking collar giving him up now, but huge beads of sweat forming on his brow were culprit. The harder he tried to conceal his feelings, the more his fear turned on him. He was ice cold. He knew what was coming.

Miguel turned toward the table for the first time and began a slow walk. "We have opportunities we never had before...our families are taken care of and the Cartel has always been generous to us." The nervous Colombian sitting at the table reached for the glass of water. *Look calm*, he thought. *Act natural*, he kept telling himself. He was self-destructing right in front of everyone.

"So why would anyone take from the Cartel what isn't theirs?" He shook his head. "I will never understand this, will you Hector?"

He stopped pacing and turned toward the Colombian. Water spewed from his glass as his hand quivered at the thought of what was about to happen to him. "This meeting is over. The rest of you can leave."

The statues opened the door and the members exited quickly and quietly. "Come, Hector...we're going to see how far we can spread you over the countryside."

"Please! ...dear God, please! ..." The Colombian cried uncontrollably as he got on his knees and grabbed at Miguel's legs. "Please," his voice became muffled in the trousers.

"Carve this pig...you disgust me!"

Phillip Ward entered an adjacent room. His model-like physique and good looks defied his age.

"Alena!" He was shocked to see his fiancée sitting there. "What are you doing? I told you to wait at the hotel. You shouldn't be here!" His rapid fire concerned her.

"Phillip, why are you so nervous?" She hesitated. "I heard someone crying. What's going on?" There was no response. "You told me you wouldn't be involved in this anymore. You promised."

"A little longer, that's all I need and we'll never have to work again." He sat down, placing his arm around her shoulders. He gave a slight laugh, "Our great grandkids won't have to work." He caressed her back. "Come on, honey. Can you imagine the two of us doin' whatever we want to the rest of our lives!" He hesitated. "I'm doing this for us, can't you see that?"

"I don't need *that* kind of money." Phillip slowly started shaking his head. "Phillip." He turned away. "Phillip!" she positioned herself closer and gently pulled him closer. "I just love you so and I want us to be together, now! We have more than enough...we don't need anything else." She paused. "Let's get married and get away from all of this."

"What about Mr. IRS?" he replied. She frowned.

"Don't worry. I'll take care of him."

The Colombian in the meeting room next door began a low moan, then crescendos into a sickening scream.

"What's going on in there?"

"Let's get out of here."

As they were leaving, one of the bodyguards intercepted them. "Mr. Ward." Phillip looked up. "Mr. Rosario will visit Miami in two days. Be there." Ward reluctantly nodded. As financial advisor, Ward would be held accountable for replenishing the Cartel's coffers. Lost revenue via skimming was his responsibility. Would there be any other punishment, he wondered.

***

High-rise across from Rosario's penthouse

"Damn it! Rosario didn't show again." The muscular DEA agent kicked back in his chair, ripped off his earphones and threw them but kept the tape recorders on. The room was full of agents who stopped what they were doing and looked up waiting for the Agent-in-Charge's instructions. Before speaking to the group he turned to a rather tall, slender man with long dark hair sitting quietly in the corner. "Rico, do we take 'm?" The slender man turned his head slightly, paused and shook his head no. "Damn it!" He stood up and paced in frustration. "Get a wire in Ward's office." He stopped and turned toward the group. "I know every voice in there except one," he shouted. "Does *anyone* know her?" He glanced around the room. Everyone either shook their head no or shrugged their shoulders. "Will *someone* find out who she is and how she fits in...and what they meant by..." He glanced at a piece of scratch paper, "... 'What about Mr. IRS?' and 'Don't worry, I'll take care of him.'"

1

The sun began its late afternoon routine of splashing vivid colors of gold, yellow and crimson onto the downtown Fort Lauderdale skyline while ribbons of traffic laced the city inching their way homeward. West of the city, a copious cigar-smoke filled back room of a ghetto bar was quickly reaching maximum capacity for the Thursday night ritual, Pit Bull fighting. The clattering of the beer mugs, laughter and conversation taking place between the dog owners and spectators muffled the incessant growling and whining of the grotesque beasts. The carnival-like atmosphere seemed inappropriate for the carnage that would soon take place between the dogs in a back room referred to as the "bull pen." This was entertainment at its finest for some and a veritable moneymaker for the winners and the bar.

Aside from the fact that this was a slice of Fort Lauderdale nightlife no one ever read about in a brochure at the Greater Fort Lauderdale Chamber of Commerce and the tourists somehow overlooked, this was a lucrative section of town, especially for dog owners like Willie Walker. Willie, a man of slight stature who was never without his black golfer's hat and a Cuban cigar stub hanging from his lips, was the most revered owner at the bullpen. He and Baby, his 120 pound, earless American Pit Bull Terrier had won more fights than any other owner.

There are two main types of dogs that can be categorized as Pit Bulls; the American Staffordshire Terrier, which averages 65 pounds, and the American Pit Bull Terrier which can attain a weight of over 100 pounds. About fifty years ago there was only one breed, the Pit Bull Terrier. An English bulldog and the now extinct English Terrier were crossbred in Staffordshire County, England in the seventeenth century and the Pit Bull Terrier was born. They were popular among sportsmen for their strength, agility and courage.

Willie also appeared to be a man of modest means, but his financial holdings were many before his encounter with the Internal Revenue Service. His keen business acumen enabled him to invest his earnings—the earnings he made off breeding Pit Bulls and fighting Baby were very lucrative—into his plumbing business and several carefully concealed assets even the IRS had not discovered.

It was too early yet for the fighting to begin. There were several barrels of beer waiting their turn to be consumed. The bar only took a small percentage of the wagering providing liquor and beer sales were good, which they always were. A lone, vigilant doorman remained posted at the warped oak door to forewarn the bar owner of any trouble, especially the kind of trouble police caused on this side of town.

While the first "show," as the dog owners referred to it, was being lined up and the wagering was methodically being recorded, IRS Revenue Officer William Murdock turned the corner onto Broward Boulevard and headed west from the now silhouetted skyline of the city into the dark ghetto. As he crossed railroad tracks an irritating, white light of a bank clock glared out its message: "7:43 p.m. ... 91° ... Have a nice day!"

"Ninety-one friggin' degrees..." thought Murdock out loud. Murdock, who was a tall, well-built man in his mid-thirties, and had an all-American look, was cramped in his small, Italian import.

As he continued his westward drive he searched for a telephone. He remembered he was supposed to give Frank Laccetti, his partner, a call to remind him tonight was "on." The first three telephones he located had been vandalized with one of the receivers missing, exposing the multi-colored wires.

"Lil' savages," he mumbled. The fourth telephone booth reeked of urine, but the phone was operable. Carefully holding the receiver with his fingertips and several inches from his mouth, the call was made.

"Hello, Melissa, sorry to bother you, but did Frank get word 'bout tonight?"

"He left twenty minutes ago," she replied in a distinctly irritated tone.

"I apologize for bothering you but..."

"I know, Bill...Frank wanted to be sure he didn't miss anything. Goodbye!" she announced.

Frank and Melissa had been married a dozen years and, while she had been a loyal wife, she was a nag. Melissa wanted her husband to work the safe eight to four-thirty job he promised her when he resigned from New York's finest. Frank, a medium built man who strongly favored his Italian ancestry, resigned from the NYPD after a confrontation with a convenience store purloiner left him with only one leg. He had stumbled upon a robbery-in-progress when a close range blast from a sawed off, twelve-gauge shotgun ripped into his right leg leaving only his upper thigh intact. Melissa was also annoyed by the fact that while Frank's salary with the NYPD wasn't great, he took a substantial cut in pay to join the Feds in the Sunshine State.

Murdock squeezed into his car and continued his westward drive into the slums. He pulled into a nearly empty mall parking lot. The dome light cast a faint light on his overstuffed, black attaché case. Rummaging through the case, he found a white, 5" x 8" card which had bold red letters printed on it: **"Warning Notice-United States Government Seizure."** After printing Willie's name on the first line, he scratched his signature on the card. Frank's old VW van crept slowly toward him head-on and parked parallel as he had done so many times as a Bronx police officer.

"How ya' doin', Bill?" His accent was unmistakably New York.

"All right, I guess." What's our new number? Eight zero zero two?"

"Nah, they removed that extension today," laughed Frank. "All the unnecessary lines were disconnected."

"Unnecessary!"

"Well, the way I heard it was we're running too close to our budget, so they pulled some lines out to cut costs."

"You're kidding me?" Frank shook his head. "...that leaves one line for the two of us. Why don't they..." Frank interrupted.

"...for the four of us to use."

"Anderson and Williams are sharing the line with us?"

"That's-a-right," joked Frank using his Italian accent.

"Anderson's a certified loony tune who's about to go off the deep end and Williams ties up the lines talking about how she keeps getting passed over for promotions. How does anyone in their right mind think we can operate with one line? Unbelievable!"

"Come on, get your stuff together and let's roll," urged Frank. Murdock gathered his papers and double-checked the contents of the seizure box. He opened the bright red tool box which contained chains, bolt cutters, locks of various shapes and sizes, seizure tags and tape. Murdock picked up several heavy chains and underneath was a 3" x 5" card with the likeness of Star Trek's Mr. Spock pointing his finger stating, "I'm looking at you, Mister!" Murdock grinned and placed the box in the VW.

"We'll turn down what I think is Fifth Street and wait for Willie," explained Murdock. Frank pulled out of the parking lot and proceeded in the direction Murdock pointed.

"Where are the street signs? How do you find Fifth out here?"

"Just inhale," replied Murdock. "...when you smell the grease pit, that'll be Red Rooster's Chicken Take-Out, hang a right at the next street—that's Fifth." There was no value in owning a street atlas when you worked the ghetto since ninety percent of the street signs were either missing or spray painted beyond recognition. The two revenue officers approached Willie's neighborhood. Murdock slipped his broken glasses onto his sweaty face and searched desperately for the aroma. As they crossed another set of railroad tracks a trace of grease was detected in the air.

"We're getting close," responded Frank.

"A little farther." Without warning Frank careened his VW across the oncoming traffic. The screaming tires braking on the hot pavement, horns and shouting of the motorists alerted a small group of locals who had gathered under a tree away from the mercury street lights.

"What are you doin'?" Murdock's grip on the door handle turned his knuckles white. Frank laughed.

"Hang on, we're 'bout to have some real impact out here." The small gathering split into several different directions, yelling obscenities and uttering remarks about someone's mother. The VW rode a short distance on the sidewalk and, again, without notice, Frank cut through traffic and back into his lane.

"Dealers...hate 'em."

"Is that what this is all about?" asked Murdock still gripping the door handle. "I guess you know you're not back in New York, don't you?"

"I know, I know. It's just that old habits are so hard to break. I love putting streaks in their shorts." The two laughed.

"Turn here, Frank."

"Ah yes," he replied in his W.C. Fields' impression.

"Pull in behind this store. We'll have a clear view of Willie's place." Murdock pulled out a large pair of infrared field binoculars and focused them onto the duplex where Willie resided.

"Let's see 'em." Murdock passed the bulky glasses to his partner. "These are nice. Where'd ya' get 'em?"

"Souvenir of Nam, unfortunately." Movement in a car parked across the street and several houses down caught Frank's attention. He quickly focused the binoculars onto a married couple stripped of their clothing and in the back seat of a dark-colored car. A street light beam illuminated the interior of the car enough for Frank to view the couple gently caressing and embracing.

"It's gotta be 120 degrees in that T-bird," remarked Frank.

"Whata ya talking about?"

"That couple in the T-bird."

"What couple?" demanded Murdock.

"There's a couple really working up a sweat a few cars up." He continued his voyeurism. "She's ..." Murdock quickly interrupted. "All right! All right! I don't need to hear it." Murdock grinned.

"You better make up with Melissa fast."

"You're asking the impossible," replied Frank. "Here, take a look." Frank passed the glasses.

As Murdock lifted the binoculars to observe the unsuspecting couple, an eerie feeling overcame him. His stomach tightened into a knot and breathing was difficult. He hadn't experienced these symptoms together since Nam. Back then the symptoms served as a sixth sense forewarning him of a visit from "Charlie." But why now? Was it the similarities of the nights in Nam to this one that brought the pain. The stillness...the heat...the tropical setting...the nervous anticipation of some uncertain event. He searched his mind for the cause of his discomfort.

A couple of cars passed slowly by them. Murdock's shirt began to stick to him as the sweat continued to roll off his forehead and down his florid cheeks. He rubbed his burning, bloodshot eyes and his head throbbed from the pressures of the long day which had almost passed.

"Frank! You can't even roll down the window!"

"Sure ya can. See the vise grips on the floor?"

"Yeah," he replied cautiously.

"Clamp 'em on the little metal rod and turn."

"Unbelievable." He fumbled with the pliers and managed to roll the window down. The balmy ocean breeze which had finally made it inland into the ghetto immediately greeted Murdock. The wind gently rustled the large, majestic-looking coconut palms which appeared, he thought, as much out of place in the ghetto as they did.

"So, when's Wee Willie going to show?" asked Frank. Murdock squinted his tired eyes and held his wristwatch up.

"It's quarter to eight now. Can ya give it another thirty minutes or so?"

"Why not? Melissa can't get any madder than what she is."

"She's upset 'bout tonight?"

" 'Bout everything. She wants me to come home at four-thirty, I tell ya. She hit the ceiling when I told her I wasn't getting anything for working tonight."

"I kinda picked up on that when I called."

"Sorry. She keeps telling me how many bills we got and how she thought government workers were supposed to have it so easy. Guess she thought things would be different down here."

"What did you say?"

"I told her they are! No one is shooting at me anymore and I don't have to work late unless I want to. That one slipped out. Boy did she explode. Never knew a voice could shake the walls."

"It's good she didn't hear about the revenue officer who got shot last month." Frank nodded. Unlike police work, the tight bonds of camaraderie among IRS employees does not exist, but there are exceptions. A few families do socialize but, fortunately for Frank, the Fort Lauderdale office didn't because if they had, and Melissa heard about the shooting, she would have demanded Frank resign.

"I'm not sure how much more she'll take. Suppose she's right in a way. If Congress really cared they'd at least stop taking our benefits away. Working thirty years at this and freezing our salaries year after year just won't cut it if they expect good people to stay on."

"Who said we're any good?" joked Murdock. "I'd like to forget about this tonight and just go home, but I'm not sure when I'll get around to catching up with him again."

"What's your case load at?"

" 'Bout 117," replied Murdock. He was a senior revenue officer and, at his level and case complexity, he should not have had any more than about forty investigations assigned to him.

"What's Willie owe us?"

"I've got 'em down to $11,300. Collected about $50,000 so far, but that was almost a year ago."

"Why so long ago?"

"He left the area last year after the police caught up with him and his gambling. They raided a club not too far from here. Willie was busted and they contacted us because of the amount of cash he had."

"How much?"

"Eighty thousand dollars."

"That's more than just gambling money," replied Frank.

"No one ever caught him with drugs. Anyway, he had a safe

deposit key on him which he refused to talk about. I traced the key to the Landmark Bank and seized the box. Got a writ and drilled it."

"Whadya get?"

"A couple of loose, pear-shaped diamonds and..."

"How big?" interrupted Frank.

" 'Bout two carats each. One jeweler in Miami said they were glass—two jewelers in Fort Lauderdale said they were the real thing and worth nine grand. Can you believe that guy in Miami trying to con me and then showing up at the sale to buy 'em!"

"Anything else?"

"A warehouse receipt. The detective working the case went with me and we found a custom Cadillac, loaded—color TV, bar, and electronic gadgets you wouldn't believe. Willie nearly passed out when I told him I found it. He had warranty deeds in the glove box to three nice lots along the west coast. Fort Myer's office seized and sold 'em for me."

"For a guy in the ghetto, he has a lot," remarked Frank.

"He had some ocean charts," continued Murdock.

"You find his boat?"

"Didn't have one."

"Why the charts?"

Murdock shrugged. "What puzzled me is why put 'em in a safe deposit box?"

"They must've had value to him," replied Frank. "You still have 'em?"

"Yeah." There was a brief moment of silence between them. "After all I've seized, he's still better off than most of us."

"How'd ya find out he's back?"

"Believe it or not I passed him on Sunrise Boulevard. He's driving a new van with a custom paint job. I checked out the plates and it's in his name. No lien on it, either. It's worth about twenty-one thousand."

"Wonder why he's back?"

"Don't know but this oughta be interesting," replied Murdock as he slumped further down into his seat and closed his eyes.

"Ya know, we're like shadows," Frank interrupted the silence.

"Do I have to hear this one?"

Oblivious to the question, Frank continued, "We're always with the people we investigate, come out when the sun's up, disappear when it goes down and when..."

Murdock was beat. He interrupted Frank, "I'm gonna think twice next time about asking you along."

***

By 8:12 p.m. the first show had taken place leaving one animal quivering in a dark red pool of blood in the bullpen. The crowds were wild with excitement. The owner collected his winnings while the animal was dragged out with a meat hook. The winner taunted the other owners to fight his dog, but no one accepted the challenge. Everyone knew that his dog, being in an excited state, fully aroused with his adrenaline flowing, was even more aggressive and powerful than before. The owner called to have the blood-stained animal returned to his cage. The dog, hesitating long enough to parade around the arena one more time, entered his steel cubical.

Willie and Baby were next on the agenda. Baby was locked in one of the wooden stalls which lined the rear wall. Willie teased Baby with a kitten by dangling the animal from a rope. Moments before his fight he let Baby devour the kitten which would send his dog into a frenzy. Baby's cage was placed tightly against the stall and a sliding door opened, allowing her to charge into the steel cube. The cube was then positioned next to the bullpen.

The once vociferous crowd was now only a murmur as the spectators and owners exchanged comments about how possessed Willie's "Devil Dog" looked. Willie stepped up to the platform where Baby's cube was placed. Rubbing his chin, he looked the crowd over contemplating the tax-free money he'd make off Baby tonight. The owners' deferential nods pleased Willie. He leaned over and began whispering to Baby in which she responded by salivating and making a high pitched cry. Pieces of kitten fur and meat clung to Baby's massive teeth.

"You better watch him! Watch him, Baby, watch him!" he yelled over and over. “He’s gonna getcha! You better get ’em, he gonna get ol’ Willie.” Willie spat on Baby’s face during this pep talk. Baby responded with several acrobatic flips. This went on until the cash had been collected and the bets recorded.

Suddenly, the silver doors were lifted and the two beasts immediately butted heads. The somewhat reticent crowd roared as the animals went into a crazed frenzy, growling and trying to sink their fangs into each other’s throats. Baby was only slightly larger in size but her experience far outweighed her opponent’s. Not being able to clamp into Baby’s neck, the opponent turned its large, grotesque head slightly and clamped onto Baby’s front left leg. Baby threw her head back and gave a high-pitched cry that quieted the crowd. Baby was hurt. Willie found it difficult to swallow as he looked on. The opponent exposed his neck and in a fraction of a second Baby lunged those powerful, vice-grip jaws into the neck of the inexperienced dog and violently shook him. The betting was as intense as on Wall Street as Baby held her position. The other owner, realizing the precarious position his dog was in, conceded just as the first stream of bright-red blood erupted into Baby’s face. Willie called to Baby, but it was too late. The Devil Dog was in a trance, possessed. Her only response was to the stream of warm blood pulsating in her face as she sunk her teeth even deeper, forcing the release of the opponent’s hold. The dog, struggling for its final gasp of oxygen, began to gargle in its blood, coughing continuously until it dropped just a few feet from the owner who was livid. Baby’s fur was drenched in blood. She looked at the crowd and took several leaps at the patrons, almost bringing one of them into the arena. Willie called to her but she continued her acrobatics and growling. He retrieved a long plastic pipe, especially made for this occasion. A steel, plastic-coated cable ran through the pipe forming a noose at the end. Willie lowered the rod several times before snagging Baby around her tremendous neck. As he tightened the chain he yelled, “You done good, you done good, Baby! Papa’s proud of his Baby! Come on now, let’s go home.”

Baby continued to back up, dragging Willie back and forth along the railing that separated the two. Another owner held Willie in place while he again tightened the chain. With help from two patrons, Willie was able to pull his dog to the cage. The pipe was passed through the front cage door and out an opening in the back. Baby, only then, was influenced to enter the cage which was promptly loaded into his van. Willie quickly collected his percentage and started home.

***

"Did you call the wrecker?" inquired Frank. A tow truck would be needed to transport Willie's van to the storage yard once it was seized.

"Yeah, but it took some doing," replied Murdock. "The towing service we were dealing with ended up owing us $60,000 in payroll taxes."

"What's gonna happen?"

"Think we're gonna have to seize them this week. I got a hold of an independent wrecker who's new to the area. Got a good rate. Should be here any minute."

"What time is it?"

"Eight-twenty."

Moments later a royal blue wrecker turned down Willie's street. The small, dark orange lights that outlined the top of the cab and sides gave the truck an ominous look as it slowly proceeded by Willie's house. Frank flashed his headlights several times before catching the driver's attention. The wrecker pulled in along side Murdock. A tall, trim man wearing a worn, brown cowboy hat and matching boots greeted both of them, "Howdy boys. One of you Billy Munchkin or..." squinting his eyes and holding the small piece of notebook paper closer he continued, "...Munster?"

"It's Murdock, Bill Murdock," pronounced Murdock. "And you are?"

"Bobby Joe," replied the driver.

"I could've guessed that one," whispered Frank.

"What's your last name?" inquired Murdock.

"Parker. Owner and operator of Parker Enterprises...at your service. 'Preciate y'all callin'. I'm on twenty-four hour call and no job is too big or too small for ol' Bobby Joe."

"Well, Bob..." Murdock was interrupted.

"My friends call me Bobby Joe," replied the driver in a stern voice. Murdock looked over at Frank.

"Bobby Joe, we're waiting on a man driving a custom-made, '80 van. Should be here any minute. It's black with wide silver stripes."

"You boys sure you got the right address?" the driver glanced around with a dubious look.

"What do ya charge if he doesn't show?"

"For you boys, nothing. Just remember to call ol' Bobby Joe. I still have some family back in El Paso I gotta send for. Don't cha know I could sure use the money." As the driver explained his first impression of South Florida, Willie pulled into the gravel driveway which arched through his yard.

"It's showtime," stated Murdock as he straightened his back and gathered the items he would need. "Think you can get this van of yours started?" With a couple of tries the VW engine sputtered and finally responded. "Bobby Joe, wait for me to signal before you hook up, okay?"

"That's fine, Billy."

Frank turned to his partner, "Billy?" Frank pulled behind Willie's van. The driver backed his wrecker in with the rear floodlights on. Willie poked his face out trying to get a glimpse of the unexpected guests but the bright lights blinded him.

"Who's dere? I ain't done nuttin'. Who is it?" Willie's voice began to tremble.

"Bill, you have to open the door from the outside." Murdock was concentrating on what Willie's reaction would be and didn't hear Frank's instructions. "Bill, you wanna get out of the VW?" Murdock turned to listen. "Open the door from the outside."

"Unbelievable."

Since there was no response from the visitors, he began to talk to Baby as Murdock struggled with the door.

"Baby, you gotta watch him! He's gonna getcha! Willie's gonna get hurt! Get 'em girl, get 'em!" Baby, barely settled from the show, responded immediately to her master's familiar request and began crying to him in the high pitched squeal. Willie lifted the bolt that secured the door to Baby's cage as the two figures slowly approached each side of the van. Holding a leather, wallet-like case containing his badge, Murdock greeted Willie.

"Good evening, Mr. Walker. Revenue Officer Murdock with the IRS. I believe we have some unfinished business to take care of."

"Oh, thank God, it's only you. Thank God!" Willie rested his head for a moment on the steering wheel. "You almost gave ol' Willie a heart attack pullin' up like dat." His heart was pounding. "I thought you'd be somebody else. Well, I'll be." Willie laughed and shook his head.

"There's still about eleven thousand dollars due and owing which I need to collect now," explained Murdock.

"I be working hard just to puts a roof over my head and take care of my chilluns. How does ya' expect a po' man likes me to pay dat kinda money. You already tooks what I got. De ain't no mo." Frank was recording the van's description and other necessary information on the seizure forms.

"Bill, I'm ready to inventory the inside," yelled Frank from the other side.

"Fine. Mr. Walker, please step out so we can inventory. We're seizing the van." Murdock stripped a page from one of the forms and handed it to Willie through the window of the vehicle.

"Does we have to go through dis again? Der must be another way, Mr. Murdock." Murdock looked up and the remainder of what once was a cigar cast a soft, orange glow on Wee Willie's ebony cheeks.

"Willie, I don't get paid any extra for doing this. To be honest with you, it's a lot more work. By the time I sell your van I'll have completed more forms than I care to and I'll be lucky if we can get what you still owe us."

"Dis van worth a lot mo den what I owe. You cain't do dis again!" pleaded Willie.

"Can you pay the amount now?"

"You gots to give me time, Mr. Murdock...time."

"Time?" Murdock's voice raised a couple of decibels. "You've had since early '78. Most people pay their taxes and I think they want you to pay, too. Go ahead and start the inventory." Frank twisted the handle of the side door downward. They didn't need permission to go in since the vehicle now belonged to the United States Government.

"Don't do dat!" shouted Willie.

"We don't have a choice," replied Murdock.

"I mean Baby's loose in der." The thought of what would happen if they opened the door made Willie quiver. Frank jerked the door open.

"No, Baby, no!" shouted Willie but it was no use. Baby was still pumped from the bullpen and more than willing to take on a new opponent. The beast leaped out knocking Frank to the ground. Baby's growl was enough to send anyone into shock.

"Oh God! GOD! Help me!" yelled Frank at the top of his lungs. Frank lifted his knees to his chest and began kicking the underside of the dog's powerful body. Baby lunged several times at Frank's face but he kept kicking, screaming and hitting Baby as hard as he could lying on his back. Willie raced over to Baby, but she was too engrossed in what she thought was another show. Frank struggled to keep his hands around her massive neck but was losing. Baby kept lunging for his throat hoping to get a death grip on it and end this fight. She hesitated for a moment before digging her jaws into Frank's leg, at the knee. Murdock found a board in the yard and cracked it over the dog's arching back without budging the animal. Baby kept shaking her head relentlessly as she drove her teeth deeper into the limb and then locked her jaws. Lucky for him it was his prosthesis.

Frank, trying desperately to detach the leg, called to Murdock, "Bill, get a crowbar from the rear of my van!" As Murdock searched for the steel rod in the dark VW, the driver reached under the seat of his wrecker and pulled out a chrome-plated, government model, .45 caliber semi-automatic pistol. Quickly ejecting a round, he calmly walked over behind the large, unsuspecting animal.

"I don't like Pit Bulls and I sure don't like no dog biting on my customers before I get paid." He screwed the muzzle of the miniature canon in the earless hole in Baby's head.

"Adios!" The blast from the pistol shook the ground and, like an overripe tomato being splattered on pavement, sent Baby's head into what seemed to be a thousand different directions. Her carcass lay quiet for the first time that night as it drooped over the lifeless limb which faintly resembled a human leg after the attack.

"Frank! Frank!" shouted Murdock as he ran over to him. "Are you all right?" Frank was motionless and slowly opened his eyes which had been covered in blood. His ears were ringing from the blast.

"I'm doing just fine for someone who's been splattered with dog brains and lost his rubber leg to a dog with no ears." Frank started to laugh notwithstanding the traumatic experience. Murdock tried to hold the laughter in but the long hours and tension overcame him and he burst into laughter.

"And to think we're doing this on our own time," laughed Frank hysterically. Both of them, now sitting down juxtaposed, uncontrollably laughed.

"Bobby Joe, thank you." Frank could barely catch his breath. "I gotta find a hose and get these guts off me." Frank struggled getting up and slowly hobbled over to the house. He pulled his shirt off, sat down and drenched his sweaty, bloody body with cool water. "Ahh, this feels good," sighed Frank as he continued showering himself. The humid October night created an insatiable thirst in both of them which was quickly quenched by the garden hose. The bright floodlights of the wrecker revealed Willie's silhouette sitting by Baby's side, gently stroking her headless carcass as he wept.

"Why do we do this? I mean, it's not like we couldn't do something else," wondered Frank aloud. Murdock, nestling his head in his folded arms which were supported by his knees, looked up momentarily.

"I'm not sure. Thought about changing after my first year on the job. Once I even..."

"Ah!" The driver's resonant voice disrupted the unusual quietness which followed the explosion. "Ahhh!" This time his voice echoed between the houses.

"What's the matter?" asked Murdock as he slowly got up.

"That dog crapt all over my lizard skin boots when I popped his top. If that dog wasn't dead I'd run over his stinking butt."

Murdock looked over at Frank, triggering uncontrollable laughter. Upon hearing this, Willie began crying a little louder. Murdock extended his hand to Frank and helped him off the ground. Frank leaned on Murdock and climbed into the VW.

"My leg!" Murdock's head snapped in his direction. "I forgot my leg!"

"Well, we can't have that happen," replied Murdock. The two looked at each other, triggering more laughter. The leg was passed through the window.

"Willie, meet me at the storage yard if you have any personal items you want from the van," shouted Murdock after catching his breath. Willie knew the procedure all too well and nodded his head.

2

The unrelenting 4:45 a.m. alarm pulsated throughout the condo disrupting the early morning silence. Murdock struggled to locate the clock, turned a couple of knobs and plopped his aching body back into bed. The aroma of freshly brewed coffee from the automatic coffee maker permeated the room beckoning Murdock to rise which he did, but under protest.

"Can't believe it's time. Feels like I just laid my head down," thought Murdock. He slipped his teal-colored jogging pants on along with a sleeveless T-shirt and felt his way to the kitchen, being ever so careful not to wake his wife and children who were ages four and two.

After several sips of the redolent brew, Murdock regained control of his senses. He sat down and propped his long legs onto the opposite chair, took a deep breath and exhaled. His mind began to prioritize the daily events he had to accomplish. He finished his coffee and began walking toward the beach foregoing his usual jog. The streets were bare with the exception of a lone street-sweeper slowly making his way down Las Olas Boulevard.

Murdock arrived at the beach. The darkness of the morning created a sense of unity between the heavens and earth. Only the distant lights of a few fishing boats offered any point of reference in the void. Murdock walked north along the shore toward the

Fort Lauderdale strip, a stretch of hotels and establishments peppered the oceanfront. They seem to lay in silence awaiting the arrival of dawn. A few more yards and he sat down, propped his body up with his elbows, and buried his feet in the cool, soft sand.

The sounds and smells of the ocean overwhelmed him, creating an almost euphoric feeling which chased the tension from his body. Murdock's love for the ocean and its mystique had grown stronger with the passage of time. He knew he could never leave the coastal area since he used the morning as therapy and the ocean was his therapist.

Rays of golden light, like fine tuned lasers, began to pierce the blanket of clouds which had covered the night. A distant rainstorm drifted aimlessly across the horizon. Murdock watched as ripples from a large school of silver-sided, glass minnows cracked the mirror-like ocean surface. The commotion attracted several seagulls in search of their morning meal. The distant luminescent lights, the cry of the seabirds and Murdock's thoughts greeted the dawn. He took one last glance about him, absorbing all that his senses could, as if this would be his last witnessing of God's magnificent creation, and then proceeded home.

"It's me, Beth."

"Good morning," she replied cheerfully despite the early hour. "Sorry I wasn't up when you came home last night. What time was it?"

" 'Bout ten-thirty. You were dead to the world."

"Audrey and PJ had an exhausting day. Yours must've been rough."

"Not too bad. I'll tell ya about it when I have more time. The ocean was beautiful this morning, wish you could've seen it."

"When have you gone to the beach and not thought that it was beautiful?"

"True." Murdock smiled.

"What would you like for breakfast?"

"Just coffee...and a bagel, I guess. Barely have enough time for a shower." Murdock showered and slipped into his clothes, gave his daughter a kiss on her pink cheek and thought how precious she looked cuddled next to her purple doll. PJ was sleeping with his bottom in the air. He gave him a hug and smelled his fine hair hoping the scent would stay with him.

"Here, make it last. We paid car insurance this month." She handed him a crisp twenty-dollar bill. The two kissed good-bye.

"Thanks for the bagel. I'll call ya later today."

"Try and have a good day!" yelled Beth.

Murdock arrived at the downtown office just in time to receive a call from Frank.

"Hey Bill, can't make it this morning. I feel terrible...splitting headache. I'll try to make it in a little later."

"Don't worry about it, I'll get someone else to help me. Just take it easy and I'll see you whenever."

"I told Dick about last night. He's a little bent out of shape over it," said Frank.

Richard Davenport, the group's manager often referred to as "Dick," which he despised. No one liked him because he rarely supported his revenue officers during case decisions, especially if there was controversy. Murdock respected the difficult position of managing a group of twelve field agents in a large metropolitan city, but not Davenport. Murdock was convinced that Davenport would have been the kind of officer in Nam that his troops would have hung.

Davenport was sipping coffee from his favorite mug, an obnoxious looking, three-dimensional likeness of a face similar to his own. A large, red nose protruded from the cup and droopy eyes stared at everyone. He took another sip and caught a glimpse of Murdock.

"Murdock!" shouted Davenport from his glass-walled office. "Get in here." Murdock proceeded to the office.

"Better watch in there. He's in one of those affectionate moods this morning," cautioned Pete Michaels, another revenue officer in the group.

"Thanks for the advice, but he's really a wimp." Pete smiled and turned to his typewriter.

"Have a seat," ordered Davenport. "What are you guys trying to do now? We got a green hornet this morning on those shenanigans you two pulled last night." A green hornet was office slang for a congressional inquiry into an investigation usually initiated by a disgruntled, non-complying taxpayer. The official form for such an inquiry was green and, depending on the circumstances, the outcome could sting.

"What do you mean shenanigans?"

"I'm not through!" yelled Davenport. Murdock hesitated. "I don't know what you two were trying to prove last night, but it won't happen again. You didn't even clear working after hours! I've been on the phone since six-forty-five trying to answer questions about something I didn't even know was going down. You've given me my last headache." Davenport was incensed as he took a swig of Maalox. "I'm through trying to explain things like seizing the wrong race horse..."

"That wasn't mine," interrupted Murdock.

"... the diamond rings from the woman while she ate lunch."

She was eating at Pier 66, a posh hotel, a restaurant and marina where the who's who in Fort Lauderdale gather for lunch. This one particular taxpayer Davenport alluded to owed about $45,000 in unpaid income taxes. Murdock had secured a financial statement which revealed very few assets. While inspecting a yacht at the marina belonging to a corporation that owed taxes, Murdock discovered the lady dining with friends and wearing one of the largest diamond rings he had ever seen. Having the 97% of the public in mind who struggle but voluntarily pay their share of taxes, Murdock and Frank confronted her only after she swallowed the last morsel of linguine and had picked up the tab for everyone at the table. They seized the ring and every congressman and senator she could find complained to the IRS. Davenport was the one who had to answer and he didn't like it.

"... What about the catfish farm? Remember the catfish farm? Well, I do! I still get questions on that one. And how about the TV crew that zoomed in on the cows with the seizure stickers on their tails...how 'bout the funeral home? I could go on and on and now I can add this dog you shot to the list!" Davenport was fuming. The veins in his neck pulsated. "I've worked twenty-eight years and ten months. I can smell retirement and I don't need the boat rocked! Understand!" While Davenport was correct in the cases he cited, these were only a few out of the thousands of cases Murdock had investigated in which concerns arose.

"Understand this," replied Murdock. "Willie ought to be lucky we didn't get him for assault and interfering with a federal investigation. His dog almost killed Frank and we had nothing to do with the shooting, although shooting the dog was the right and only thing to do." Murdock was intense.

"All right, all right, settle down," instructed Davenport at the top of his lungs. "I want a fact sheet on what happened last night. Times, names, the whole nine yards. Got it?"

"Yeah, I got it," Murdock stood up.

"One more thing..." Davenport leaned back in his high back, brown leather chair. "... neither one of you will get any overtime for working last night. You didn't clear it with me so forget it."

"I don't care about the overtime..."

"Careful Murdock," interjected Davenport who would have loved to get him on insubordination.

"... I did what I had to do to close this investigation and move onto the next case. I've only got a hundred and seventeen of 'em. Ever think about reducing my inventory? I'm carrying fifty cases more than any of the others." Cases were assigned based on complexity and dollar amounts. The more complex cases were given to the General Schedule 12 officers which was the highest level an officer could attain without going into management or staff work.

"And you ought to be thankful I'm not formally reprimanding you. Now, get out of here!" ordered Davenport. Murdock shook his head and left. As he closed the door behind him he mumbled, "See ya, Dick." The secretary giggled, but quickly gained her composure when she saw Davenport staring out of his glass cage. He began pacing with the phone to his ear and a handkerchief in his hand, patting his profusely sweaty brow.

"Pete, can you help me for about an hour? Frank can't make it today."

"I'd love to but I've got someone up front. It'll be awhile," replied Pete.

"Hey Julia, can ya give me a hand?" Julia Black was also a senior officer with an excellent reputation for case investigations. She was a little heavier than her petite frame would comfortably allow. Her hair, auburn-colored, was wavy and shoulder length. She was always upbeat, something the office sorely needed.

"Sure, but I've got to go to Hollywood and check out a warehouse. Hollywood PD is standing by on some stolen goods they think belongs to one of my taxpayers."

"Mine can wait 'til this afternoon," replied Murdock.

"I'll sign us out."

"We better leave before I strangle him."

It was 8:30 a.m. when the two exited the office and already, a loud, motley crew had formed in the reception area awaiting their tax questions to be answered. The most noticeable ones were the quiet, pale couples sitting against the wall rehearsing their lines for the auditor.

"Hang in there," declared Murdock to the receptionist who half smiled and rolled her eyes.

"I've got a government car today," stated Julia. They were hard to come by since there were only two for the entire office of thirty officers.

"You sure you want one?" asked Murdock skeptically.

"We just got this one from the shop."

"Now I know I don't want it." The two climbed into the spacious automobile and proceeded to Hollywood, a thirty minute drive south from their office.

"What was the green hornet all about?" Murdock told her the story.

"It's amazing how these spineless congressmen even support people who refuse to pay their taxes."

They pulled into a warehouse section of Hollywood where an unmarked detective's car was parked on the curb. A man in his late twenties was sitting in the rear seat, arms behind his back.

"Even this part of Hollywood is clean," commented Murdock.

"They have to or the Mafia complains." Murdock grinned.

"Good morning, you must be Detective Kendrick," observed Julia.

"Please, call me Ruth. You two must be the feared IRS." Julia smiled.

"Julia Black and Bill Murdock. Thanks for the call."

"Come on in before we cook out here," noted the detective. "I've got a load of stuff in here you just might be interested in." They entered the warehouse through the main office, a small disorganized room with papers scattered everywhere. "I'm with the white-collar crime unit. We've been watching this one for some time now. He entered the register company in Lauderdale and loaded his truck up and brought it here. Caught him selling this stuff. He's got a rap sheet a foot long."

"How'd you know I was working with the register company?"

"Found your business card on the ground. The individual we arrested said a Lewis Farmer asked him to move the cash registers here."

"Farmer is the president of the register company," replied Julia.

"He said Farmer hadn't paid him so he was selling it. I knew something was up when I found your card. So, are you interested in them?"

"You bet. We read the riot act to Farmer a couple of days ago. He was scheduled to pay us or we were seizing his business. These registers will satisfy some of the corporate liability. You know anything else about Farmer?"

"No, I ran a check, but no hits. I don't know him."

"I'll give you an inventory list since, technically, you're in possession," informed Julia. Murdock nodded in agreement.

"So you two do the confiscating for the IRS?" asked the detective.

"That's a big part of our jobs, but not all of it," explained Julia.

"You work primarily with businesses?"

"No, we pick on everyone," replied Julia with a smile. "Corporations, partnerships, individuals, people in penthouse condos all the way to the ghetto."

"Sounds like you earn your pay. Any overtime?"

"There's a lot of overtime, but no pay with it," responded Murdock.

"Guess you're busiest around April fifteenth."

"The Service Centers are, but we're busy year round. We handle the civil aspects of a case, non-filing, paying, that sort of thing.

We don't audit per se, that's left up to another division."

"Better get started on this inventory before the warehouse turns into an oven," stated Murdock.

"Heard it's going to be ninety-eight today. I can feel it already," determined the detective.

The three entered a final set of doors which opened into a sizable, dusty room. The torrid, heavy air inside the warehouse pressed on their chests. Light seeping through the cracks and crevices in the steel structure spotlighted the millions of airborne particles in flight. Murdock immediately removed his tie, rolled his sleeves up and pulled out a yellow legal pad.

"Julia, I'll call out the model and serial numbers if you record them." Murdock opened the front and rear bay doors. A cross breeze made it through the labyrinth of warehouses which covered numerous blocks. Over the next two and a half-hours they combed through every register recording numbers and descriptions. Murdock found 1930's bar registers and a National Register dating back to 1905 most interesting. The six 1930 bar registers were black with an unusually wide and heavy base. These registers were popular just after Prohibition was repealed. The 1905 model appeared to be in perfect condition. The embossed designs and delicate workmanship were from a bygone era in which artisans put a piece of themselves into their work.

"Do you want to leave these registers here or find a way to get 'em back to the store in Lauderdale?" asked Murdock.

"We'd better take 'em back. I don't want to pay rent at both places. He still has some items I can sell back there."

Julia spoke to a couple of Latin Americans. "Spanish comes in handy for you?" asked Murdock.

"I don't know how you get along without it down here."

"It's easy. I know when they're swearing at me and that's when I pull out the ol' locks and chains. Miraculously, someone in the business starts speaking English and I get on with my questions. It's amazing how locks can breakthrough the language barrier." Julia smiled.

They followed the workers back to the main store where the registers were arranged into thirty-two different categories called "lots." Items were usually, but not necessarily, grouped by similarities. Murdock began to tour the once productive business searching for any clues as to Farmer's whereabouts. Large vats in the rear of the shop were filled at one time with a liquid solvent. The registers would then be lowered into the vats for cleaning and lubrication before completely disassembling them. Another section of the store contained thousands of parts, tools, and computer chips used to repair the machines. Murdock meandered through the shop, inspecting and appraising how much a particular item might bring while Julia began drafting her sale notices. A small rear office had boxes of paper everywhere. Murdock rummaged through the open boxes, hoping to find bank statements or a list of his accounts receivables he might be able to collect.

After searching several boxes and finding very little useful information, he spotted a sealed envelope toward the back of a box. Inside was a warranty deed which described a house in Key Largo, Florida. The house had been transferred from Farmer to a corporation called Sea Unlimited, Inc. of Miami Shores, Florida, for "love and affection." No money had exchanged hands. The document was signed John L. Farmer. Searching a little more, Murdock found a vehicle registration and title to a 911 Porsche. The car, however, was still in Farmer's name.

He flipped back to the warranty deed and the date of transfer read "February 14, 1980." The transfer of the house raised a dozen questions in Murdock's mind when he was startled by a man wearing a white construction helmet with the City of Fort Lauderdale symbol, a red sun and blue sailboat juxtaposed on the front center of the hat.

"Did you know your water bill hasn't been paid for the last two months?" inquired the city employee.

"No, I'm with..." Murdock was interrupted.

"Just as I thought. We plan to shut the water off today if you don't pay immediately," continued the confused city worker. "I'm going to take a quick look around here for any leakage because your bill is especially high this month. Here's what you owe. I'll be right back." Before Murdock could explain anything the small, slender man began his methodical search. Murdock observed the man as he extended a long, flexible cable from the flashlight which had a minuscule light at the tip. Murdock grinned thinking how odd acting the man appeared.

"What's he want?" asked Julia with a quizzical look. Murdock laughed.

"He thinks we own the place and he's squeezing me for a water bill. Says he's gonna turn the water off if I don't pay today."

"I need to shut the water off anyway. Didn't you tell him who you are?"

"He wouldn't let me." The city worker returned.

"Well, I didn't find any leaks. Guess you just used a little more than usual," squeaked the frail man. "Any reason for the increased usage?"

"I've been eating a lot of Mexican food lately and the stuff goes right through me. Especially those refried beans. Suppose I've been using the toilet more than usual. Would that explain it?" Murdock kept a straight face.

"Well, yes, I guess it would. That would contribute to the additional water usage." The petite man pulled out his check sheet and, not being able to categorize this problem, quickly scratched something at the bottom. "You prepared to pay up?"

"No," replied Murdock.

"I'm turning the water off as of five o'clock this evening. If I were you I'd stop eating refried beans. You wouldn't want to create a health hazard. Good day!" The man exited the shop with a brisk walk as if he couldn't wait to perform his duty. Julia laughed.

"Do you believe him?"

"I can't believe either one of you," Julia continued laughing.

"Anyway, I took care of disconnecting the water. Here's a couple of interesting items." Murdock passed the warranty deed and title to her as she sat down and began studying the crisp documents. Julia passed Murdock a worn address book which had several pages torn from it. Thumbing through the book he recognized the name Douglas Warbington. He concentrated and tried to place the name. "Warbington," mumbled Murdock.

"What?"

"This name." Murdock wheeled his chair over and pointed to

the neatly printed name. "Does it ring a bell?"

"No."

"Why would Farmer transfer his house and not make a dime on it when he needed the capital for his business and us? Doesn't make sense does it?" Julia shook her head.

"I told him two months ago we were going to close him down since he couldn't even keep current. The corporation owes about a hundred and fifty thousand dollars. He was paying me fifteen hundred a month until sales picked up. He acted as though he was going to come into some money, but he wouldn't say from what."

"Maybe he thought he could unload the house before you caught up with him," thought Murdock. Julia shrugged her shoulders. "Wait a minute, he transferred the house four months before you even contacted him according to your history sheet." Each investigation has its own record chronicling the officer's actions. Julia reviewed the sheet.

"You're right. Maybe a Final Notice from the Service Center prompted him."

"Then he should have given the property away, shortly after the letter was received."

"Makes sense. What if the transfer was repayment of a debt to Sea Unlimited?"

"Possible," replied Murdock. "If that's true, then there should be some record of the loan at the courthouse. I'll check it out." Murdock made a note in his portfolio.

"It'll be recorded if the loan was legitimate," replied Julia. Murdock rubbed his eyes as he tried to think his way through the information.

"These three names were written at the same time. They're together," interjected Julia. She passed the book back to Murdock and pointed to the neat, block-styled names:

DOUGLAS WARBINGTON
PHILLIP WARD
RAMON MARTINEZ

"What are you getting at?"

"These names were written at the same time while the other names were scratched in at some other time," explained Julia.

"As if they belong together," added Murdock.

"Right!"

"So."

"Maybe it's nothing, but I got a feeling they've got something to do with this." If property were transferred to another party for less than fair consideration during the time taxes accrued and went unpaid, a revenue officer would explore the fraudulent transfer aspects of the case. If they determined that the intent was to place the property beyond the reach of the government, the officer would initiate a report to transfer the property back to the first owner and the property would be seized and sold.

"There might be a common thread here. If I could only remember where I saw the name Warbington. Tell ya what, I'll check out the names with CID on my way to the van Frank and I seized last night." CID, or just CI, refers to IRS Criminal Investigation Division. Until recently, the IRS has had six divisions; CID which works the criminal cases; Collection, which is assigned civil investigations worked by revenue officers; Examination, who conducts the dreaded audits; Resource Management who supplies and assists the employees; Information Services who the public might look upon as the computer nerds and Taxpayer Service. "You 'bout ready?" asked Murdock.

"Sure, I can do this paperwork anywhere," replied Julia. "Farmer has a boat somewhere. I'll check with the Coast Guard."

"Why do you think he's got a boat?" asked Murdock.

"Found these maps."

"Ocean charts," replied Murdock. He unrolled one and studied it.

"Does it mean anything to you?"

"I'm not sure." He paused. "That plumber I worked last night."

"The one with the dogs?"

"Huh-ha. He had charts, too, but no boat." Murdock rolled the map. "You mind if I keep this?" asked Murdock

"Here's his business card." Julia passed the white card to him. "Guess Farmer asked him to do some plumbing."

"Maybe. Think I'll pay him a visit...or call him," responded Murdock.

As the two were locking the front door, a man in his early fifties entered the rear door. He was well dressed with his jet-black hair combed straight back; each hair was in place. His shirt was unbuttoned exposing several heavy gold chains. An Italian horn charm rested on a thick carpet of chest hair. Slowly removing his sunglasses, he stepped inside.

"Where's Farmer?" he asked politely.

"I'm Bill Murdock with the IRS. That's what we want to know." Murdock raised his badge never taking his eyes off the mysterious visitor. "Where do you know him from?"

"He's been working on my registers. Said they're ready. So we're here to pick 'em up." Two abnormally large men, sharply dressed, stood on each side of the automobile.

"Which registers?"

"The black '33 bar registers. They've been in the family for a long time. My father first used them in his restaurant in New York. Now they're in my restaurant."

"Which restaurant?" asked Julia.

"The Vineyard," replied the visitor proudly. The Vineyard was a private nightclub and restaurant where only the very affluent could get a reservation. Although the club maintained a low profile in the community, it was known for its organized crime connections.

"Can you furnish us with any proof of ownership?" asked Murdock reluctantly.

"Of course not! They were especially made for my father, a gift!" The visitor's voice raised in tone and the two watchdogs waiting by the car took a step forward, poised and ready to leap.

"I'm sorry, but we can't just return the registers to you without documented proof of ownership."

"Do you have any idea what these registers mean to me?"

"I think so. I'm sorry. Let me explain the best I can do. We'll notify you of the sale and you or a representative can place a bid. The highest bid takes them," explained Murdock very cautiously.

"Let me see if I understand you, Mr. Murdock. I'm going to have to bid on my own registers?" He turned to his watchdogs and gave a slight laugh. "They want me to buy my registers back. Can you believe it?"

"I apologize, sir, but that's the best we can do."

"You know where Farmer is?" questioned the mysterious man.

"No idea."

"I understand that you have rules to follow. I'll be at the sale and I'll find Farmer."

Julia locked the store as Murdock jotted down the license number of the navy blue Mercedes.

"We'll check him out, too. Got a bad feeling about him."

The two arrived at CI. There was a flurry of activity going on. Several special agents were standing next to a long oak table covered with numerous files and documents which were neatly stacked. They could barely hear above the computers exchanging and correlating data. The printers responded by spitting out sheets of information.

"Hi Bill!" greeted an attractive secretary with long blonde hair and the greenest eyes Murdock had ever seen.

"Morning Marlene. How do you stand all this noise?"

"It does get a little hectic around here once in a while."

"What's goin' on?" The office looked like a newsroom that had just received a hot story.

"There's a grand jury convening in a couple of days."

"I don't believe you've met Julia Black." Julia extended her hand and smiled.

"So, what can I do for you?"

"Any chance of running these names for us ASAP?"

"You know I'm supposed to clear this through Carmichael?" David Carmichael was CI's group manager.

"He seems a little tied up right now and I really need the information." Murdock was begging. He knew the request would sit on Carmichael's desk for days owing to the grand jury convening.

"Well, don't tell anyone. As soon as the computers are free I'll slip this in. It'll probably be tomorrow though."

"That's fine."

"I'll bring it to you."

"Thanks...a lot."

Murdock and Julia traveled to the storage site where Willie's van was parked the night before. After the inventory was completed, Murdock used the tow truck driver's telephone and called a special telephone number established for the IRS at the Department of Motor Vehicles.

"This is IRS one-nine," informed Murdock.

"Go ahead," replied the man's voice on the other end.

"Seventy-nine Porsche nine-one-one, license plate number Echo, Delta, Alpha, one, two, one and a Mercedes, year unknown, number Juliet, Oscar, Tango, four, seven, five. Both are Florida plates."

"Hold the line." Murdock waited for the information. He looked over and saw the animated driver proudly re-enacting last night's events.

"The Porsche is registered to a J. L. Farmer of Lighthouse Point."

"Any liens showing?"

"None. The Mercedes belongs to a Carl Genovesi of Bal Harbour, Florida. No liens. Anything else?"

Murdock thanked the nameless voice on the other end. He inspected the van and was surprised at how clean the driver was able to get it.

"The van smells so fresh inside. What did you do to it?"

"I also recondition cars, so I cleaned it up a bit."

"Bet that dog smell was hard to get out."

"Not as hard as getting Willie's odor out. Whew, talk about nasty!" explained the driver. "Willie does like his Cuban cigars," replied Murdock.

"Billy, it wasn't his cigars, just him." Murdock grinned and thanked the driver for his help. A tentative date of sale was set.

"My stomach's growling." Murdock paused for a moment. "I know this place along the New River that's not expensive and what a view. Wanna try it?"

"How could I say no?"

They pulled up to Shirt-Tail Charley's, a rustic-looking restaurant situated right on the water with a view favoring downtown.

The surrounding banana and coconut trees gave a decisively tropical flavor to the eatery. The million dollar yachts and sailboats lie motionless awaiting the return of their owners. The gentle, sultry breeze swept soft, puffy clouds away which allowed a full viewing of the azure skies and invited the sparkling sunshine to dance upon the water. Several bikini clad tourists were mesmerized by the glistening light as they gathered at the center of a nearby bridge to model their evenly tanned, lightly oiled bodies.

"Isn't this something?" commented Murdock. "I've lived here all my life and it still does wonders for me."

"You mean the girls?" quipped Julia.

"No, of course not," Murdock grinned. "Doesn't this do anything for ya?" asked Murdock.

"Yeah, it reminds me I forgot my sunglasses at that cowboy's place."

"Call him from here. He'll probably deliver them."

"What about the cars?"

"The Porsche is free and clear. Farmer's got a Lighthouse Point address. Do you have it?"

"It's his mother's address. I've talked to her already. She doesn't know where he's at. I didn't push it, she's in her eighties," informed Julia.

"Our mysterious visitor at the shop was Carl Genovesi. He's in Bal Harbour."

"Where's that?"

"South toward Miami Beach. He bothers me a bit," confessed Murdock.

"I noticed you were quick to identify yourself. I didn't think anyone could bother a big guy like you."

"It was the quart of oil in his hair." Julia laughed. "You gonna be in the office next week?"

"In and out," she replied.

"I'd finish the Hundred Percent as quickly as possible since, if we find the Porsche, it'll bring in some bucks."

Julia agreed. "I'll give you a hand transferring the house back to Farmer."

"Thanks. I'll do the homework on Sea Unlimited," stated Julia.

The One Hundred Percent Penalty—now named Trust Fund Recovery Penalty—is a collection tool used only by revenue officers when dealing with corporate taxpayers who cannot satisfy their unpaid taxes. The IRS looks first to the corporate assets to liquidate the unpaid tax and, if that is unsuccessful, they can take a percentage of what the corporation owes and assess the amount against the responsible officers and employees of the business. This assessment then allows the IRS to pursue the responsible corporate officers and employees' personal assets: their house, car, boat, jewelry, etc. The Trust Fund Recovery Penalty is not a penalty. It represents all of the taxes withheld from employees' paychecks. The employees believe the withholding is for taxes, but the employer fails to deposit the withholding at the bank and, instead, reinvests the withheld money back into the business or their pockets. Very illegal, and will get the IRS after those who do it.

The two finished their fresh filet of baked grouper and tangy conch fritters and proceeded home trying to figure out why the owner of a failing business, who was desperate for money, would rather transfer his Key Largo house to another corporation for "love and affection" and then disappear.

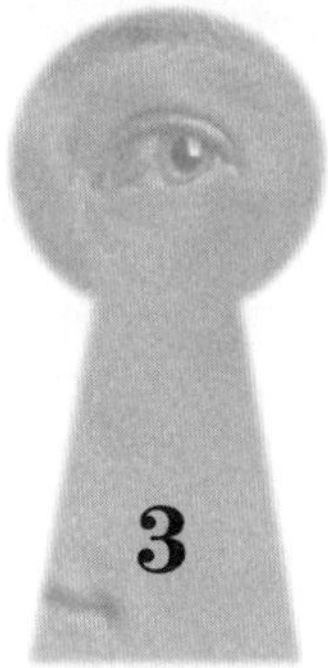

3

The walls were made of cherrywood with paintings of mountainous rural scenes, worth a fortune, being displayed. Persian rugs, the most expensive found, covered the imported white, marble tiled floors. Furnishings, hand picked from Italy, filled the opulent commodious room. Alena Muller sat patiently in the luxurious office she shared a year earlier with Phillip Ward. She was bright, petite and pretty with shoulder-length ash blonde hair. Ward owned the office which cost more than the average house in Miami. Peanuts for a man who had acquired enough money to span three lifetimes. At the rate Ward was buying properties around the world, his bank accounts would soon be exhausted.

A year ago, Alena was working in the adjoining offices as an attorney reviewing contracts for corporate mergers. She worked with Ward for two years before she learned about his clientele and the role he played. But it was too late. She was in love. In love with a man who wanted to own the world.

His clients were wealthy Colombians and Panamanians who relied solely on Ward for his financial expertise. They had one peculiarity—they each dealt exclusively in the importation of an illegal white, powdery substance and had never been convicted, albeit several indictments had been handed down.

Ward had a strong business which, in 1980, netted him

$450,000. After a business associate gave him $300,000 to do four hours of legal work for a Colombian who had been indicted on possession and distribution of cocaine, he changed. In his first case with the Cartel the DA had the defendant's cash sent to the forensic lab for analysis. When the testing was completed the results were presented as an exhibit. Traces of cocaine were found embedded, proof, the DA claimed, that it was drug money of the Cartel. Ward slipped a note to his associate informing them that the DA's cash should be tested to prove a point. Drug money was in such wide circulation that it was possible for traces of cocaine to be found on anyone's money. When the DA's twenty-dollar bills returned, the results stunned the jury. The two bills had traces of cocaine embedded on them. The defense argued that this was not an isolated incident, but that if each of the jurors' money was tested it would also indicate that, at one time, the currency had been involved in a drug transaction.

The allure of easy and substantial income changed his life and what he wanted out of it forever. During the following two years, he became a vital link in the ring of lawyers that served the Rosario Drug Cartel. He played an important role in developing investment strategies, laundering and coordinating the "meetings" in which the drugs and currency were distributed.

Ward established a network of corporations to help in the laundering of drug money. Sea Unlimited was the first in a series of such enterprises. The cash would be flown to Sea Unlimited. A deposit would be made to one of several Caribbean banks. The money would then be wired back to another Sea Unlimited account in the States and would appear as a legitimate business transaction. The wash cycle was completed and the money was clean, clean enough for the IRS to tax. The wired money hit the account toward the end of each month which made it very legitimate. Ward would invest most of it and arrange a meeting for payment distribution.

As Alena continued flipping through magazines waiting for Ward, the meeting with Carlos Rosario was almost completed. Rosario was a distinguished looking man with grey curly hair. He was wearing a navy blue blazer with 18K gold buttons. His hands sparkled with diamonds and emeralds—fruits of his labor.

"The five hundred thousand you wired me was nice...," he puffed on his cigar. "But far short of what we were expecting." Three of Rosario's bodyguards stood like statues near the door.

"I'll have the balance soon. You have all of the funds in my accounts. I'm selling my oceanfront properties. The proceeds will more than satisfy the balance."

"You don't understand, I'm not waiting. If you don't have the balance now, I'll take the properties."

"The property will sell quickly and it's worth a lot more than what was taken."

"Good," replied Rosario taking another drag of his cigar. "The Cartel was inconvenienced by this so we need a little extra to forget about the problem." He continued sucking on the short cigar.

"How soon can the property be transferred to the Cartel?"

"Tomorrow morning. I'll have the deeds here."

"Good, I didn't want to introduce you to my associates anyway. I like you." One of the statues smiled.

"We're done." Rosario rose and the two shook hands. He and his entourage left the office. Two men in front of him and one behind.

"Alena!" Ward was surprised to see her this time of day. "Come in." Ward hid his nervousness. "You look gorgeous." Alena, without speaking a word, entered the office. Her head was down. "What's the matter?"

"I told you, I don't want you involved in this anymore. It's not worth it."

"A little longer and it's over...I'm out," explained Ward.

"No! I want it to end now! It's just not worth it...it never was."

"Nothing has ever happened and it'll be just fine."

"I've just got this terrible feeling." Alena paced about the room.

"Please sit down and relax."

"I'd like our daughter to know her father." Ward paused, turned and looked at her.

"I'm pregnant."

"Alena!" Ward's voice softened and he went to her side. They embraced each other tightly. Tears filled both their eyes.

"What do you think?" asked Alena, making a face, unsure of

Ward's response.

"I think it's fantastic! You know I've always wanted children with you."

"How long have you known?"

"A month."

"It's a girl?"

"I don't know, but I'd like a girl. Is that okay?"

"I'd love it! I want her to look just like you." Ward held her warmly. "Let's have about seven and we'll live way out in the country with snow-capped mountains surrounding us, a lake nearby with horses, and fresh air. We'll have a fabulous life." Alena smiled.

"I just want our baby to know her father. Can't we just leave...now? We'll move so far away no one will find us."

"Honey," Ward placed his hands on her shoulders. "there isn't a place far enough away when it comes to the Cartel. I've got to come clean with them and earn some more money to last us. Just one more time...I promise."

"When can we get out of here and start our lives?"

"Soon."

Ward embraced Alena again. Tears filled her eyes. She gazed out of the window at the turquoise bay feeling very helpless and unable to get over the feeling she had that something very bad was going to happen. Ward walked over to his speakerphone.

"Roberta, I'm taking the afternoon off." Then turning to Alena, "Let's have lunch on the boat."

They left the plush office and picked up some Chinese food on the way to Ward's catamaran at Dinner Key Marina nestled in downtown Miami, minutes from his office. They sat close on the deck looking out.

"Ward, I love you." He smiled a warm smile back and gave her hand a gentle squeeze.

"I've never loved anyone like I love you," reassured Ward. "From the moment I met you I knew you were special. You've touched feelings I never knew I had." Alena's eyes teared. "I've never had this kind of closeness with any other woman. I love you and nothing is going to keep us apart."

"I needed to hear you say you loved me again." Alena and

Ward's eyes teared as he embraced her, standing with his cheek against her hair.

There was silence between them as they absorbed the moment, hoping that it would not pass too quickly.

"My father doesn't want me near you."

"I know. I'm sorry because I can't live without you. Telling him about us and the baby won't be easy."

"I'll think about it, but it doesn't matter. I know what I want and how I feel. I'll talk to him in a couple of days."

"I'm sorry."

" 'Bout what?"

"Having to deal with your father about this."

"Don't worry, he'll have to understand." The two continued hugging as a gentle ocean breeze meandered into the bay area and through their hair.

As the afternoon came to an end, two men from a van clicked dozens of photographs of them.

An obstacle they didn't realize was that Ward was a target of the IRS Criminal Investigation's *Operation Liberty,* an interagency initiative with the Justice Department, FBI, and the DEA, which focused on drug attorneys. Two years ago, the IRS was under intense fire by Congress to bring in more money. The twenty-three billion dollars the agency had collected the year before was simply not enough. The IRS began searching for ways to secure the additional dollars and appease Congress. They finally came up with a good, but nearly impossible task of tapping into the subterranean economy. The IRS placed most of its resources into beefing up a campaign to attack certain industries notorious for unreported income. One target, they surmised, were drug attorneys. The DEA pulled a lengthy list of names of those who had been indicted for possession or trafficking in narcotics. Agents from the three agencies combed through court records identifying the lawyers representing these felons. Phillip Ward's name was snagged when research on the Rosario Drug Cartel revealed three attorneys working for them. Phillip Ward was the third and last one hired by the Cartel.

The IRS began pulling income tax returns and determining the attorney's standard of living. While most of them were smart enough to live modestly, Phillip Ward wasn't one of them. Not because he wasn't intelligent enough because he was—he was brilliant in law school having graduated in the top five percent at Yale without really trying. Ward's problem was that his self worth was tied to materialistic things and coming from a poor family, he had much to prove to himself. So he purchased properties from around the world. This lifestyle far exceeded the income expressed on his tax return and pushed his name to the top of the list. His holdings were staggering: controlling interest in an Arabian horse ranch, owner of a multimillion dollar yacht equipped with helicopter, a Donzi speedboat; he owned or was a partner in oceanfront hotels and houses in the States, Brazil, France, Spain and Hawaii.

These assets were like waving a red flag before the bull, and the bull was charging hard until December 19, 1979, when, suddenly, the agency stopped dead in its tracks. Unknowingly, Murdock crossed the bull's tracks when he began investigating the three names listed in the directory he found at the register company. The bull was about to become extremely nervous...and dangerous.

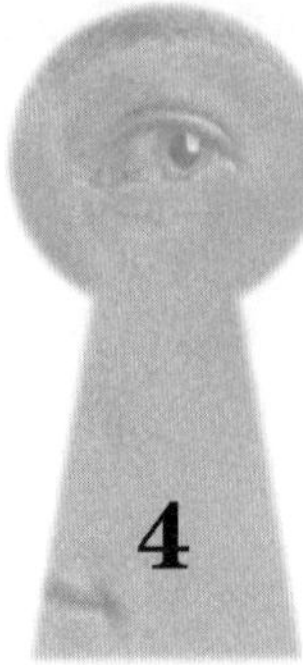

4

Murdock arrived at the office at 6:34 a.m., Thursday. He followed Hank Goffman, a revenue officer of thirty-two years, who was shuffling his way down the corridor of the Federal Building with his usual morning paper tucked neatly under his left arm. He was the oldest revenue officer Murdock knew and probably the oldest in the district if not the Service. A district is usually the equivalent of a state and each district has a director who has the overall responsibility of the six divisions. The larger states may have more than one district and, of course, director. The Jacksonville District, which, until about 1986, encompassed all of Florida. Presently, there are two districts in Florida, Jacksonville and Fort Lauderdale.

Hank transferred to Florida under *Operation Sunshine,* a program to increase the number of revenue officers and agents to help resolve the increase in tax cases. Hank had been a flying ace during World War II and retired from the military with a chest full of ribbons and medals. At the age of seventy, he was slightly hunched over and looked at the world through coke bottle lenses. This morning, like most mornings, Hank could be heard singing the same tune.

"Zippa de do da, zippa de day, my oh my what a wonderful day. Plenty of sunshi..."

"Morning, Hank," greeted Murdock.

"Uh, oh, morning Jim or...Pete...," replied Hank uncertain of himself.

"It's Bill."

"Right, right, Bill. How are you doing?"

"Just fine." Many employees thought that Hank was just one good reason why there should be mandatory twenty-year retirement for revenue officers instead of the thirty years they currently must work. Although Hank had two impeccable careers with the government, he was quickly deteriorating since the loss of his wife a couple of years ago in New Jersey. The Service was sympathetic and granted him a transfer to Florida to live closer to his children and assist with the growing number of cases. Hank, prior to Davenport's three-hour group meetings, would be seen turning his hearing aid off which, Murdock thought, was evidence that Hank still had his wits about him.

Murdock made his way to the office flicking the fluorescent lights on as he passed the various divisions of the IRS which were separated by six foot dividers. He pulled a couple of case investigations out of his cabinet drawer and found a worktable. The employees believed that these worktables were a less than brilliant solution to conserving space and funds. The regular desks with drawers had been stockpiled in the Government Services Administration warehouse and replaced with the small, drawerless tables. File cabinets were then purchased for each employee and placed against the opposite wall of the large office, making the job even more inconvenient. The rationale, if there was any, was that since the position of revenue officer was "in the field," permanently assigned desks were not needed. The number of desks could then be reduced because, on any given day, only a few people would be in the office, leaving plenty of room. What the National Office in Washington, D.C. failed to realize was that at Murdock's level, a significant amount of time was needed in the office reviewing documents, researching legal reference guides and analyzing case issues. Murdock had to get into the office early if he were to get a table at all. There were only fifteen tables for twenty-five revenue officers. This, and the recent removal of telephone lines to cut costs, upset many.

Everyone reported to the office today. Becky Williams was an officer everyone thought slipped through the cracks. This morning she immediately tied up the single telephone line reporting what she thought were discrepancies in her duties to the union. IRS employees have the option of paying membership dues to join the National Treasury Employee Union. This union will represent them in performance and conduct-related concerns. If the union is unsuccessful in resolving the issue with management, they can seek arbitration which is binding on both parties.

"Buenos penis, everyone!" shouted Frank as he hobbled into the office. Becky Williams, who had just put the telephone receiver down, immediately began dialing upon hearing Frank's greeting.

"Say, your Spanish is coming along nicely," complimented Pete Michaels.

"I think so. Those little Spanish businesses along Bay Boulevard are really helping me," explained Frank proudly.

"How are ya feeling?" asked Murdock.

"Wonderful!"

"And Melissa?"

"She's spending a little time back north with her father." Murdock looked at him without saying a word. "All right, she found my chewed-up leg in the closet and started crying. I thought I hid that thing better than that. Suppose she needs some time to rest her nerves," replied Frank.

"Why don't you come over for dinner tonight?" asked Murdock.

"I'd like that but...I'm getting good at heating soup." Murdock grinned.

"Ol' Davenport hit the ceiling when he saw my request for the reimbursement on my leg."

"What'd he say?"

"He thought it was a little steep. I asked when was the last time he priced one."

"I bet he liked that," responded Murdock.

"Told him I acquired this deep tan since working in Florida and thought it would be fashionable to have a matching leg." Murdock laughed wishing he had been there to see Davenport's face flush with fury.

"I checked several places and gave him the lowest price. I told him if he didn't sign the paperwork, I'd come into the office just to wave my stump at him."

"It worked?"

"Yeah, the weak-stomached jerk immediately signed it."

Murdock shook his head in disbelief. He admired Frank for having the strength to deal with Davenport. Frank's character was such that telling people what he thought, whether it was solicited or not, came naturally.

Murdock began sorting through his mail and found a pink envelope addressed to him. Bold black letters covered the front, **"To Be Opened By Addressee Only."** Inside he found a yellow slip of paper annotated, *Give me a call, quick.* Murdock turned the page and found three names printed on silver-colored computer tape:

Philip Ward - Restricted Access
Ramon Martinez - Restricted Access
Douglas Warbington - Restricted Access - Inactive

Murdock immediately called Marlene. The confidentiality of the information intrigued him.

"Marlene, I've got the names. What does it mean?"

"I can't talk here. Meet me at eight-thirty at the snack bar balcony."

"All right." Marlene's secretiveness puzzled him.

Murdock studied the computer printout again. In all of his years working with the Service he had never encountered a restricted access. The fact that CI did have files on the three names confirmed Julia's suspicions that the three were related. But how?

"Bill," interrupted the group's secretary. "Mr. Davenport would like to speak to you." Murdock watched as she informed Frank, Pete and Ernest Shelton who was Davenport's right hand, of the same invitation. The four trickled into the glass cage and sat down.

"I'm glad each of you are in the office today," smiled Davenport. Frank looked over at Murdock who was glaring. They knew something was coming. "...and thank you for making yourselves available for some details."

"Dick, before you go any further, I can't afford the time right now," advised Murdock. He knew Richard Davenport despised the name Dick.

"I'll talk to you in private after this meeting," informed Davenport. "Laccetti and Michaels, as of Monday, you'll be reassigned to coaching a training group. Eighteen trainees are arriving. You'll work across the street at the Landmark Building for about a year. Two other coaches will join you from the North Miami office. Wrap up as much as you can by Friday. Take some of the easier work with you. Any questions?" Davenport looked at Frank and Pete.

"Just a comment. Thanks for the extra time to prepare for them," remarked Frank. "How can we do it? We have too much going on."

"You boys can do it," replied Davenport smiling. Davenport turned and looked at Murdock.

"You and Ernie will be detailed to the South Miami office. They're heading up a task force to clean up the Keys. Thought you might be interested in it." A smirk covered Davenport's face. "Close what you can this week. I'll tell you Friday who to transfer the work to."

"You mean someone else is actually going to receive additional cases?" replied Murdock acrimoniously. "I want a travel advance and overtime when needed...all the mileage back and forth on weekends paid," demanded Murdock hoping Davenport would refuse so that he could decline the detail.

"No problem," replied Davenport in a calm voice. "You can head out Monday morning for the Key West office. They'll be expecting you. You three can leave," ordered Davenport as he looked at Frank, Pete and Ernie.

"Murdock," said Davenport as he stood and walked slowly around to the front of his desk and sat on the corner, close to Murdock. "I received a call from Carmichael in CI. He wanted to know...and now I do, too. What's your interest in these people?" Davenport handed him a half sheet of paper with the three names

Murdock had become familiar with during the last twenty-four hours. He had not seen his boss this serious. A stressful, sick-to-your-stomach kind of nervousness.

"The names came up during one of the investigations I'm helping Julia with. Somehow they're connected to her taxpayer and assets that were fraudulently transferred."

"Well, they're a little concerned you're going to screw up their investigation...but then, you're gonna be in the Keys a while, aren't you?" Murdock smiled within knowing the assignment would allow him to look into the transfer of the Key Largo house. His only concern was Ernest, who could easily interfere since he reported directly to Davenport.

"So the three are under investigation?"

"Apparently so and they want you out of it ."

"It's odd, the case didn't have CI's code," stated Murdock. A revenue officer, trained in the civil aspects of an investigation, might unknowingly weaken the criminal potential of CI's case if they weren't aware the case was under criminal investigation. Therefore, CI inputs a code into the system which alerts the revenue officer. The case was not coded but rather, had a peculiar and unheard of "Restricted Access" code.

"Not our concern, Murdock. Be a good soldier and follow orders. I want you out of here come Monday morning, got it!"

"Dick, I'm going to think about this detail. If I haven't overlooked a date I can't break, I'll do you the favor." Murdock knew Davenport's blood pressure was rising. Murdock stood, towered over him momentarily and left for his 8:30 rendezvous with Marlene.

She was gazing out when Murdock approached her.

"Marlene." She quickly turned around.

"Bill, who are those people I made inquiries on? Carmichael asked me twenty questions about it and stormed off. I've never seen him like that. Who are they?" Marlene was extremely nervous. "I've never seen this kind of security with our system." She was frantic.

"I'm not sure who they are...yet," replied Murdock.

"Carmichael left the U.S. Attorney's office for this, and he never...*never* leaves the U.S. Attorney's office before the grand jury convenes."

"How'd he know you accessed the names?"

"When I tried to bypass the restrictions, the computer locked. The entire system shut down. I've never seen anything like it in all of my years retrieving transcripts."

"But how did he know the system shut down?"

"Apparently, an advisory was sent to his computer." Marlene was noticeably nervous.

"You think Carmichael restricted the files?" asked Murdock.

"I thought so at first, but he got too excited over it. Like someone else was going to find out or something. I called a friend in Miami who's been around a long time and she's never heard of it either. She thinks someone higher than Carmichael had to have done it—a lot higher."

"What about the word 'Inactive' next to Warbington's name?"

"It means he's deceased. We had him under investigation but he died."

"Anything else about the names?" probed Murdock.

"One other thing. I don't know if it'll help you, but Carmichael had me establish the same file code on all three."

"What does that mean?"

"Everyone being investigated in the same case is assigned the same case code."

"So they're definitely connected?"

"That I'm sure of," replied Marlene. "Carmichael really grilled me. Be prepared for lots of questions," warned Marlene.

"Davenport already asked. I'm sorry for all the problems," Murdock said apologetically. "I'm entitled to any information if it's on a need-to-know basis."

"Is it?"

"Yes!" answered Murdock defensively.

"Well, I'll see you in a month or so." Marlene looked puzzled. "They put me on detail to the South Miami office. Keep me out of trouble I guess."

"You stay out of trouble?" she commented. Murdock grinned. "I better get going. Sorry I couldn't help and good luck." Marlene turned and proceeded back to her office.

"You did help," shouted Murdock. "Thanks."

Murdock requested the last filed Form 1040, income tax return, on each of the three men. Before he could retrieve the returns, he'd have to ascertain their social security numbers. To do this, Murdock entered a unique command code into the IRS computer known as the Integrated Data Retrieval System, or IDRS, and then the names. The numbers appeared on the screen which Murdock jotted down. He then entered a second command code to view the return. The first social security number was entered. Within seconds the screen flashed: DATA NOT AVAILABLE. The second social security number was typed in: DATA NOT AVAILABLE. The last number was inputted: DATA NOT AVAILABLE. Murdock entered a final command code. This would let him know if the returns had even been filed. If the 1040s had not been filed then IDRS made some sense; after all, there couldn't be any data available if the returns had not been filed. Moments later the information on the screen aroused Murdock's tenacious curiosity. Form 1040s had been filed by Douglas Warbington and Phillip Ward, so where was the information?

Murdock left the IDRS room and saw Hank Goffman standing by his table holding the half sheet of paper Davenport had scratched the three names on. Tilting his head slightly back with his arms extended, Hank studied the first name on the torn paper.

"Haven't seen this name in a while," stated Hank.

"Which one?"

"Douglas Warbington."

"What do you know about him?" asked Murdock anxiously.

"When I transferred down here all you could read about in the paper was this cloud of controversy over his death. The paper carried it for days."

"The name sounded familiar but I couldn't place it," stated Murdock. "Wasn't he a banker suspected of fraud in Miami?" The name was coming back to him.

"Miami was after him, but he was indicted in Houston for laundering drug money," recalled Hank with an almost photographic memory. Murdock was amazed with Hank's recall abilities.

"Didn't he die about three years ago?" asked Murdock.

"Two and a half," replied Hank with certainty in his voice. "A gruesome death. He was burned beyond recognition. No teeth or fingerprints to use."

"How did they identify him?"

"Found him on his yacht at Bahia Mar."

"Do the other names mean anything to you?" questioned Murdock.

"No. I was trying to place them but, no, I've never seen them."

"Was the IRS involved in the investigation?"

"Not that I recall, but you would've thought so based on the laundering scheme, wouldn't you?" Murdock nodded in agreement.

"Thanks. I've been trying to place the name. Fort Lauderdale PD must've had their hand in on the investigation. Think I'll stop by and talk to 'em."

"Talk to Miami, too," advised Hank.

"Hank, one more thing. Any idea how I can get my hands on returns when there's no data available?"

"They were filed?" Murdock nodded. "Get the information through the Service Center's computer branch. It's formatted a little differently, but all the same information is there," replied Hank.

"How do I get it?"

"Get Davenport to sign a request and you'll have it in about two weeks."

"What if I wanted to bypass Davenport...got any ideas?"

"Give me the social security numbers. I know someone who'll pull it. This is on a case isn't it?" Hank knew the penalties for browsing information on unassigned taxpayers was stiff.

"The names came up during one of Julia's cases. Somehow they're related. If I could find 'em I might be able to locate the owner of the company we're working. He's disappeared. Davenport wants me to let it go but...and it's just a gut feeling I've got, but something's not kosher." Hank listened. "Hey, I don't want to get you in any trouble with Davenport."

"It's case related...I'm not concerned and besides, he'll never know."

"I'm going on a detail to South Miami for a month or so. Can you hold the information?"

"Sure will."

"Thanks again." Hank nodded and immediately sat down and began tapping his foot to another Disney tune.

The secretary had just paged Lawrence Anderson, another revenue officer, on the intercom and informed him that someone was waiting for him in the lobby. He was considered by his peers to be a certified loony tune. He was visiting a psychiatrist for his uncontrollable and sudden outbursts of anger and vulgarity which he usually directed at his taxpayers. The Service had given him a leave of absence to seek help. Lawrence returned to duty but, again, was slipping back into old habits. He was a short, heavyset man in his late twenties. The women in the office admired his coal black, curly hair. Davenport was documenting his observations of Lawrence as well as what the public had to say about him. If professional help didn't correct the problem, Davenport was going to submit disability papers for him. Some wondered if there was really anything wrong with Lawrence although, what sane person would do some of the things he did?

"Lawrence," interrupted the intercom again. "I know you're over there." The secretary was getting frustrated. She had found him on other occasions hiding from her under his worktable. "If you don't come out I'm telling Mr. Davenport." The office laughed.

"What does that slob want now?" he mumbled. He stood up and slammed his pen down on the table causing several work papers to flutter about. "Can't get anything done." He passed Julia who was just arriving from the field. She heard his incessant mumbling and tried not to laugh. Lawrence looked the crowd over in the lobby searching for a familiar face. "Anyone here to see me?" shouted Lawrence at the crowd who was anxiously waiting to have their tax questions answered. The blue-haired crowd rushed and inundated him with their questions.

"Get out of here. I'm not answering your stupid questions," he yelled. His face was flushed. One elderly lady demanded that he answer her questions or she would report him to the authorities, as she put it. Lawrence squatted to attain eye level with the woman.

After getting into position, he promptly thumbed his nose at her.

"Did you see that, Irving? Did you see what he did to me? Catch me Irving. I think I'm going to faint." The little woman placed the back of her hand on her forehead and sat down.

"Mr. Anderson," stated a deep voice from behind the crowd. Lawrence turned toward the man with a look Peter Lory might have in Frankenstein. A tall lean man handed him a folded piece of paper.

"I'm a processor and you've just been served to testify on behalf of Mrs. Clark in her divorce settlement."

"This is a federal building and you can't serve this here." He shoved the document back at the processor.

"Sorry, I've done my homework. I can serve you all day long in the reception area. You have a nice day!" The processor quickly exited the area.

"Come back here you worthless ..." He shouted a slew of obscenities at the top of his lungs. The crowd went silent. He proceeded to chase the man through the front doors and into the corridor but lost him. He caught the last glimpse of the messenger trotting down the courthouse steps. He propped the door open with his foot, cupped his chubby hands around his mouth as he continued his shouting. "You no good... ! I've got better things to do than help some tramp clean her ol' man out. You...you...you ..." Another barrage of obscenities erupted.

A pin could have been heard dropping as he reentered the lobby area. All eyes were on him. As he passed the lady that demanded the answers he again thumbed his nose at her.

"Oye vay! He did it again, Irving. I'm going to faint this time."

Occasionally, revenue officers would be issued a subpoena to testify about a spouse's financial holdings. The officer would have the knowledge if he or she worked with the couple on their delinquent taxes. Since Lawrence had conducted an extensive investigation into the Clark's financial affairs during one of his tax delinquency investigations, or TDI's as revenue officers refer to them, he had a wealth of information.

Frank and Pete had just returned from their new offices across the street where they would coach the trainees.

"Eat your hearts out everyone," announced Frank. The group of revenue officers gathered around them. "You're not gonna believe this, but we've got our very own..."

"And very private..." injected Pete.

"Offices on the east side?" asked Julia.

"He means with an ocean view!" stated Pete.

"We're not slumming with you guys anymore," claimed Pete.

"You sure it's the east side?" asked Julia.

"E-A-S-T," spelled Frank. They both laughed. "Like, I don't want to rub this in but, did Pete mention we could see the O-C-E-A-N?"

"Not to mention Bahia Mar and all those beautiful babes...I mean boats."

"Yep, they're even putting brass name plates on the door," stated Frank.

Lawrence uttered a litany of obscenities at Frank.

"Larry, this is gonna set you back a few weeks in therapy but, it's true," Frank's voice raised.

"You're lying again. That's all you ever do."

"Go under your table and have a nervous breakdown, okay!" Lawrence proceeded back to his area mumbling about him.

"Bill, I've got a sale scheduled at one. Can you make it?" asked Julia.

"Got a taxpayer coming in at two. I'll be there after the interview."

"Well, there's four of us. That should do it. Oh, I almost forgot. Ran a check on Sea Unlimited. Phillip Ward was the registered agent. I'm waiting on some other stuff." Registered agents establish corporations on paper and were usually, but not necessarily, attorneys.

"You were right about the three names being related," stated Murdock.

"What's the connection?"

"Still not sure, but CI opened a file on Ward and Martinez. You can bet Farmer is in on it, too."

"What about Warbington?" asked Julia.

"CI had him under investigation with the other two but he's dead...murdered 'bout two years ago. I'm gonna read up on it at the library," replied Murdock.

"I didn't find any loan being recorded at the courthouse by Sea Unlimited or Farmer," remarked Julia.

"So the house transfer wasn't repayment of a debt."

"It could have been an unrecorded debt," replied Julia.

"I hear ya, but it's not a legitimate debt. Something else is going on."

"You're probably right."

"Guess it doesn't really matter since he transferred the house when he owed taxes." Julia agreed. Regardless of whether or not a note had been recorded, property transferred for less than fair consideration was fraudulent if the transferor owed or was accruing federal taxes.

Julia left with Frank, Pete and Lawrence. She had to take Lawrence since everyone else was either tied up or out of the office. She was selling the entire contents of a drugstore which required at least four people due to the volume of products. Lawrence rode with Julia while the other two took the government car. She took this opportunity to talk to Lawrence concerning his conduct at the upcoming sale. She also thought that if Lawrence went with Frank and Pete they'd kill him. After explaining specific instructions on the do's and don'ts, Lawrence held his head down and nodded his chubby face as if he understood and would comply.

When they arrived at the drugstore there were three dozen people standing in the heat of the afternoon sun waiting to place their bids. Julia, with the help of Frank and Pete, had divided the merchandise into sixty different lots or groupings ranging from footpads to hairnets and everything in-between. The four decided Julia would auction the feminine products since the three men could not bring themselves to do it. The owner had two other stores in his chain. He sacrificed this one to pay his $18,000 tax liability. He had been withholding the social security and income taxes from his employees' salaries, but during difficult times, had felt it less painful to divert the entrusted funds back into his business rather than to the Federal Reserves.

As the bidders filed in they signed their name and address. Lawrence was given the innocuous task of passing out numbers which they would raise and place their bid. Julia allowed the people to wander about inspecting the lots against the sale notice. The four answered questions which took some time but made the auction go a little smoother and faster.

"Who's in charge?" inquired a rather rotund woman.

"Mrs. Black is, but I'm sure we can answer your questions," replied Pete.

"No, I must speak to Mrs. Black," demanded the bidder. Julia was talking to an older black woman at the time of the request.

"She's standing right over there," informed Pete as he pointed.

"I see her." The large woman proceeded directly to where the two were standing and started talking to the black woman. Pete, seeing the confusion between Julia's last name and the color of the woman's skin, began making wagers with Frank on how many people would make the same mistake.

"Are there any items in the back room for sale?" inquired a man. Pete and Frank knew the answer, but the bet was on.

"Why don't you talk to Mrs. Black," informed Frank as he pointed in Julia's direction. The man, without hesitation, interrupted the black woman and started asking her questions.

"That's a beer for me, Frank." Pete smiled. Each question was directed over to Julia and the black bidder. Lawrence was pacing up and down the aisles trying very hard to obey Julia's instructions. He passed a section where the rotund woman was counting feminine douches and comparing the number to what was listed on the sale notice.

"Excuse me, but there seems to be an error in the number of douches," explained to lady.

"Now, what seems to be the problem, lady?" asked Lawrence.

"Looky here..." The woman pointed to the sale notice. "...it says 500 douches."

"So?"

"Well, do you see 500 douches on this counter?" The woman's tone was completely inappropriate for Lawrence.

"Let's see," observed Lawrence, as he looked around trying to maintain his composure. "I count fifty, not five hundred. I'll inform Mrs. Black that there's been a typo."

"What do you mean, typo?" shouted the woman not realizing she was poking a tiger. "I traveled from Pompano Beach for this and now you're telling me it's a mistake!" Lawrence looked around again and started mumbling to himself, *remember what Julia said. I don't want to disappoint her. Relax, take a deep breath.*

"Hey buster, look up when I'm talking to you. Do something about it! Are you even listening to me?" Well, are ya?" shouted the foolish woman as she poked him with her finger on his shoulder.

"Lady, if you don't like 'em, don't bid on them. Find something else that will help you." The bidders were gathering around them. "On second thought, why don't you..." A barrage of obscenities followed. The woman, still in shock, stormed out of the store shoving people aside. Lawrence was in hot pursuit when Julia intercepted him. She had a way no one else had with him.

After apologizing, Julia proceeded with the sale without any further incident. The four took turns auctioning and by five that evening the last item had been sold. The final count came to $21,000. The difference would be refunded to the taxpayer. Julia offered to buy dinner as a way of compensating the revenue officers who assisted her. A tradition at the Fort Lauderdale office.

"Meet me at Ernie's...rooftop. I'll be along after I get the cash converted," declared Julia. Most of the $21,000 was in one hundred dollar bills which had been remitted by the "forty thieves," a name given to a small, but wealthy band of regulars that attended most of the IRS sales. They were partners in large scavenger liquidation companies which fed off the remains of dying corporations. Revenue officers tolerated them since, in many instances, the Service would not have obtained the minimum bid, the lowest amount that could be accepted at a sale, without them. If the minimum bid was not reached, the IRS would have to purchase the items and credit the taxpayer's account and try to resell the seized merchandise. Not a cost-effective procedure.

Lawrence rode with Julia. This time to offer additional protection because of the large amount of cash.

The four met on the rooftop bar of the two-story restaurant which wasn't far from the office. The establishment's food and uniqueness attracted all types of people; from business executives to drifters. They gazed out over downtown Fort Lauderdale drinking frosty mugs of beer, eating the restaurant's specialty, conch fritters and Bahamian bread, and listened to Frank and Pete's wagering story.

Murdock finished his research at the library which confirmed Hank's information. Both Fort Lauderdale and Miami PD's conducted joint investigations into the money laundering schemes and banking fraud which had ties to Houston. Warbington was murdered before the grand jury convened. Murdock felt something was missing from the articles, but he couldn't put his finger on it. Not completely satisfied that everything had been reported in the paper, Murdock stopped at the police department. A large Marlin mounted over the entrance to the main lobby indiscriminately greeted both thugs and good citizens alike. Murdock was an avid fisherman and studied the monstrous fish before meeting with homicide detectives. He entered the building and waited patiently outside the homicide division.

"Bill Murdock?" asked Detective Dana Streeter.

"How are ya?"

"Just fine, thanks. Come in," instructed the good-natured detective. "I want you to know I reported all of my moonlighting income last year," remarked the detective smiling.

"Too bad, but I'll be sure to mention it to the auditors." The detective laughed as they turned a tight corner and entered his cluttered cubicle.

"You're interested in the Warbington file?"

"I know he died, but are you investigating anything else on the case."

"No, I'm surprised anyone from the IRS is asking us 'bout this."

"Why?" asked Murdock as he crossed his legs and tried to find a comfortable position in the steel, padless chair.

"One of our white collar boys was assisting the IRS in the bank fraud aspects of the case when, out of the clear blue sky, they didn't need us anymore. This was over a year ago."

"Who called?" The detective opened the dense file and flipped through a couple of pages.

"Carmichael," replied Streeter.

"What did he say?"

"No explanation other than they didn't need us."

"Why didn't you pursue it?" asked Murdock.

"We couldn't. The Feds had jurisdiction and besides, we were short-staffed."

"Why did we ask for assistance?"

"Matt Jacobson is retired now, but he was one of the best paper trail chasers. He worked with the Treasury Department on a few other cases."

"Did Carmichael request the help?" Streeter nodded.

"Then a year later they abruptly ended the investigation," stated Streeter.

"Was that unusual?"

"I've never worked with the IRS before, but it sounds strange doesn't it? I know Matt was ticked at the sudden change in direction."

"Any chance of contacting Matt?"

"Hold on, you're in luck," stated Streeter as he glanced at his watch. "Suppose to meet him in forty-five minutes. The Kings are running." Kings were Kingfish and they were making their seasonal migration which occupied most fishermen's thoughts this time of year. Murdock looked about the office at the nautical furnishings reflective of the detective's lifestyle. Streeter made the call and Matt Jacobson was more than happy to accommodate Murdock.

He followed Detective Dana Streeter in and out of the tangled afternoon traffic. They reached a secluded section of Fort Lauderdale off the west end of the New River. Gas-styled lanterns on poles marked the driveway's entrance and exit. A single strand of heavy rope was strung between the poles. A forest of banana trees covered the property from the street almost to the canal which bordered the rear of the property. Jacobson was on his 24-foot boat which appeared more like a floating laboratory with all of the sophisticated electronic equipment affixed to it. After the introductions and small talk about the boat and neighborhood Murdock began his questioning.

"So why did you stop working the investigation?"

"They flat out told me to back out! Adamant about the whole thing."

"Did you ever see 'em back out of a case like this before?"

"Never! It was like they were concerned I was gonna see or hear something I shouldn't. They told me they had other priorities."

"What priorities?"

"That's what I asked, but no one gave me a straight answer. I had plenty of other work to do but, just as this case was unfolding...gettin' interesting they pulled the rug out from under me."

"And Carmichael asked you to stop?"

"Demanded I stop!"

"Any other IRS officials pop up?"

"No, but I could tell Carmichael was getting the word from someone else."

"How do you know?"

"He was just too nervous and squeaky over the whole thing."

"Squeaky?" asked Murdock.

"Yeah, when the brass starts squeezing real hard it forces the air out of your butt so fast it squeaks." Murdock grinned.

"I've got a squeaky boss," commented Murdock.

"They should've solved the case. Heck, I could have solved it myself."

"Did they have enough evidence?"

"We had enough to bury Warbington. A little longer and I could have linked this other guy..." Jacobson hesitated and looked out. "...his name escapes me right now...but I was about to tie him to Warbington."

"This other guy, was his name Farmer?" asked Murdock.

"Nah."

"Ramon Martinez?"

"No."

"What about Ward?"

"Paul Ward!" replied the ex-detective.

"Phillip Ward," corrected Murdock.

"That's it!" exclaimed Jacobson. "What do you have?"

"Ward was probably the attorney who established a corporation called Sea Unlimited. Ya ever hear the name?"

"No."

"I know the names are related, but I don't know how. Assets were fraudulently transferred from Farmer to Sea Unlimited."

"If Warbington was involved, count on drug trafficking, too. The low-life got what he deserved," said the retired detective as he finished stringing thirty-pound test monofilament fishing line through the last eye on his hefty glass boat rod.

"Warbington was laundering?"

"Not that I could prove, but Houston said he was. IRS knew this 'cause they told me! The whole investigation has been an enigma. Something stinks, but I don't know what. Kinda glad I'm out of it but, if you could, let me know how it turns out? It's a loose end for me." Murdock nodded.

"Never knew Florida bananas could grow so big and yellow," commented Murdock. He inspected the large bunch of bananas.

"Guy next door said I could eat all I wanted. Nice guy, huh," replied Jacobson.

"They any good?"

"Oh, they're tasty all right. I use to eat them in cereal, by themselves and with peanut butter on 'em. So, one day I asked him how he did it. The jerk told me he didn't do nothin' cause the tree was over his friggen septic tank! Can you believe it?" Murdock laughed. "I'd been eating these things which were nourished by an unlimited supply of crap for over a year before I asked. Haven't eaten any bananas since." Streeter and Murdock laughed again. Jacobson revved the throaty twin outboard engines. They were whining to go chase schools of Kings. Murdock thanked the detective and plodded his way back through the miniature tropical forest.

Murdock finally made it home after grappling with the afternoon traffic. Beth, Audrey and PJ were in the small front yard playing catch with a beach ball.

"Hello everyone!"

"Papa's home!" His two children came running toward him screaming with excitement.

"Pick me up, pleeease," urged Audrey.

"Come here ya little beggars." Murdock picked them both up

and they wrapped their arms around him and squeezed.

"Audrey... PJ, your Daddy had a busy day. Give him a chance to rest."

"It's okay. They help me take my mind off stuff, don't cha?" Murdock buried his face in them. "Let's go for a quick walk." The four walked down the Isle of Venice which was lined with condos and apartment buildings to a nearby canal which branched off from the Intracoastal waterway. Sailboats dotted the canal. They sounded like an orchestra tuning before a concert as the wind rattled the ropes and clips which were attached to the rigging masts.

"Isn't this nice?" Murdock studied the scenery. Beth smiled and placed her arm around her husband's waist. "We came close to moving to Rio de Janeiro today," stated Murdock.

"What are you talking about?"

"This offshore company turned over a six hundred and fifty thousand dollar cashiers' check payable to me! Can you believe a multi-million dollar corporation doing that?"

"You've got such an honest face. Why Rio?"

"No extradition agreement. No one could touch us. We'd build a house overlooking the beach." Beth laughed.

"And give up this rented condo?"

"It'd be tough, but if we really worked at it, just maybe." Beth laughed. The sunlight clung to the aluminum sailboat masts and the two again looked out. Julia had called as they opened the front door.

"How'd the sale go and did Lawrence behave?"

"Got everything I needed and yes, he behaved...well, almost."

"What's up?"

"Thought I'd call since you're leaving next week. Find out anything?" Murdock talked to Julia over the next ten minutes explaining all he had found. AJ, his daughter, was still attached to his neck.

"Did you say Warbington was reported murdered in seventy-seven?" asked Julia a little puzzled.

"Yeah. Why?"

"The book of names we found was published in seventy-nine." Murdock hesitated. "What do you mean?"

"That particular style book was first printed last year."

"You sure?"

"Nineteen seventy-nine is printed on the book. I called the publishing company. It's the first edition." Murdock was silent. His pulse quickened.

"You think Warbington's alive?" asked Murdock.

"What else could it be? Warbington's name appears about two years after he was allegedly murdered. Unless there's another Douglas Warbington."

"Maybe." Murdock hesitated. "The police never got a positive ID on the body," continued Murdock.

"He could've staged his death to avoid prosecution," said Julia.

"Whatever it was, sounds like the IRS knew," said Murdock.

"Or was in on it," responded Julia. That possibility silenced them.

"Why? What would we have to gain?" asked Murdock.

"I don't know," Julia replied exasperated. "...but I'm going to find out. One more thing, call me if anything comes up on the Largo house."

"Will do. Take care of yourself, Julia."

"You too, Bill." Murdock's stomach began to tighten as his sixth sense kicked in thinking about Warbington, the IRS' possible involvement in a murder/cover-up and that Julia would be left here, alone, to investigate that lead.

"Bill...supper's ready," shouted Beth.

"AJ, go tell mom I'll be there in just a minute."

Murdock flipped through his case investigations until he found Willie's telephone number. He dialed Willie.

"Mr. Walker?"

"Dats me," replied Willie.

"Murdock, with the IRS. I wanted..."

"I needs my charts back," interrupted Willie.

"That's why I'm calling. Why do you need them?"

"They belong to someone and I needs 'em back."

"What's the significance of them?"

"I just needs 'em back and that's all I knows 'bout dem."

"Who are you holding them for?" There was silence. "Who do

they belong to?"

"I can't say."

"Why not?"

" 'Cause dey wouldn't be happy wid Willie. When can I have 'em?"

"I'll get them to ya in a few days."

"Don't take too long, will ya now?" As Willie hung the phone up someone was waiting for him in the shadows of his house.

5

Only sixteen trainees reported Monday morning to be sworn in as revenue officers. Two got smart over the weekend and decided the IRS was not what they wanted to do with the rest of their lives. After all, investigating tax delinquents and having Congress chastise them for enforcing the rulebook Congress wrote didn't sound like a whole lot of fun.

"All right, everyone..." instructed a rather heavy-set man in his mid-fifties known only to the group of trainees as "Ralph." While his black 1960-ish tie matched his horned rimmed glasses, it barely reached the fourth button down his white shirt. "...stand up and raise your right hand." He scanned the room. "Your other right, honey." He then pointed to someone else on the other side of the room. "...the other right, God gave you. Great! Thank you. You're a fine group...future leaders of this organization." A few laughed.

While the group was being sworn in Pete and Frank put the final touches on the paperwork they would use to auction a personal residence. The sale would introduce the recruits to one of the more difficult aspects of their occupation. A facet of the job that was, unfortunately, quite common and, equally unfortunate, necessary.

The trainees were now official and could accompany the more seasoned revenue officers on case investigations while waiting to attend the next opening of Phase I Revenue Officer Training.

They waited in the room like lost sheep in need of a shepherd. Ralph exited the room.

"Thanks, Ralph," stated Pete.

"Sure...good luck with 'em..." Frank half smiled.

"... you're gonna need it with this crew."

Pete and Frank stepped into the room.

"Have a seat and Frank's going to brief you on what to expect this morning."

Frank hobbled up to the front of the room and delineated the circumstances leading up to such a serious enforcement posture as selling a person's home. He also reviewed the legal requirements that had to be met and the authority that allowed them to conduct such a sale.

"You mean to tell me that this person received three phone calls and six letters from the IRS and he still didn't respond?"

"Sad, but very true," responded Frank, struggling to recall the trainees name."

"It's Bob."

"Thanks, Bob. Not only that, Mr. Coolidge failed to respond to both of Pete's personal field visits."

"How do you know he got the messages or letters?" inquired another sheep from the flock.

Pete stepped in, "The case history sheet indicates that the Atlanta Service Center spoke to him, no letters returned to the Center as undeliverable and, at the second visit I made he refused to talk with me." The trainee acknowledged with a nod.

"What's our job at the auction?" asked another one.

"Primarily, we just want you to observe a typical sale. We'll need someone with decent handwriting to take the name of the bidders and issue numbers. The rest of you can be spotters."

"Spotters?"

"Point out the bidders so we don't miss anyone."

"Will Mr. Coolidge be there?"

"No. You have an address and a map to the property. See you there in about thirty minutes."

Pete and Frank rode together and actually arrived after a couple of cars full of the trainees. The once beautifully maintained house in Harbor Beach backed up to a finger canal which lazily found its way around Pier 66 and then merged into the Intracoastal waterway.

"You passed your first test," teased Frank.

Potential bidders were peering into windows and examining court and IRS documents while others studied the layout of the property.

"You two can start registering the bidders and passing out these numbers."

Pete announced to the crowd to sign in and then reconvene at the rear of the property. A huge patio and awning offered the only shade near the property. The once lush landscaping withered, indicative of Mr. Coolidge's state of mind and attentiveness to his affairs. Following the meandering canal west of the property brought Pier 66 into full view. The residence, even in its current condition was worth half a million dollars. The first mortgage was down to $89,000 and there were no other liens except the Notice of Federal Tax Lien for $286,000. Someone was going to get one profitable deal compliments of the IRS and one recalcitrant taxpayer.

A crowd of thirty-two people gathered under the patio canopy. Only eleven were registered bidders. Pete read the opening statement and answered the usual questions. The people were slow to bid, typically cautious as they looked around. The bidding got stuck at $150,000.

"Surely this property is worth more than a hundred and fifty thousand! The lot alone is more than that! Ladies and gentlemen..." Pete was on a roll. He was a gifted orator. He turned toward the canal, gazed up at the Pier 66 monolith, arms extended as though he was delivering an intense sermon from the pulpit. "... behold this beauti..." his words stopped flowing and he turned pale. A feeling of nauseousness overwhelmed him.

"What's the matter?" asked Frank. Within seconds the answer was given. Mr. Coolidge had arrived. He took a few more steps and the entire crowd gasped.

"Don't anybody move or I'll take you out!" His light blue T-shirt was splattered with blood. "Bloody vultures. That's what you are...all of you...scavengers. Trying to turn a buck at my misfortune. But not today! TODAY IS MINE!" thundered Coolidge.

He brandished the shiny black, pump 12-gauge shotgun. Frank slowly stepped backward working his way into the crowd. He needed cover to retrieve his Smith & Wesson .38 special he had strapped to his ankle. As a Bronx cop, he had been in a similar situation and learned two things—don't be seen reaching for the pistol and time wasn't on his side.

Coolidge walked closer to the group which immediately responded by pulling tighter together and back against the rear wall of the house. When the crowd contracted, Frank was leaning over and dropped his .38. They were wedged so tightly that breathing was even difficult let alone attempting to retrieve the revolver. The crowd inched all the way back, isolating Frank from the only remedy.

Pete was an island, alone and isolated. The first and primary target. Somehow he regained his composure enough to speak.

"Mr. Coolidge..." Coolidge snapped his head so quickly in Pete's direction that his sunglasses went airborne, revealing his bloodshot, crazed-looking eyes encircled by purple rings. There was a murmur in the crowd as someone began to weep.

Coolidge's crew cut hair dripped sweat. "You must be Mr. Michaels." He walked over to him, keeping an arm's length distance. "You're worthless...did you know that?" Pete swallowed as if there was something stuck in his throat. "Say something!" Coolidge gritted his teeth and displayed them like a rabid dog. He raised his shotgun and pointed it at Pete's head and waited. "What's the matter-cat got your tongue?" The rabid dog turned maniacal. Five more seconds, like eternity, passed. Frank used his crutch to try and pry the human sardines apart, but to no avail. He knew what was about to happen and there was nothing he could do except watch.

Pete was ghost white. His hands and arms trembled. The moss green shirt turned evergreen in color as his body responded to the intense stress.

"Well, look at that...he's pissing in his pants. Big IRS man pissing in his pants. You're just like my ex...take, take, TAKE!" he shouted. "It's time for this to end. Got the old lady this morning, now it's your turn, Michaels. What's it feel like?" There was no response from Pete. Pete was literally coming apart. "That's right, close your eyes real tight," tormented Coolidge. "You're thinking about what else you should've done with your stinking life! WELL, IT'S TOO LATE!" His shouting continued. A few more seconds passed in silence. "What's it feel like?" No response from Pete except tremendous shaking. "I asked you a question and I better get an answer." He asked the question in a melodic tune. Pete began mumbling. "What did you say?" Pete continued a little louder. "I STILL CAN'T HEAR YOU! WHAT ARE YOU MUMBLING?" Coolidge shouted as loud as his barrel chested lungs would allow. "You better say it loud you worthless SCAVENGER! SAY IT! ...SAY IT!" Coolidge pumped the shotgun allowing a shell to enter the chamber. The time had come. He was shaking as much as Pete.

"You better say it now!" Pete responded, shaking even more violently, eyes squinting shut as if the pressure would suck them into his skull. He cried as he continued mumbling louder and louder. "THAT'S IT! FOR ALL TO HEAR!"

"...Thy kingdom come...thy will be done..." Pete continued trembling. "...on Earth...as it is...in heaven..."

"That does it!" interrupted Coolidge. "...you worthless..." a slew of obscenities erupted from him.

What happened next shocked everyone. No sooner had Coolidge uttered those words when he stuck the barrel of the shotgun to his heart and a deafening ring shattered the confusion of the day, sending Coolidge's body into the canal. The crowd was showered with all of the venom and hatred kept inside of him.

Pete's body wouldn't stop trembling. He continued the Lord's Prayer, crying. Frank and one trainee were the only ones that remained. The others ran as fast as they could, knocking into each other.

"Pete." There was no response. Frank gently rubbed Pete's shoulder. "Pete...it's over. Everything is all right." Pete, without opening his eyes, held on to Frank and sat down. Frank sat beside him placing Pete's head on his shoulder. Pete continued crying as Frank stroked his hair, telling him that everything was going to be okay.

Frank turned to the only remaining trainee, “Bob, get an ambulance out here...and call the police.”

6

Murdock was thirty minutes into his drive to the Florida Keys when the early morning sun began to dodge between the wall of evergreens which lined the lonely stretch of interstate. His dwarfed automobile was overstuffed with luggage, skin diving equipment and, unfortunately he thought, Ernest Shelton. The fishing rods sliced the wind, whistling a lonesome tune. Murdock was rapidly gaining on the four hours of highway that lay ahead of him. With the help from his car radio, he relaxed in his seat and enjoyed the journey amidst the incessant complaining of Ernie.

Ernest was a computer whiz who worked for the IRS's Information Services prior to crossing over to the Collection Division. Everyone was surprised when he reported to work his first day since he didn't fit the revenue officer mold. Ernie was conservative, an introvert and overall stuffed shirt who took the job and Davenport too seriously. He wore horn-rimmed glasses and looked as though he would be comfortable wearing a bow tie. His blond hair was 1950-ish short. Murdock regretfully broke his silence.

"Ernie, you fish?"

"No!"

"I didn't think so."

"What's that supposed to mean?" asked Ernie.

"This is gonna be a memorable trip," mumbled Murdock.

A welcomed silence fell upon the two. They pulled off the interstate in downtown Miami. The pungent aroma of coffee and what smelled like burned toast permeated the area and announced to visitors that they were in Little Havana.

"Buenos dias, amigos. Fill 'er up?" asked the station attendant.

"Oui," replied Murdock.

"Don't get us shot," demanded Ernie nervously.

"Feels like we're in another country doesn't it? I just don't feel safe here," said Murdock as he looked back at Ernie who was looking over his shoulders. "Hey Ernie, all the billboards are in Spanish."

"Say it louder why don't you! Pay the man and let's go, please." Murdock paid the attendant and the two were back on the string of highway which was leading them to a veritable tropical paradise.

The interstate highway had now tapered into a single lane as the nine o'clock sun edged the top of the trees and began to evaporate the moisture-saturated air. A majestic-looking bald eagle soared high above in the warm air currents, scanning the area he once ruled. Unable to prevent the southward migration of developers, he defiantly roosted atop a telephone pole.

Murdock slowly turned off the highway and into Tommy's Restaurant which was nestled quietly in the midst of luxuriant mangrove trees. The bush-like trees grew in thick clumps and served as a sanctuary for numerous waterfowl and fish.

The two climbed out of the car and walked along a decrepit wharf which lead to a weathered boathouse. The structure cast a shadow over the wooden boats used by the "conchs," as the residents were called, for crabbing and fishing.

"Have you ever seen such clear water?" asked Murdock. Ernie could care less.

"What are those long silhouettes?" asked Ernie.

"Barracuda. You see the red starfish over here?"

"Here's a yellow and brown one," responded Ernie as he began to take an interest in the abundance of wildlife. Murdock grinned at Ernie's new found appreciation.

"I hope the residents can stop the high-rises going up," stated

Murdock.

"Who would want to build in the swamp? Bill, what are those white trees over there?" A thousand trees were solid white and looked like a snow-covered mountain.

"Those are mangroves covered with bird-crap."

"You're kidding?" Murdock shook his head no. "Amazing."

The two were quickly seated next to a large picture window overlooking another section of the mangrove swamps. They glanced out the window just in time to see a large blue heron gracefully in flight. Ernie began reading the history of the Keys which had been reproduced on the menu.

"It says that Key West was used by pirates as a refuge until the area was settled in the 1820s and that the island was originally named Cayo Hueso for Bone Island by the Spanish. Did you know that?" asked Ernie.

"No." Murdock lied. He had read the same menu a dozen times. "Anything else interesting?" asked Murdock.

"There's about fifty islands which make up the Florida Keys and most of them are of limestone. In total, they're one hundred forty-five miles long and one hundred thirty-four square miles. Key West is also the southernmost city in the U.S."

"Interesting," replied Murdock. "There's more, Bill." Murdock grinned. "In the mid 1880s Key West was the major manufacturer of cigars in the U.S. They even grow almonds here!"

"Seeing that you're so interested in the area Ernie, I'll tell you some things that aren't on the menu. Florida East Coast Railroad was the only link from the mainland to Key West. A hurricane hit in 1935 and destroyed the tracks. You'll see some remnants of those tracks when we pass through Bahia Honda. People use it as a fishing pier now. The overseas highway was constructed years later and we'll drive across a bridge seven miles long."

"Really?" Ernie was excited.

"One last item. When we pull out you'll see a silver pipe about two feet in diameter on the left side of the road. It'll run the entire length of the Keys."

"A gas line?"

"Water line. It was built during World War II."

"Expensive water."

"The most expensive water in the U.S."

"Don't forget our delicious Key Lime Pie that originated here," interrupted a cute, portly waitress awaiting their breakfast orders.

"There's a lot of history here," offered Ernie.

"We've seen it all," replied the waitress. "From pirates to treasure hunters to slave and rum runners and now drug smugglers. We've got our share of writers and painters who have settled here. No place like it anywhere. Now, what would you boys like to eat this morning?"

***

Davenport strolled into the new offices across the street wondering if they should keep the space and try to hire more people. The window of opportunity to hire would only be open another week and a half. Not enough time to do quality hiring, he thought.

Davenport met Frank at the training office.

"Who put these here?" he asked pointing to brass nameplates on the doors.

"You mean you didn't?"

Davenport didn't respond. He had a demure look about him. "I want you to resign!" Frank looked at him as though he were listening. He wasn't. "You don't belong here."

"We didn't have anything to do with what happened. Coolidge was a nut. You read the police report," replied Frank, sternly.

"Think about it, Frank." Davenport looked dejected, turned, placed his hands in his pockets and walked away. Frank watched him as he left and, for the first time, felt sorry for him.

***

Murdock pulled along side the road and checked his street atlas.

"There's only one way to Key West," quipped Ernie.

"Was that on the restaurant menu, too?" The tension quickly mounted again. "I've got to check this place out for Julia."

"What place?"

"Just a case she's working on. Her taxpayer owned a house here. I thought I'd save her some time. Here it is, Fourteen Ocean Breeze Drive. Looks like if I go to mile marker number ninety-two and veer off to the left I oughta be in the general vicinity." Murdock didn't want to tell Ernie anything since Davenport had instructed him not to work the case. They passed several mobile home trailer parks. Each of the homes were white, in neat rows and situated on pilings. The owners had magnificent views of the turquoise-colored water that surrounded the area. Numerous boatyards occupied Key Largo as did airstrips for small, single-engine aircraft.

"There's Ocean Breeze," informed Ernie. They turned down a shell-covered road. Each house was at least two stories and situated on deep water canals. The manmade waterways enable the boaters to easily navigate the often shallow waters of the Keys.

"I didn't realize there were so many people here," stated Ernie. The signs hanging from the mailboxes displayed Hispanic surnames.

"There's an especially heavy concentration of Spanish in the upper Keys. There's the address," said Murdock. The octagonal designed, two-story house was made of cedar and a spiral staircase in the center appeared to be the only entrance and exit. A screened deck encircled most of the dwelling. The nameplate was missing from the mailbox.

"What now?" asked Ernie.

"Take a look around. You can stay in the car if you want. I won't be long." Murdock walked around the house toward the canal side. That part of the house which faced the water was made of smoked glass. Several wind chimes made of thin oyster shells glittered in the sunlight as they stretched from the rafters. The chimes sounded like an orchestra of triangles, each playing a different composition.

Murdock turned a corner and proceeded to the front when he noticed a neighbor watching from an A-framed house next door. Before he could knock an elderly man with grey hair answered the door, leaving the screened door tightly shut.

"What do you want?" inquired the man cautiously as he talked through the screen. He was dressed in a sleeveless, white T-shirt which revealed his potbelly. Checkered shorts and knee socks covered the rest of him.

"Any idea who lives next door?"

"Why should I tell you anything?"

"I'm with the IRS, Bill Murdock."

"Got something that says that?" asked the man as he raised an eyebrow. The tone in his voice sounded as though Murdock couldn't prove who he was. Murdock opened his leather case. The man pulled out his glasses and studied the finely printed words on Murdock's credentials.

"It looks official enough. All right Mr. Murdock, we'll talk." The neighbor opened the aluminum door and propped it open with his foot.

"So, who resides next door?"

"I don't know. Several different people show up from time to time. Can't tell who lives there."

"Is there someone you see more than others?"

"It's hard to tell and kind of odd I suppose, but the only time anyone ever shows up is at night...late," he added. "I've never seen any faces. I just hear the voices...a woman's voice, too...and that car. Gee, it's loud."

"What kind of car?"

"It's one of those...you know...expensive foreign race cars."

"Porsche?" asked Murdock remembering he had found the title to one while helping Julia at Farmer's register company.

"I think so. Sounds like the turbine engines I used to work on before I retired from the airlines. The engine keeps me up at night."

"Is it black?"

"Black...I suppose. It's dark. What kind of trouble is he in?"

"Federal taxes."

"That's something I've always taken care of. It's the least I can do to live in this great country of ours."

"How long do they stay at the house?"

"A few days towards the end of the month. Like clockwork.

There's a crowd of 'em for the first couple of nights and then they leave...except for the Porsche and the woman, and they stay another couple of days." He paused for a moment. "...and then no one returns until the end of the next month."

"They haven't been here this month?"

"In another week or so they'll be here. I'd like to see you run the riff raff out."

"Would you call me when they show up?"

"I'd love to," replied the man with a smile on his face. Murdock gave him a business card.

"Okay, thanks."

"Have a nice day!" shouted the man as he waved goodbye through the screen door. Murdock turned toward his car and shook his head at hearing that phrase again.

"Find what you needed?" asked Ernie as he patted his forehead with his white handkerchief.

"Not really. Guess we better get rollin'," replied Murdock.

"This oughta save her quite a bit of time," stated Ernie.

"She's helped me out with my cases," replied Murdock.

"Me, too, she's an excellent technician. She's so pleasant, never too busy to help," continued Ernie. Murdock was surprised Ernie, being Davenport's own shadow, could have such kind thoughts about someone.

"Maybe there's hope for ya yet," stated Murdock.

"What do ya mean by that?"

"Nothin'."

Three hours later and with very little conversation having taken place, the two traveled the last stretch of Highway US 1, crossed the forty-third bridge that linked the keys and entered the one time pirate haven, Caya Hueso.

Everywhere they looked the town was empty. Once busy charter and drift boats lie dormant. Sidewalk corners that once exploded with color from the island artists were bare.

"Where is everyone? I expected crowds and festivities this time of year," remarked Ernie.

"There's your answer." Murdock pointed to nine touring buses packed with Cuban refugees. Hand painted signs taped to some of the buses expressed the conchs' sentiments. *Castro's Sewage,* read one sign. Another bus read, *White House or Bust!* "They're going to 'Tent City' in Miami until they can figure out what to do with them," explained Murdock. Tent City was an area fenced off underneath I-95 and military tents were erected to house the refugees.

"They're criminals aren't they?"

"According to the news many of them are, but not everyone. I like that one over there." Murdock pointed to a bus which had a sign stating, *Next Stop...Plains, Georgia.* "This fiasco is gonna keep Carter out of the White House. He's a humanitarian, but there comes a time to draw a line," remarked Murdock.

"What about 'give me your poor, your tired...'" Murdock cut Ernie off.

"The statue is an anachronism," replied Murdock.

"I can't believe the flag waving, pro America, Viet Nam Vet volunteer..." Murdock cut him off again.

"That's enough, Ernie! Don't talk 'bout Nam!"

"I'll talk about anything I choose," replied Ernie sharply.

"I did what I thought I had to do," shouted Murdock. Ernie pushed a sensitive button on Murdock. "I didn't run and hide in some college library until it was safe to come out. You missed this in your library readings and so I'll tell ya, there was a time when we needed people and their diverse skills to build this country. Those days are gone, we're not a welcome mat for this nonsense!" The two were silent for a couple of minutes. "Ernie..." Murdock hesitated. "I didn't mean to get carried away."

"It's okay."

"No, it's not. Sorry."

Entrepreneurs gathered outside their small, one-room shops to discuss the topic of the day and the cause of their plight, the Cuban invasion. The Mariel flotilla, as it was named due to Mariel, Cuba being the point of deportation. According to the news releases, over 100,000 Cubans arrived in the Keys with a quarter of them being hardened career criminals. Perplexed by an ever-growing prison population, Castro had opened his sewers and flushed many of his problems out to sea and into the U.S. Hundreds of thousands of tax free dollars were illegally earned during a very short period of time by boaters who participated in the flotilla. Captains were charging and getting $10,000 per person for a ninety-mile ride. By the time the U.S. responded to the crisis, the bomb had been dropped and the damage done—the Keys lost their main industry, tourism, and the area's crime rate soared as South Florida absorbed the shock waves and fallout. South Florida was changed forever.

Murdock, unable to find the office, asked one of the locals for directions. The office was tucked in behind a small post office near an old lighthouse constructed in the mid 1800s. The obelisk, with its entourage of date palms flanking the structure and surrounding blue skies, was post card perfect.

The office was small and dingy in appearance with off white bricks covered with moss. Cocoon eggs laid by large roaches had been deposited between the cracks in the bricks. Ernie opened the glass door labeled, "United States Treasury Department - Internal Revenue Service" and entered the musty, poorly lighted room with Murdock following. Thick dust layered a couple of wooden desks and chairs. Hundreds of small, grey water bugs, a type of crustacean, carpeted the yellowed terrazzo floor.

"Geeze! I hate bugs!" cried Ernie. Ernie tiptoed between clumps of them.

"Don't worry Ernie, they don't bite." Murdock laughed as Ernie continued his hopscotch-style walking. As the two approached a dark hallway, voices were heard.

"A full house, boys. Cough it up," demanded a stocky man smoking a Cuban cigar and wearing his accountant-styled glasses on the tip of his nose. His sandal-covered feet were propped up on a large blue and white cooler as he scooped the dollar bills from the other two players.

"Hello," expressed Murdock.

"Murdock and Shelton from Lauderdale, right?"

"That's right," responded Murdock. The stocky, bald man introduced himself as Jake Democko. His dark beard was neatly groomed and close to his face. He placed the deck of worn cards on the table and shook hands.

"Hi Jake," greeted Ernie.

"Please, my friends call me Palmetto." Murdock grinned wondering why he wanted to be called the name of the ugliest insect in South Florida. "Meet Harry Whittaker or 'Cricket' as he likes to be called." Cricket was medium height and had thick black hair. His high cheek bones and other handsome features were definite indicators that someone in his family, during some generation, was an American Indian.

"Glad you're both here," greeted Cricket. "We've got a lot of work cut out for us."

"This is Carlos Hernandez," informed Palmetto.

"Which insect is he?" asked Ernie.

"Call him Beetle."

"Welcome," said Beetle. Murdock nodded as he wondered about the motley crew.

"Anyone care for an ice cold, frosty beer?" Palmetto reached into the ice packed cooler.

"Love one," replied Murdock. Ernie declined.

"We've got soda if you'd rather have one. We always carry a little on account of we gotta limit Cricket's intake of alcohol," added Palmetto.

"Goes back to his great grand-daddy Running Bull," explained Beetle.

"Enough of the chitchat boys, pass me a brew," demanded Cricket. Palmetto tossed a beer over to Murdock and Cricket. Ernie reached for a carbonated beverage.

"Have a seat, guys. So, how are things at the country club?" asked Palmetto.

During the 1960s, the Fort Lauderdale office was first named the Country Club due to its pleasant surroundings, generally nice areas and overall country club atmosphere. Back then, Fort Lauderdale was a very laid back beach community. Only two roads existed and the commercial areas extended about five miles inland from the ocean. The sea breezes blew stronger and further inland back then. The advent of skyscrapers didn't occur until 1970 with the construction of the Landmark Bank Building. Fort Lauderdale would weather another decade before the erection of another monolith. Somehow, the country club name stuck with the old timers even though the pace had quickened, destroying the country club ambiance.

"Some of us are busy," replied Murdock. "How 'bout South Miami?"

"Oh, we've chased down about all the migrant tomato pickers we could handle. Told the boss we all needed more work," said Palmetto.

"Sounds like nonsense, Jake," replied Murdock.

"Please, it's Palmetto."

"You three screwed up just like I did," said Murdock. They laughed.

"Well, suppose you're right." Palmetto rubbed the sweat from his forehead while Beetle downed another frosty, cold beer and allowed a deafening belch to escape.

"So why are you here?" asked Ernie. Palmetto glanced at the clock.

"Let's go down to the dock and get ready for sundown. I'll tell you what happened then." Palmetto packed his belongings.

"At the risk of appearing ignorant, what's so special about sundown?" asked Ernie. The three insects looked at each other in disbelief.

"You really don't know about sundown here?" asked Cricket.

"Come along my son and ye shall learn," informed Palmetto as he put his arm on Ernie's shoulders.

"The answering machine on?" asked Murdock. He was hoping the neighbor next to the Key Largo house would call.

"It's on. We'll split the inventory tomorrow," opted Palmetto.

"Maybe we should go check-in first," expressed Ernie.

"Do whatcha want, but we reserved the rooms for you."

"Let's check-in," agreed Murdock. "If you saw my car you'd understand."

"All right, but hurry. We'll save ya spot at the dock." The five of them left the tiny sweatbox and proceeded to the hotel which was only a five-minute drive from the office.

"Bill, there's something about the area," mused Ernie. "Can't put my finger on it...the island is so out of touch with time."

"Seems that way doesn't it," agreed Murdock. The narrow cobblestone roads took them by beautiful two story homes built during the turn of the century.

"You almost expect to see a pirate's ship come floating into the lagoon," remarked Murdock. Ernie nodded.

The hotel resembled one of the antebellum houses they had passed. Freshly painted, sky blue shutters and trim complimented the oyster-white building which was located right on the ocean. A turquoise lagoon flowed around the right side of the hotel and a single lane, old stone bridge crossed the inlet. A thin line of coconut trees gave the lagoon the appearance of a South Pacific island. Neither of them had ever seen so many palm trees in one area.

As they opened the screen door to the hotel, brass lanterns barely illuminated the hallway. Mahogany veneer covered the walls. A large, tapestry rug lined the interior. The air in the lobby smelled old and dusty. Two large brass ceiling fans rotated slowly, gently fanning the many palms which invaded the lobby. As they approached the check-in counter the clerk was reading her bible which was as worn as the hotel.

Both rooms overlooked the lagoon with a partial view of the ocean to the left of the balcony. They decided to walk to the dock since it was only a quarter mile away. As they walked along the beach, a large, black Manta or "Devil" Ray shadowed their every movement, gracefully gliding in the shallow, lucid water.

"What do you think of 'em?" asked Murdock.

"I'm not sure what to think about the insects, except strange."

"I've heard from others that they're good at what they do," stated Murdock.

"I'm not sure what that is right now," replied Ernie. Murdock grinned. Ernie was right. They sounded like flakes, but could so many back home be wrong about them?

"Glad you boys could make it," greeted Palmetto as he tossed a dripping wet can of beer Murdock's way and handed Ernie a soda. The dock was lined with tourists and conchs alike. It appeared to be a rather large block party under the quick setting sun.

"It won't be long now," announced Palmetto. Ernie looked about and wondered what the king of the insects was referencing.

"So let's hear your story," Murdock said. "What dastardly offense did you guys commit to get ya banished?"

"Better let Beetle tell it. He bought the ticket that got us here."

"My case...your idea," replied Beetle as he crushed another beer can between his thick hands. "This jerk of a city councilman was running for re-election in Miami. I had two accounts on him for 1978 and 1979. He kept giving me the run around and then finally paid the seventy-eight."

"How much?" asked Ernie.

"Only six grand, but the guy's check bounced. When I approached him about it he starts yelling about how important he was..." Cricket interrupted.

"...like he was the great and powerful Oz himself."

"...then he starts in on how he could have my job for this and, well, by that time I heard enough and left. I knew he had a car almost paid for that I could seize...everything else was mortgaged to the hilt. I sent him his copy of the lien we filed."

"Guess you got his attention after that," commented Murdock.

"You would've thought so, but not a word," replied Beetle.

"So you seized the car," surmised Ernie.

"Well, I was gonna 'til Palmetto came up with this brainstorm of an idea." Palmetto shrugged his shoulders. Cricket laughed. "An anonymous phone call was made to his opponent that a lien had been filed. Called the Miami News and gave them the same stuff. The next morning it made the paper."

"...and he lost the election," interjected Palmetto. They chugged another beer.

"What's wrong with Cricket?" asked Ernie.

"Nothin'. He just goes into a trance when he's been drinking a lot."

"We watch him and slip him a soda once in a while," noted Beetle.

"How'd they know you called the paper?" asked Murdock.

"They didn't 'til some dime-dropping idiot in the office told," replied Beetle as he crushed another can.

"Yeah, but once the lien was filed at the courthouse it's public knowledge. They can't do anything about it," explained Murdock. Palmetto and Beetle looked at each other.

"We're here aren't we?" replied Palmetto.

"And will be for quite some time if my Ouija Board is right," gulped Beetle. Murdock was correct. The lien was public knowledge and anything on the lien could be discussed without violating Privacy Act laws.

A nearby radio played a Jimmy Buffet tune. Something 'bout a pirate and being born 200 hundred years too late. The crowd of conchs who had gathered at the dock all sang along. Clearly, Jimmy Buffet was the island's local hero.

"What's that dark spot moving across the water?" asked Ernie. A large, cloud-like mass proceeded steadily toward the dock.

"It's a school of baitfish. Watch these guys work the nets," informed Murdock. Ten-foot nets soared through the air like saucers bringing in fifty or more baitfish ready to be sold.

In a matter of seconds the crowd at the dock was silent. Beer cans and glasses of wine, whiskey and champagne were held high into the air.

"What's happening?" asked Ernie.

"What everyone comes here for this time of day. Look straight ahead," informed Palmetto. The blood-red sun began to quickly melt in the vast sea, turning the water before it a reddish-orange. The clanging of cans and glasses followed as the crowd toasted the descending fireball. When the sun disappeared, they downed their drinks and applauded mother nature for her wonderful display. Several women sitting on the railing then exposed what mother nature had given *them*. The crowd, again, toasted and applauded mother nature. Ernie stared in disbelief as his pants grew tighter and tighter.

"Hey Ernie, don't take 'em too serious, you'll bust out of your shorts," yelled Beetle. They laughed as Ernie pulled his shirt out and covered what was revealing his innermost thoughts.

"Don't worry about it," said Palmetto. "They're excited too, but you'd never know." Everyone roared with laughter, even Ernie.

"What is that?" A white haired man with a crew cut was covered with iguanas in assorted sizes. Each lizard had its own leather harness and thin chain as they crawled all over the man's body.

"Just one of the things that makes Key West what it is," announced Murdock.

"And what's that?"

"Key West!"

Other interesting people began strolling and performing in the island streets. A few more drinks and songs later, the dock patrons blended into the alleys and took what remained of the day with them.

***

The aroma of a Sunday meatloaf permeated the house. Alena's father faithfully prepared the dinner each week for the two of them. Before sitting down he handed his daughter a manila folder.

"What's this?"

"Something you should know about. Tell me what you think," he replied as he walked back into the kitchen.

Alena studied the 8" x 10" black and white photographs affixed to the left side of the file. There were enlargements of her fiancé, Phillip Ward, and several Colombians. Her look answered his question. "Where did you get these?" asked Alena forcefully as she flipped to the next photograph.

"I can't tell you that." There was silence. "They were taken three nights ago. Nice company he keeps. The first photograph...do you have *any* idea who that man is standing next to Ward?"

She shook her head, "No."

"Does the name Carlos Rosario ring a bell?" Her father was clearly annoyed.

"Vaguely."

"Let me refresh your memory...the Herald mentioned extortion, racketeering, kidnapping, conspiring to traffic in narcotics and eleven...*eleven* counts of murder!"

Alena slowly placed the file on the coffee table, stood and walked over to the bay window. The view of Biscayne Bay didn't look as good as it did before. She started to softly cry as if to keep it from her father. He leaned against the doorway of the kitchen and stared at her, not knowing how to respond.

"Why is there always something wrong with the people I love?" Her gentle sobbing continued. "First mom, and now this! Will it ever end?" Looking downward, she cupped her face and progressed into a deep, heartfelt crying.

"I told you not to go near him, didn't I?" His voice carried. "You always have to do it your way, though. Never listening. Just like..." He stopped short of completing his thought. He shook his head slowly, still standing in the doorway."

"Just like who?" demanded Alena, turning around. She was livid. "Just like mom?" Alena struggled with her composure. "And you always have the right answer, don't you?" she asked sarcastically. "Wonder what your answer was when mom told you she couldn't take it anymore and left. What did you have to say then?" bitterly mused Alena calmly, but accusingly. "I have a pretty good idea why mom killed herself. And all these years I thought it had something to do with me." She snickered.

"Don't you talk to me like that!" raged her father as he stormed out of the kitchen. "I did the best I could, it wasn't me."

"Truth bothering you?"

"Truth! I'll tell you the truth! Your mother loved alcohol more than she loved us! *That's* the truth!"

"Don't you mean, you? This never had anything to do with me." The shouting continued. Words never meant to be spoken were shot like flaming arrows. Alena turned from the window and picked up her purse. "Dad..." she began crying. "... I'm never coming back." Alena's pace quickened as she proceeded to the front door. Her father intercepted and grabbed her by the arm. She shrugged him off and pulled away. "I'll never know why you enjoy hurting me so." Just before she slammed the door she cried, "One more item and I'm through with you...guess whose baby I'm carrying?"

"Nooo!" shouted her father. Alena slammed the front door. "Don't go, Alena," he pleaded as he opened the door. Alena closed the door to her car. "Don't go," he cried. Off she sped. "I'm just trying to help you..." he said looking down the street as his only child left him. "...I love you more than anything...don't leave me," he sighed with remorse. Alena's father returned to the kitchen, pushed the plates aside and buried his face in his hands. Would he ever see his daughter again and, if he did, how would he fix it *this* time, he thought.

7

Murdock awoke to the roar of diesel engines and the screaming of gulls begging the fishing boat captains for their morning breakfast. Occasionally, a handful of old baitfish would be thrown to them as a token they eagerly accepted. Murdock opened the French doors leading to the veranda and inhaled the fresh salty air. Porpoises, like children playing and teasing one another, rolled before the large boats on their journey out to sea. The eastern horizon was stratified with colors of crimson, orange, then yellow, and finally blue.

By 7:00 a.m. the five finished breakfast and were at the office dissecting the Keys into territories. Murdock studied the large map of the Florida Keys which was hung on a wall.

"If you don't mind, I'll work the northern end of the Keys. From Key Largo down to Islamorada," asserted Murdock.

"That's fine, but it's gonna be a lot of driving for you," replied Palmetto as he continued sorting cases.

"I could work next to Bill's area...say from Islamorada south to Marathon," said Ernie.

"Good, we'll take the heaviest concentration of cases southward to Key West. It'll offset the driving you guys will be doing," informed Palmetto. "Leave where you're staying at on the recorder. We'll be in touch. I almost forgot, we have a contract with

Island Wrecker Service. They're all over the Keys." Palmetto passed each of them the wrecker's business card.

Prior to leaving, Murdock and Ernie spent three hours of extensive, tedious courthouse research on the largest dollar cases. They listed as many assets as they could find. Warranty deeds were photocopied and mortgage holders carefully recorded since, if equity existed, the property would be seized immediately upon the persons failure to fully satisfy the delinquent taxes. The taxpayers they were working were part of the three-percent of the population who not only refused to pay Uncle Sam, but who stiffed everyone else. Prior to assigning the case to a revenue officer, the IRS had telephoned and written the taxpayer on numerous occasions, but to no avail. These people were why Murdock and the 5,500 officers nationwide were hired and carefully trained in financial, investigative and various legal matters. Their administrative powers were awesome. With two forms and only the concurrence of their supervisor, the revenue officer could seize and sell just about anything they deemed appropriate. Anyone could be summoned to appear or produce documents without receiving any judicial approval. No other agency could do this. No other position within the IRS had this level of authority, only Murdock and the others like him. The revenue officer was the judge, jury and, unfortunately, the executioner at times.

While at the courthouse, Murdock retrieved the Quit Claim Deed which transferred John L. Farmer's right, title and interest in the Largo house to Sea Unlimited, Inc., for "love and affection." The house was valued at $210,000.

"Another transferee?" asked Ernie.

"What?" replied Murdock who was in deep thought.

"To think some people believe they can actually beat the IRS by transferring property," asserted Ernie. "Did he transfer the property while taxes were accruing?"

"Yep."

"You got 'em."

"By the time we get the house transferred back to Farmer, we'll have the One Hundred Percent Penalty Assessment done so we can collect back to. We should be able to pay off the corporate personal assessments when we sell the house." Murdock didn't mind discussing the case since Ernie didn't know that this was Julia's investigation. He didn't want Ernie to know too much since he might be inclined to tell Davenport who had instructed Murdock not to touch the case. "I'm through here. Guess I'll head out...see ya later."

"Okay," replied Ernie. Murdock climbed into his car and proceeded north on US 1 to his new territory.

"Ernie, we're leaving too. We've got some seizures lined up. Take care," commented Palmetto. Palmetto was the quasi-manager while they were in the Keys. Murdock and Palmetto were the same grade and had similar levels of expertise, but owing to the number of years Palmetto had, Murdock listened to him. Palmetto made good, sound decisions and knew all of the intricate facets of case investigations. Off the job was another story. But that was typical, too, because revenue officers have the most difficult and demanding position in the Service and work long, stressful hours; consequently, they happen to play hard. This is one way they maintain their mental stability in their very unbalanced world. "...and be careful. Make sure you got one of us with you when you work a protester case." Ernie nodded.

Tax protesters were people who wrote "Fifth Amendment" across their tax returns or sent letters to the IRS stating why the money they earned was not really income. In both situations, special codes were input to identify these people so that revenue officers would be extra cautious when contacting them.

Beetle and Cricket packed up their cases and proceeded to their first stop, Joseph Miller, an illegal tax protester or ITP as they were called by the IRS. Miller, in addition to owing the IRS, had filed a "Fifth Amendment" tax return for 1980. Each revenue officer received a computer-generated list with the ITP's name, residence, employer and assets. Often, each office would have one specialist whose primary duty was to either convert them into responsible taxpayers or seize their wages and all of their worldly possessions, if necessary. This was often a long and tiring assignment which would rotate to another revenue officer after a year's tour of duty.

Most of their time was spent researching courthouse records for improper transfer of properties. When they weren't in the courthouse, they were checking with banks, employers or observing the protester to ascertain whether they worked. Often protesters held secret meetings which always caught the interest of IRS.

"What's Miller's address?" asked Beetle who was driving the rented Oldsmobile.

"North on US 1 until you get to Pirate's Cove. There's a bait and tackle shop to the right."

"I know where it's at. Should we call the Sheriff's Office?"

"Nah. No history of violence, just philosophical differences."

"Does he have anything?" Asked Beetle.

"He owns the bait shop...no equity though. The inventory is worth 'bout twelve thousand...and a VW."

"We'll take the VW first and see if we can't get him to borrow the rest. He owe anything on it?"

"It's free and clear." Meaning no liens were recorded.

Cricket continued perusing the thick files. He started listing the car's description on a seizure form Palmetto had previously signed as Acting Group Manager.

The highway leading out of Key West was barren except for an occasional busload of refugees bound for Miami. Cricket looked out the window and watched several lobster boats laying and checking their traps.

Twenty minutes later the two passed Pirate's Cove and turned onto a shell-covered, narrow road which led to a yellow, single story, concrete building. Bright blue letters, three feet high, were painted on the building, "Fresh Bait." No vehicles were parked anywhere around the building, but a sign hanging in the window indicated they were open.

"You ready?" asked Beetle. Cricket nodded and closed his black folder which contained the seizure paperwork. Beetle opened the squeaky door and pulled out his leather credentials. A woman bulging out of her blue jeans and cotton top greeted them. Her black and gray hair was braided down her back and she looked to be in her forties. Her face and hands were characteristic of someone who had been working on the ocean most of their life.

"You boys don't look like you're fishing. What can I do for y'all?"

"Is Mr. Miller in?" asked Cricket.

"He's down on the bridge. Just left a few minutes ago. He'll be there all day."

"Is that the next bridge north?"

"Yep. You distributors? Cause we don't need any more rods 'n' reels."

"We're not distributors, we're the IRS and you might say it's..." he hesitated, "...Miller time. Is he your husband?"

"Yes, but he won't talk to you."

" Now, why is that?" asked Cricket.

"He thinks your Communists."

"You mind if we look around?"

"I sure do, but seeing that you're the tax man, guess there ain't nothin' I can really do." They looked the inventory over. Hundreds of rods and reels for all types of fishing were displayed. Freezers full of cut bait were in the back and live bait wells filled with shrimp and pilchards lined the wall.

"You live here?"

"Where else?" replied the woman. Cricket took notes as he walked around. Beetle called the wrecker service.

"I really hope your husband talks to us."

"Well, he won't."

Beetle and Cricket waited near Pirate's Cove for the wrecker. Fifteen minutes later the three arrived at the bridge. The orange VW was parked on the shoulder. The driver was briefed on what was about to happen. The wrecker driver backed into position. A huge man was standing at the center of the bridge.

"I hope that ain't Miller," commented Cricket.

" 'Fraid so. The license plate matches."

"God help us. He's gotta be three hundred and fifty friggen pounds!" exclaimed Cricket in awe. The big man was wearing overalls with a dark green T-shirt. His straw hat was down low on the brow of his shaven head revealing several thick wrinkles of skin on the back of his neck. He looked like a character out of James Bond.

"We'll just be careful and everything will be fine. We'll be in and out, right?" whispered Beetle with a forced note of optimism.

"Right," replied Cricket. Miller spotted the two and stared.

"Mr. Miller?" asked Beetle clutching his badge like a security blanket.

"Yes," replied the overgrown man in a very high-pitched and-very effeminate voice that tickled Cricket so much he almost laughed. Almost. Beetle identified Cricket and himself and asked that the taxes be paid and a proper return be filed.

"I'm not paying anyone and certainly not you."

"Is there something we can explain to you to help clear up any misunderstandings you might have?" asked Beetle.

"Why is it you always pick on the common folk? And why should I pay you anything when all you do is send my money to Egypt, huh?" It was difficult for Cricket to take the man as a threat with that high pitched voice.

"Talk to your congressman about where they send the money, not us."

"I just don't like the way things are set up."

"You're confusing Congress and the IRS. We do what Congress tells us to do. That's what gets me about you protesters. You're fighting the wrong people. You ought to be writing your congressman." The big man was silent as if he were thinking about what was just explained to him. "We're going to give you one more chance to pay before we take enforcement action."

"I don't have anything so I don't really care," replied Miller. Beetle signaled the wrecker driver who started the hook-up.

"Mr. Miller, we're taking possession of your car. May we have the keys?"

"No. And, I'm reporting you." Beetle and Cricket ignored the words and proceeded to issue the two forms they had previously completed.

"You can't take Betsy, can you?"

"Don't want to, but li'l Betsy's going for a ride." The wrecker driver was backing his truck to the front of the VW bug when he struck the car.

"Hey! Easy with her," shouted Miller.

"It's not your car anymore," explained Cricket.

"You're crazy!" The VW began to creep backward a few inches.

"You're a couple of nitwits just trying to get at us poor folk." The VW slipped a couple of inches backwards again as the wrecker driver attempted to get his winch working. Beetle and Cricket turned toward the car and began walking toward it just in time to see the VW roll back a foot and then stop.

"The car's rollin'!" shouted Beetle. The wind was blowing on the bridge so hard that the driver couldn't hear him. The two quickened their pace, never taking their eyes off the car. The car began inching backward with every stride the two revenue officers were taking. They burst into a sprint while the wrecker driver kept his back to the car as he continued working on his faulty winch.

"Stop...my car...Betsy!" yelled Mr. Miller waddling as fast as his plump legs would carry him. The driver freed his winch and turned around just in time to see the tiny car drop over the edge into the crystal clear water. "Betsy!" cried Miller. The VW was gone, bobbing up and down in the deep channel like a rubber ball.

"What are we gonna do? We gotta think quick!"

"Give the car back to him," stated Cricket.

"And tell him we changed our minds?" replied Beetle

"You're catching on." Beetle contemplated the solution.

"Can't."

"The current is gonna take it out to sea." The car bounced like an apple in a barrel as the four looked over the edge.

"I'll have you in court over this. I've got you by the gonads and I'm a squeezing," shouted Miller as he dramatically raised his hand into the air, clenched his fist and shook it.

"You better help us get your car cause if we can't, we're gonna seize something else," explained Beetle. Cricket took off his shoes and shirt, emptied his pockets and removed his watch.

"Hand me the rope." The driver passed him a roll of heavy rope. "Wish me luck," he shouted and then hollered as he ungracefully jumped into the warm, tropical waters. Once the car reached the end of the point, strong rip currents traveling parallel to the shore would quickly push it out to sea. While the accident was clearly not their fault, the protester would look for anything to use against them.

Cricket caught the runaway VW still bouncing and turning

around like a child's play toy. He struggled against the currents as he tried to tie one end of the rope around the bumper. A few more minutes and the car would be beyond reach. Cricket finally tied the rope and began his long swim back.

"My winch can't pull the car up all the way. It'll burn the motor out."

"Don't worry, I'm gonna let the VW float around the point so that you can pull her up over there." Beetle pointed to a flat spot away from the embankment. The driver nodded. "Good work," yelled Beetle, breathing a sigh of relief. The strong currents began to move the car with great speed.

"Start walking the car down the shore," explained the driver.

"Mr. Miller, you'd be wise to help us. You're gonna lose a lot more than this if we can't get the car out." Miller thought about it for a few seconds.

"Wonder how much all those fishing rods are worth?" asked Cricket still catching his breath.

"All right! I never thought I'd see the day I'd be helping the Infernal Revenue Service. Give me the end," demanded Miller. He anchored himself on the shore like a beached whale and began slowly pulling his car out of the sea.

"Don't worry 'bout the engine, my shop will flush it out," shouted the driver. "It'll run like new." Half an hour later the car was hooked to the winch and ready to be towed. Only a little water entered the car but seaweed was everywhere.

"We're gonna take care of your car and get it running again. Pay us the amount on the paperwork and we'll release the lien and you'll get the car back."

"How long do I have?" asked Miller exhausted after his battle with the ocean.

"Next Friday and then it's gone."

"Then my taxes are paid and I'm done."

"Wrong. You've got to file some legitimate returns and then you're clean. Let's go."

"What about me? Who's going to take me back?" asked Miller.

"This is highly irregular, but seeing that you helped and you look like you're gonna drop dead any minute, we'll give you a lift."

They started talking about the ordeal and, somehow, the three began to bond. Even Mr. Miller laughed. He realized that perhaps he had been protesting the wrong group of people.

"Thanks for the lift and I'll see what I can do to come clean with y'all."

Palmetto had a slew of cases to choose from during his detail. Investigations at his level were much more involved and complex. His cases ranged $25,000 on up. Once he had a case for 80 million dollars. He screened each one of his assignments and found the ideal case; a doctor who had been previously indicted in Miami for health insurance fraud and failure to file and pay income tax returns. The doctor had not reported his income to Uncle Sam since his graduation from medical school in 1965. He had served some time at a minimum security prison, but had not paid what was still due the government. The doctor was detected when a small band of revenue officers conducted a "cold canvass." Cold canvass was the term used for going door to door conducting compliance checks of all returns required to file. In the case of the doctor, personal income tax returns and business returns were checked.

Palmetto remained at the office pouring over the two inch thick file and learned that in '78 and '79 an audit assessed $115,000 as additional tax. After tacking on fraud and failure to pay penalty along with interest, the amount totaled $202,000. The file revealed that he was an officer of a closely-held corporation in which the business received all of his income and assets. Very little was left in his name. He alleged that the corporation made the money and not him personally. The IRS, a U. S. Tax Court and a Federal judge took exception to that claim and concluded the doctor's income had been illegally channeled into the corporation. All of his assets were co-mingled with the business so much so that the corporation became the doctor's "alter ego." The two were inseparable based on the revenue officer's investigation.

The doctor's house, valued at more than three-quarters of a million dollars had a mortgage totaling only $60,000 and was still in the corporate name. He hadn't learned his lesson since all of his income was still being funneled back through the business.

Palmetto would spend many long hours compiling evidence to prove the alter ego status. A Federal tax lien would be filed showing the alter ego relationship and then the house seized and sold. But for now, he needed something quick since the alter ego paperwork could take some time. He wanted something that would make an impact not only on the doctor, but in the area. Two average looking vehicles and the household furnishings were listed on the financial statement.

Palmetto arrived at the entrance to the doctor's exclusive Island Resort community and was stopped by a security guard posted at the entrance of the bridge. This was the only way on or off the small island.

"Good morning!" exclaimed the guard dressed in a summer uniform comprised of navy blue shorts and a light blue shirt. His silver hair and matching beard was close to his face. He looked as though he should have been a ship's commander. "And who are you visiting this morning?"

"Dr. Franklin."

"Is he expecting you?" The guard looked over the roster of expected visitors.

"Not exactly. I'm with the IRS."

"May I see your ID?" Palmetto presented the leather case containing his credentials confirming his identity. "I'll call and let him know you're coming." The guard walked back to the air-conditioned booth. Moments later he returned to gather and record vehicle information, length of time he expected to be at the residence and his badge number. A visitor's pass was issued and he was advised to display the paper on his dashboard. Palmetto was given a map of the area and an explanation on how to get there.

The island was "U" shaped according to the map. Each residence was a palatial estate neatly tucked in behind a forest of vegetation with a security wall protecting every house. The doctor's house was the next to last residence on the "U." It, too, was a mansion with wrought iron gates, security cameras, and tropical plants and trees everywhere. As Palmetto pulled up to the gate, a security camera zoomed in and recorded his every movement. Within seconds the gates opened, allowing Palmetto access. Palm fronds brushed his car as he turned onto the cobblestone driveway and up to the entrance. Cats in assorted sizes and colors darted back and forth across the driveway and into the brush. They were everywhere. Palmetto hated cats—their eyes, their carefree independence and especially their fur. He had a phobia about fur. The thought of touching fur would, at times, make him nauseous. He waited a minute until the cats disappeared before getting out of his car. The two-story house was beige stucco and had royal blue canvas awnings. Mammoth clay pots containing orange trees were on each side of the doorway. The cobblestone continued up to the eight-foot solid wood door which was accented with brass hardware. Palmetto noticed the red light on another security camera had observed his presence and paralleled his movements. As he approached the door, a small, round man with thick curly white hair, looking over his gold wire glasses, opened the door.

"Jake Democko, IRS."

"Come in," replied the doctor who was dressed in his stocking feet and was donning a silk robe. "I'd be at work today if it weren't for these sinuses of mine. All this beautiful weather and I've got a sinus infection. Please, come in." The two walked into a spacious living room with cathedral ceilings and unique skylights. The rear of the house had a large bay window overlooking the island. Tied to the dock was a 42-foot sport fishing boat. Palmetto looked, but couldn't see the boat registration. The living room floors were made of imported Italian marble. Turn-of-the-century paintings decorated the walls.

"I know why you're here, but I can't pay. Can we make a deal?"

"What kind of deal are you talking about?" asked Palmetto wondering if the good doctor was going to offer him a bribe.

"You know what I'm talking about," remarked the doctor displaying a bit of his temper.

"No, I'm afraid I don't. Why don't you explain it to me."

"You people make deals every day. Reduce the interest here, cut a few penalties there and once, an associate even told me that they accepted whatever this one guy could pay. That's right. He owed about seventy thousand dollars and the IRS wiped the slate clean for only five thousand dollars. I want one of those deals," demanded the doctor as he folded his arms and sat back in his high back Victorian-styled chair.

"You're referring to an Offer-in-Compromise."

"Well, tell me how it works cause I want one."

"You have to offer me the equity in all of your assets, the house, furnishings, jewelry, the boat, the cars and anything else of value. But..." Palmetto hesitated. He got a glimpse of the doctor's temper and knew he was going to blow a fuse when he finished explaining.

"But what?" The doctor's voice increased a few decibels. Here it comes thought Palmetto.

"Because of public policy we can't accept one from you."

"Public policy? What's public policy?"

"If accepting an offer from you to settle your tax would be frowned upon by the general public then the Director wouldn't accept one. You were convicted on tax evasion." The doctor looked around ready to explode. "I've looked at your financial statement and, quite frankly, you own some sizable assets."

"You mean the corporation owns the assets, don't you?"

"Are you going to start that line of thinking again. You served time once for it so I suggest..." Palmetto was cut off.

"I was wrongly accused," shouted the doctor as he dramatically rose to his feet shaking his index finger high into the air. "You guys wanted to target a doctor." He returned to his seat.

"I don't suppose it had anything to do with the fact that you committed Medicare fraud or that you didn't file any tax returns or the way you accounted for your money, did it?"

"You think this is such a good system we have here?" asked the doctor.

"I'm not here to swap philosophical differences with you. Either we discuss payment or the conversation is over," informed Palmetto. He had had enough of the good doctor.

"You're just like the agents I dealt with before. Get out of here, you loser!" The doctor once again rose to his feet. Palmetto stood and looked the doctor in the eyes.

"I'm taking enforcement action unless the full amount is paid by Thursday morning. Here's my card."

"Get out of here!" This time the doctor's petite wife came rushing out. "Get me my pills, my pills...hurry!" He fell back into his chair clutching his heart. Within seconds his wife returned and slipped a small white pill under his tongue.

"Please leave, whoever you are. My husband is a very sick man. Can't you see that?"

"Ma'am, this is the last effort the IRS will make to get your husband to pay voluntarily." Palmetto gave her a notice demanding the full amount or distraint action would be taken. "Pay it by Thursday and you'll never see me again. Ignore it and your lifestyle, as you know it, will change. Good day."

Palmetto escorted himself out of the house making as many mental notes as he could about the fixtures and furniture. As he walked up to his car, several large fluffy cats were comfortably resting on the hood and roof of his rental. "Get out of here you nasty fur balls. Scat...scat!" He waved his arms about, but to no avail. The cats had made up their minds that what they wanted was rest and Palmetto's car would do just fine. Palmetto, realizing the hopelessness of the situation, picked up a dead palm frond and struck at the cats, completely missing them and denting the car. "Why are there cats?" he mumbled.

Palmetto made it to the Island's entrance and walked over to question the guard. He wanted to know if there were any sensitive issues about the doctor or his family which might have an adverse impact on the IRS when he seized. Doing the right thing when it looks wrong can be fatal in the IRS.

"I take it your meeting didn't go very well." Palmetto nodded.

"Does he own any weapons?"

"Just his temper. It'll probably kill 'em one day."

"I saw a Sport Fisherman docked out back. You have the registration number?" The guard thumbed through a small box and retrieved the number. "Can you tell me what else is in the house?"

"He's got a fortune in art...he's a collector, or at least his wife is."

"Any other cars?"

"No, that's it."

"He's got to have a safe in that house. Any idea where?"

"Don't know the location, but I can give you the name of the company who installed it." The guard was anxious to help. The doctor had fussed at him one too many times. Finally, pay back.

While Palmetto would like to collect the account in full the idea of enforcement action on this tiny island was much more appealing since it would have greater impact on compliance in the area. He returned to his office leaving the front door of the muggy building open. A rear window was then propped up. A phone call to the South Miami office was made. He would get another revenue officer to secure a Writ of Entry from the magistrate so that he could enter the residence and seize the contents of the house. To seize an asset which was on private property required a writ. If the asset was located in a public area, no writ was necessary. The revenue officers would consult IRS attorneys who would review their requests, walk it over to the U.S. Attorney's office who would get the magistrate to sign. Depending on the magistrate, the revenue officer would or would not have to appear and give testimony.

Palmetto spent the rest of the day pouring over the file, courthouse records, mortgage holders, boat and car registrations and talking to the safe company.

***

It was late afternoon when Murdock turned into an overnight traveler park in Tavernier, a small community immediately south of Key Largo. He followed the one lane, blacktop road to the end of the park. Several pop-up campers, motor homes and small mobile homes shared space with coconut palms. A few people stayed year round, but most were just vacationing. Murdock approached a 60-foot mobile home which had a Florida room attached. The trailer faced a private lagoon. Lobster traps, rope and styrofoam balls, used to mark the location of the traps, cluttered the small yard. Murdock knocked on the jalousie door. The sound of the loose glass made a racket. Murdock walked around to the rear of the mobile home.

"Anyone home?" shouted Murdock who returned to the front. Murdock knocked again. Still no answer. The gentle revving of a well-maintained diesel engine caught his ear. He turned and saw an old, white lobster boat chugging its way to the private dock in the lagoon. Large black letters covered the boat's transom forming the name *Amanda*. After several minutes of negotiating the pilings, a slim, bronze-colored man wearing a red bandanna and a gold earring emerged from the boat. Murdock walked towards the man who was busy wrapping and tying the thick rope to the dock.

"Excuse me, sir," shouted Murdock. The man continued tying his knots. "Excuse me, I'm looking for some fresh lobster." The man hesitated, trying to place the familiar voice. He slowly turned and looked up through his dark, pilot-styled glasses.

"We'll, I'll be," replied the man stroking his golden beard. He removed his sunglasses and stood up. "It's been a long, long time."

"Too long," replied Murdock extending his hand and smiling.

The man was Dwight Evans, an ex-revenue officer who was hired the same day as Murdock. The two had worked closely since their assignment to the Fort Lauderdale office. Off the job, they spent most of their time together fishing, skin diving and boating, while their wives socialized with each other. The two were even with one another at the hospital when their daughters were born four years ago. The pressures of the job became too great and Dwight started drinking. His drinking began to interfere with his job and, more importantly, his wife divorced him after realizing he would never stop. She took their two children back to Ohio where they were originally from and tried to make a new life. Dwight yearned for the life he once enjoyed and joined AA in an effort to get his family back. After a year of abstinence, he pleaded with his wife to return. During the few weeks that followed, while his wife was considering the move back to Florida, their daughter was fatally injured when a drunk driver struck her car. The wife blamed Dwight for the death of their daughter and never returned to Florida. He knew if he hadn't been a drunk his family would never have left and his daughter would still be alive. A month after her death, he overdosed on pills. He would have died had his neighbor not spotted him through the screen door. After his release from the hospital, he immediately resigned from the IRS and moved to his uncle's trailer park in the Keys, seeking relief from the unrelenting pain. Murdock tried to keep in touch, but Dwight wouldn't have anything to do with it. Murdock thought he'd try again especially since the daughter's birthday was today.

Dwight had severed all of his contacts with the people he knew. The people who reminded him of the job he hated, the way he was, and the reason why his daughter was no longer alive.

Dwight finally reached out and shook Murdock's hand and the two embraced.

"Fresh lobster you say? How many pounds?"

"Enough to get me through tonight," replied Murdock. The two laughed.

"You're gonna have to work for this meal. Help me unload the boat." Murdock couldn't have been happier. He detected Dwight's enthusiasm. After climbing aboard he began emptying the holding bins. Hundreds of lobster had been caught. The copper-brown, spiny crustaceans snapped their tails and made a high pitched sound.

After a short trip to the market with the lobster, they returned to the trailer. The evening's lobster meal was the best Murdock had tasted. Perhaps, Murdock thought, it had something to do with being with his old and dear friend again.

"So what brings you to the Keys?"

"Ol' Davenport wanted me out of his hair for awhile."

"Is he still a spineless jellyfish?" Murdock nodded. Pictures of Dwight's family were scattered about the small living room. An 8" x 10" photograph of his daughter hung on the wall.

"Anything exciting going on these days?"

"Not really. Things are worse. Telephone lines being pulled, no supplies, no desks."

"No desks?"

"We've got MOWS, Multiple Occupancy Work Stations. They're tables with one small pen and pencil drawer." Dwight laughed and shook his head. Dwight's laughter warmed Murdock. He hadn't heard it in a long time.

"What about you? How's the lobster fishing?"

"It's a clean, honest living and no idiots or sad stories to deal with. At the end of the day you feel like you really earned your money. Hard work, but I like it."

Over the next several hours the two talked about old times off the job and about opening a restaurant one day. It was getting late and Murdock had another long, hot day ahead of him.

"I wish you'd keep in touch. Beth and I miss you. We're not that far away," remarked Murdock.

"I'll try. But you wouldn't believe how busy I am down here. When I'm not lobstering I'm doing some electrical work. You know, you're always welcome to visit Amanda and me." Murdock paused. He wasn't certain if he had heard Dwight correctly. Surely, Murdock thought, Dwight meant Amanda, his boat.

Dwight stood up and walked over to the refrigerator and removed a birthday cake bearing four candles and the name "Amanda." He placed the cake on the table and began lighting the candles. Murdock was motionless. He didn't know what to do. He wanted to leave. An eerie feeling came over him as goose bumps covered his arms.

"Before you go Bill, help me celebrate Amanda's birthday. She's happy you're here." A tightness developed in Murdock's throat. He was speechless...frozen. Dwight finished lighting the fourth candle, picked the cake up and walked halfway down the hall to the first bedroom. "Bill, help me celebrate." Dwight turned the light on. Murdock remained seated while his mind flashed back to Nam. It was his first flash back in nine years.

He was on patrol near the Laos and South Vietnam border, not far from Da Nang. His squad had one mission—destroy the most vicious band of VC's responsible for hundreds of the most gruesome killings of men, women and children seen in Vietnam. The killings were the VC's way of psyching out the American and South Vietnamese soldiers. Although the monsoon weather conditions reduced visibility to less than four feet, the small band of U. S. Army Rangers, led by Murdock, pushed on.

Murdock came to a clearing in the dense brush and waited for the remainder of his patrol. He signaled the others who understood his every movement and gesture. They immediately spread out. The driving southwest rain felt like needles piercing their face and hands. While walking through the clearing he saw the silhouette of a quonset hut and again signaled to the patrol. Murdock took a few more steps and slipped. Unable to catch his balance, he fell. His hands sunk into a partially decomposed body of a child. Murdock thought he would loose his mind. While the pounding rain quickly washed the remains off of him, the memory would last a lifetime. He watched the erosive rain wash away the rest of the child.

Murdock was numb, but continued toward the hut wiping his hand on his pants. Numerous other bodies were found—most of them children. Sadness and shock overwhelmed him and, momentarily, he was motionless. As he approached the hut, he could hear a woman's voice. She was singing. Notwithstanding the heavy rains, stench emanated from the quonset hut. He cautiously approached the entrance armed with his combat .45 calibre pistol. Inside, a dehydrated mother was sitting down, stroking her daughter's long dark hair. The woman was totally oblivious to Murdock's presence. She held the girl close to her as she quietly sang and gently rocked back and forth.

The little girl had been slaughtered along with the other children several days earlier. Murdock learned from a patrol member that the heads of the village men had been stuck on poles and strategically placed throughout the area. Murdock was getting close to his target. He attempted to communicate with the woman in her native tongue, but there was no response. She had been sitting in her own excrement for days and, in Murdock's opinion, she would never recover. How could she? Murdock lowered his head and left the dwelling. He signaled a patrol member who then entered the hut and a shot rang out, extricating the woman from her devastating sorrow.

Murdock cried that night. He prayed for the innocent people who had been murdered merely because they wanted to warn Murdock and similar patrols to keep away.

Murdock's flashback ended. He was in a cold sweat. He stood up and slowly walked down the hallway. He could hear Dwight faintly singing. He hesitated just outside the bedroom and collected his thoughts. As he entered the room his eyes immediately focused on Dwight who was kneeling along side a small bed which was covered with stuffed animals. The smell of smoke from the candles permeated the room. A 16" x 20" portrait of Amanda at age two was positioned against the wall in the center of the bed. Dwight, after staring at the picture for several minutes, bowed his head and cried. Murdock placed his hand on Dwight's shoulder and tried to help him up, but Dwight refused.

Within minutes Dwight fell asleep with his head on Amanda's bed, the rest of him was on the floor. Murdock helped him into the small bed and placed the cake back into the refrigerator. Unable to leave his friend, Murdock spent the night on the living room sofa and cried. This time for his friend who had lost his mind.

8

Murdock overslept the next morning. He was drained from the prior, emotionally charged night. He cautiously opened his eyes and, for a brief moment, wasn't sure where he was. A ceiling fan rattled as the circulating air cooled his sweaty body. Slowly, he sat erect on the sofa. Rubbing his hands through his wavy locks of hair, Murdock collected his thoughts.

"Dwight!" shouted Murdock. There was no answer. He knew Dwight was lurking in the shadows of insanity. Murdock had toed that fine line his last three months in Nam. He forced himself up and walked down the hallway toward the first bedroom where he had left Dwight. He peeked inside the room, but no one was there. He continued his search down the hallway to the master bedroom.

"Dwight?" He knocked on the door and still no response. Murdock slowly turned the knob and opened the squeaky door. The bed was made and the room was neat. He breathed a sigh of relief. Within a couple of minutes Murdock located a note on the kitchen table:

"Bill, thank you for caring about us. You will always be a special friend. I have to keep her alive in my mind. Whoever said time is the great healer lied. At least with me it doesn't help. I'll try and stay in touch."

Murdock folded the note and placed it in his wallet.

He proceeded back to his motel room in Key Largo and checked the Key West office's answering machine. The recording had two messages on it. The first one was from Palmetto requesting a meeting at Ernie's motel in Marathon to discuss his upcoming seizure of Dr. Franklin's worldly possessions. The second message was from Ernie informing Murdock of what he had accomplished. Murdock then called the Fort Lauderdale office.

"What's up, Frank?"

"I'm glad you finally called. How's the vacation?"

"It's gonna work out better than I thought. The weather couldn't be nicer. How are things there?"

"All right, I guess." Murdock detected Frank's tone.

"What's the matter?"

"Pete's on extended sick leave."

"What happened?"

"Taxpayer killed himself at his sale the other day. Really messed him up—he almost got it." Murdock was silent.

"Is he going to be okay?"

"I don't know. Got a feeling he's gonna resign."

"I'm sorry to hear that. Must've been really bad."

"It was."

"I'll call him in a few days," stated Murdock.

"He'll like that," replied Frank.

"What else is bothering you?" He knew Frank too well.

"All but one trainee quit yesterday."

"All of them!"

"But one," replied Frank optimistically. "...and I think he's gonna be a good one, too."

"The trainees were at the sale with you?"

"You got it."

"...and Davenport blames you?"

"Bingo!"

"Don't take it from him, Frank."

"Oh, I won't...you know me," Frank replied sarcastically.

"Something happen already?" Frank sighed.

"Guess I shouldn't have said all of what I did but...there's some good news. Davenport gave me a couple of days off to think about it. Nice of him, huh?" Murdock grinned.

"Got some bad news for ya about Willie," added Frank.

"Let me guess, he filed a protest over the seizure."

"He's dead. Not sure how he died, yet." Murdock was surprised.

"Who notified you?" asked Murdock.

"Police found your seizure paperwork on his table and called."

"Guess we'll have to wait for the coroner's report."

"Well, that's a little tricky. Police think someone clubbed him in the house and then tossed him out back. After a few days of no one feeding his dogs and Willie ripening...the dogs..." Murdock cut him off.

"Don't tell me anymore. I'm about to eat spaghetti." Frank laughed. "Just let me know if you find out anything."

"When I dropped the charts off to him he looked relieved." Murdock was in thought.

"Okay, thanks and keep me posted. How's Melissa?"

"She's still with her mom. I'm not sure when she's coming back," replied Frank disappointedly.

"She's still upset?"

" 'Fraid so. She said she can't take the worrying anymore. She did say she loved me, but just can't stand seeing me hurt again."

"You can't blame her."

"She wants me to come up."

"You going?"

"What would I do there? All I know is police work and this."

"She give you any ideas on how to earn a living?"

"Oh yeah, she's good at telling me what to do. Get this, her father wants to teach me how to run his furniture company. He'd like to keep it in the family. Melissa's an only child...you guessed that by now didn't you?" Murdock grinned.

"Could you make a living from it?"

"It's a big outfit...lots of money."

"Might not be too bad," replied Murdock.

"Yeah, but a furniture salesman?"

"You're looking at it all wrong, a furniture magnate!" declared Murdock.

"I'd lose my mind. I need the action. This is gonna sound corny, but I get satisfaction knowing I'm doing something worthwhile. I don't think I could be happy working in a furniture company."

"I hear what you're saying, but every once in a while I wish I had an out. Something else to go into," replied Murdock.

"I don't know what's gonna happen. Guess it's up to her."

"Anything else going on?" asked Murdock.

"Crazy Lawrence is being sued."

"What did he do this time?"

"An air conditioning company bounced a few checks on him and moved without telling him. He goes out early to this warehouse thinking the company was still there and locks it up. 'Bout three-hours later he gets a call from a man claiming his ice cream truck was inside, not the air conditioning business."

"Did Lawrence let him in?"

"Not 'til the next day. By the time Lawrence unlocked the warehouse, the guy's entire inventory of ice cream had melted."

"That wasn't Lawrence's fault."

"Well, the ice cream man claims he was trying to get in the day before to check his generators."

"Yep, he's wrong again," observed Murdock.

"Now the guy claims Lawrence told him it was good the Nutty Buttys melted because he was gonna shove one where the sun don't shine."

"That's our Lawrence. Maybe Davenport will appreciate me when I get back. Is Julia around?"

"Yeah, hold on. Call me sometime." Frank signaled to Julia.

"Bill who?" she asked jokingly.

"So how are ya?"

"Just fine. I'm selling those registers today. Thought I'd get CI to attend for protection."

"Good idea. Let them know Genovesi will be there. They probably know him." While CI was IRS's criminal investigators, they also provided protective service for the revenue officers when requested.

"I finished the assessment against Farmer. If you see the Porsche we can seize it," informed Julia.

"What about the house?" asked Murdock.

"I still have some paperwork to do on it. But it won't be long."

"I checked the house out. It's beautiful. Two stories, octagonal shaped and right on the water."

"Was anyone there?" she asked.

"The neighbor tells me that toward the end of each month a small crowd gathers and then they leave after a few days. Sounds like Farmer shows up."

"What makes you think he's showing up?"

"The Porsche is there."

"Be careful," cautioned Julia. "It doesn't sound right to me." Julia was concerned because she knew Murdock. She knew he would do just about anything to get the job done. While Murdock would not work outside the law, he would operate on the fringes of the gray area whenever possible and when it was needed.

"I found the deed transferring the property over to Sea Unlimited. It'll be easy to prove the house was transferred to place it beyond our reach," explained Murdock.

"Secretary of State information came back on Sea Unlimited," added Julia.

"Is Farmer an officer?"

"Close. Phillip Ward is the registered agent, Martinez is listed as the Treasurer and Warbington was President up until seventy-seven. Then the charter was amended and Warbington was left off."

"That makes sense," mumbled Murdock.

"What does?"

"Just something Hank told me."

"Hank Goffman?" Julia was a little surprised. "What could Hank tell you about this?"

"A lot, actually. Did you know he has a photographic memory? Anyway, he told me Warbington was presumed dead several years ago. He was laundering in Houston and probably Miami. They never made a positive ID on him, but there was a body on his yacht."

"Couldn't they check his dental records or fingerprints?"

"You're presuming the body had teeth and fingers," replied

Murdock.

"I had to ask," replied Julia. "The business was incorporated in Delaware."

"Delaware?"

"Yeah. Mean anything to you?"

"You ever notice how many yachts show Delaware as their homeport?" asked Murdock.

"Not really."

"Companies get a big tax break from Delaware. Maybe somewhere in Fort Lauderdale there's a yacht registered to Farmer or Sea Unlimited."

"I can get with the Coast Guard," replied Julia as she jotted some notes on her pad.

"You might want to touch base with Customs and the Florida Marine Patrol."

"You think there's a boat?" asked Julia.

"Bet ya a cup of coffee there's one," replied Murdock.

"But you owe me three cups already," reminded Julia. Murdock grinned.

"But this time I'm right."

"You're on."

"Did anyone replace Warbington as President?" asked Murdock. Julia examined the information from the Florida Secretary of State.

"Thomas Farley," she replied.

"Check him out too...and order the corporate return on Sea Unlimited." Annually, each corporation filed Form 1120 to report the income, officers and their wages paid, among other things.

"I'll do it. I still believe the Key Largo house was transferred for some other reason than to beat the IRS," stated Julia.

"It doesn't matter because we can still go after it, but what are you thinking?" asked Murdock.

"Just a hunch, but something else is going on with Farmer. I know we can seize the house, but I don't really think Farmer is even concerned about us. At least he didn't appear concerned when I last talked to him.

"Why wouldn't Farmer be concerned? He owes a chunk of

money," questioned Murdock a little puzzled.

"He had an air about him that we wouldn't be able to touch him."

"Well, we know his association with Warbington alludes to some criminal involvement. I'm anxious to get on with this case. I had the South Miami office issue a summons on the phone company. I may not know who the people are at the Key Largo house, but we're gonna find out who they're talking to."

"I'm checking with the power company to see who's being billed," interjected Julia.

"Good. Do me a favor, have Hank mail me the returns he requested for me. I'll be at this Inn for another two weeks." Murdock gave her the address when he detected Davenport's distinct yelling. What's he on the rampage about now?"

Julia laughed. "Someone took that gross coffee mug of his and won't return it. He's infuriated. Frank told him he thought he saw some old man with the cleaning crew with it."

"That's Frank, keeping things stirred up." Julia laughed.

"The funny thing is Frank told me he took it home with him and turned it into a planter." They both laughed. "He has a nice cactus growing out of it." Julia was laughing so hard her sides hurt.

"Frank wouldn't do that, would he? I do miss the zoo," exclaimed Murdock. "Odd, isn't it?"

"Not really. We all lean on each other. No one else understands what we go through on this job."

"Well, see you later."

"Be careful. Nothing is worth getting hurt or in hot water for, okay?"

"I hear you."

After saying goodbye to Murdock, Julia spotted Hank sitting at his small table tapping his foot.

"Hello, Hank."

"Hello, Jamie." Julia didn't bother to correct the mispronunciation. It was the closest he had come in months. She handed him Murdock's address and asked that he send the returns to him there. She then convened a meeting of the revenue officers who would be helping her sell the registers. Lawrence was instructed to stay close to her during the sale. Frank and Lawrence would help spot bidders in the crowd and answer questions.

Edward Kemtz, also a revenue officer, was asked to assist. Edward kept to himself with few exceptions. He was tall and stately in appearance and seemed to live in three piece suits. His brown hair and thick mustache were always well groomed. His pale skin made his brown, piercing eyes appear even darker. He had been a group manager in West Palm Beach when, two years ago, he decided the pressures of managing a group of revenue officers coupled with what he considered to be a gross lack of appreciation for him was enough, and he went back to the field. While the revenue officer position wasn't an easy one, at least he only had to concern himself with what he was doing and not the activities of twelve other revenue officers. Ed was polite, but a man of few words. His reticence was due to his perception that upper management could care less about group managers or revenue officers. Edward always gave the appearance that he was preoccupied with something which also contributed to his unusual quietness. In such a gregarious office where everyone knew each other's business, Edward Kemtz was an enigma.

Julia and the rest of the revenue officers left the office in three cars and proceeded to the defunct register company. It was another humid day with just enough of an ocean breeze to make the day bearable. When they arrived at the sale site, the temperature inside was in the mid-nineties. The registers were bunched into twenty-seven lots in total and would take about an hour and a half to sell providing everything went well.

After lunch the first of the crowd appeared. Lawrence quickly signed the man in and issued a number which would be used during the bidding. During the next thirty minutes thirty-five more bidders would appear including Carl Genovesi. He wouldn't budge from his father's bar registers. Two associates stood at his side. A slender woman in her thirties approached Julia and Lawrence.

"The 1905 register belongs to my boss. It's an heirloom...we were having some work done on it when the IRS closed the store."

"Who and where is your boss?" inquired Julia.

"He couldn't leave his work so he sent me," stated the well-dressed woman.

"I can't release the register back to you without proof of ownership. I hope you understand."

The woman removed a letter from her purse and presented it to Julia. The letter was typed and contained a message from the alleged owner. Julia read it and passed the paper to Lawrence.

"All this states is what you just told me. It isn't proof of ownership. I'm very sorry," explained Julia.

"Are you still going to sell it?" inquired the woman.

"We're going to have to if this is all you have."

"This is all he has and I don't believe..." suddenly the woman was interrupted by the sound of paper tearing. Lawrence had ripped the note into several pieces and handed them to the woman.

"This note isn't worth the paper it's written on. You'll have to tell your shyster lawyer boss to try harder," claimed Lawrence.

"I can't believe you did that!" exclaimed the woman.

"You can leave now," instructed Lawrence. The woman turned and quickly left the shop. "Don't worry Julia, I've dealt with her boss before. He's a ruthless, jackass attorney. He'll actually appreciate what I did."

"I really wish you hadn't done that," reprimanded Julia.

"Sorry. Something just comes over me when I'm dealing with attorneys. I'll behave."

Edward signaled to Julia from across the crowded, steamy room. Time to read the opening statement which informed the bidders that the merchandise was being sold "as is" and "where is" without any guarantees, expressed or implied. While almost everyone in the room had attended previous IRS sales and could recite the statement, it had to be read and questions answered. Julia finished reading.

"Are there any questions?" asked Julia knowing what the response would be.

"Are there any liens?" asked one of the forty thieves. He knew the answer. He did the courthouse research on it, but his question served a purpose.

"As I just read Mr. Friedman, to the best of our knowledge, no." Julia looked around. "If there are no other questions, we'll begin the auction."

"But I have a question," queried Mr. Friedman who was dressed in bright yellow and brown plaid Bermuda shorts, matching yellow knee socks and genuine alligator shoes.

"Yes, Mr. Friedman, what can I clarify for you?"

"Did I hear you say there are no warranties?"

"Yes, I did."

"I'm interested in the digital registers, but there's no electricity to test them. How do I know they're working?" continued the shrewd little man as he planted a seed of doubt in the minds of the bidders.

"You don't. But, I can tell you the owner of the store has completed work on them as indicated by the tag attached to the cord," replied Julia.

"But that still doesn't tell me if they're working."

"Mr. Friedman, it's just like the other sales you've attended and purchased our equipment without trying it. You must've been satisfied or you wouldn't be here now, anxious to buy more."

"So all right now. Let's get on with it...get on with the sale," acquiesced the little man.

Edward stepped up to the front of the crowd. "Lot number one is being offered. It's a one-of-a-kind treasure—a 1905 National Register in what appears to be perfect working condition," explained Edward. He was careful not to state that it was in perfect condition, only that it appeared to be in perfect condition.

Lawrence hit the sale key on the antique just as Edward finished his statement. The sale key activated the bell and sent the cash drawer flying. A corner of the drawer hit Lawrence's left testicle. Julia quickly went to Lawrence's aid as he bent over clutching his swollen scrotum. The crowd erupted in laughter with Frank laughing the loudest. Julia was able to usher him out the back door just as his first in a series of obscenities intended for the crowd were uttered. Lawrence spent the remainder of the sale lying down in the rear seat of Julia's car with chubby legs spread apart and up in the air. Lots one through eleven moved quickly.

"Lot number twelve is up next. As you can see, there are six beautiful 1930 bar registers from a bygone era. What do I hear for these rarities?" asked Edward.

"Five hundred dollars," stated Genovesi.

"Six hundred dollars," responded another of the forty thieves.

"One thousand," replied Genovesi rather calmly. The man bidding against him looked over in amazement and hesitated.

"One thousand dollars was the last bid. A generous offer but not nearly what these gems are worth. Do I hear fifteen hundred dollars?" There was silence in the room. "Surely these registers are worth fifteen hundred. I'm looking for fifteen hundred dollars."

"Eleven hundred dollars," shouted another of the forty thieves.

"I've got eleven hundred. Looking for fifteen. I've got eleven hundred dollars. Do I hear fifteen hundred dollars?" pleaded Edward.

"Two thousand dollars," replied Genovesi. He wasn't as calm. Several of the forty thieves had their calculators out figuring their anticipated profit of margin should they bid any higher. Edward, being an experienced auctioneer, did not want to give them time to think about their next bid. He wanted to generate a feeding frenzy. The forty thieves were captured by Genovesi's interest. They weren't sure how much the registers were worth, but they presumed their worth not realizing the sentimental value the registers were to Genovesi.

"Two thousand, one hundred dollars," shouted another of the forty thieves.

"Three thousand dollars," bid Genovesi. The handful of interested bidders again began to calculate. Seeing this, Carl Genovesi quickly responded and upped his last bid.

"Change that to four thousand!" offered Genovesi.

"Four thousand one hundred," stated the littlest but richest of the forty thieves who gambled he was on to something.

"Six thousand dollars," countered Genovesi without batting an eye.

"So you can have it!" exclaimed the little man as he threw his hands up into the air. Edward would have been satisfied with the $2,000 offer. He closed the bidding and sold the bar registers to an anxious Carl Genovesi.

At the end of the sale Genovesi approached Julia and Edward. He was flanked by two of the biggest and meanest looking men either one had ever seen. One man pulled out a wad of crisp one hundred dollar bills and counted out sixty of them. He still had a wad left.

"I'm pleased I got my registers back, but not how I had to go about it," grumbled Genovesi. "I'm not upset with the Internal Revenue Service. You have your jobs to do. But Mr. Farmer is a different story. Did you know he's still in the area?"

"No, we didn't," replied Julia.

"He's still around," informed Genovesi. Julia finished counting the $6,000 and issued him a certificate of sale for the registers. "Proof the registers are mine and it only cost six thousand dollars!"

"There was nothing we could do," remarked Edward.

"Believe me, I understand. I understand. It's just that Farmer annoys me." His two associates quickly and easily picked up the heavy registers and stored them in the trunk and rear seat of the Mercedes. "I'll find Farmer," sneered Genovesi, as he was whisked away.

"Nice sale, Julia. How much?" inquired Edward.

"Twenty-seven thousand," she replied with a smile. The minimum amount she needed to sell the property, based on the value of the seized property, was $13,000. This number was arrived at through two different appraisals which were then averaged. This figure was sent to the taxpayer for concurrence. A no response, such as Farmer's, was considered agreement. In arriving at the minimum bid, the IRS uses a standard formula which takes into account the age, salability and other pertinent factors. If the minimum bid had not been reached, the IRS would have had to do one of two things: bid the property in for the United States, credit the taxpayer's account and hold another sale hoping to recoup all of the credit given the taxpayer or release the property back to the taxpayer. Neither one was desirable.

"It's one-thirty. I'll buy lunch at Shooters," offered Julia.

"I'll call and see if Pete can join us," replied Frank. Edward passed since he had a few more stops to make.

"How come he won't go to lunch with us?" asked Frank.

"Don't know. Maybe it's us," replied Julia.

"Us?"

"Nah!" exclaimed the two simultaneously. Julia was bundling the last stack of one hundred dollar bills and stuffing them into a small canvas bag along with the certificates of sale she had issued. The heat was unbearable. Everyone was drenched. All twenty-seven lots had been sold and, as far as sales go, it was an orderly one.

As they exited, Lawrence was still lying down on the back seat of Julia's car, legs up in the air and resting on the front and rear seats.

"Lawrence, isn't that the dying cockroach position," asked Edward. Lawrence made an obscene gesture and uttered profanity at him.

"At least his disposition has improved," remarked Edward.

"I noticed that too. He didn't call me a WOP this time."

A stream of obscenities erupted from Lawrence. "I bruised them..." He clutched himself. "...leave me alone."

"Nothing worse than a revenue officer with bruised testicles. Anything else get it?" asked Frank.

"I'm not sure honey, come on over and take a look," quipped Lawrence with a smirk.

"Now, now, boys. Let's go," instructed Julia. "Lawrence and I are going to the bank. We'll be there."

Frank met Pete at Shooter's in the shade of a coconut palm. A waitress wearing shorts promptly took their order. The two were speechless for a moment. Her tan was awesome.

"I'd sure like to know where she sunbathes," remarked Frank.

"You'll like this one—I was out fishing last weekend and came up alongside this sailboat—these women were sunbathing with absolutely nothing on," whispered Pete.

"What's this place coming to?" Frank shook his head with a smile. "Maybe I'll take you up on fishing after all. You really see that kind of thing?"

"Kind of like fishing, you just never know when they're gonna be around." Frank smiled.

"There goes Edward," observed Frank. "Something's not right with him." Frank's police mind was working overtime again.

"I know whatcha mean. Here he is, divorced, paying alimony and child support and he can still afford to drive a new Beamer," replied Pete.

"Don't forget his Rolex or those exotic vacations. Hey, wouldn't that be something?" thought Frank out loud.

"What's that?"

"Oh nothing. I'm sure he just invests his ninety dollars a week he gets to keep after alimony very wisely," snickered Frank.

"This place sure beats New York City," noted Frank as he watched the sailboats navigate down the Intracoastal.

"You don't miss it?"

"Police work, yes—the city, no. After living down here who could go back? I tell my friends back home that there really is another way to live. They don't have to catch the Staten Island Ferry every day for the rest of their lives." There was silence between them. "To be honest with ya, I'd still be up there if this thing hadn't happened." Frank knocked on his leg.

"You ever think about leaving here?"

"Never. Florida's home for this native. Besides, I hate the cold."

"What do you do to relax?" asked Frank.

"I fish a little. Spend most of my time with Victoria. I get her Tuesday, Thursday and every other weekend. It's not enough, but what are you gonna do?"

"You gonna be okay?" asked Frank.

Pete did not look very well. "Oh, yeah," he replied.

"Why is it a revenue officer's first child is always a girl?" Pete laughed. He knew Frank was a nut. Frank continued. "It's true... 'bout ninety percent have girls first."

"And what about the other ten percent?" inquired Pete knowing Frank would have an answer he deeply believed was true.

"The kid ain't theirs."

"How long have you been like this? Ever since Melissa left?" Frank nodded yes. "I can't wait 'til she comes back," said Pete.

"You sound like Murdock. I think she's filing for divorce if I don't go back and help her father in his furniture company."

"I'm sorry, I didn't know. Just be thankful you don't have any kids—that's when it really hurts."

"I really wanted kids with her but now, it'll never be. I doubt if I'd ever marry again," replied Frank in a low voice. The two downed another cold brew and leaned back in the wicker chairs.

"You don't know, it may all work out with her. If it doesn't, you'll survive."

"If you don't mind me asking, what happened between you and your wife?"

"To make a very long story short, she wanted more than I could provide. She's very materialistic. We had a nice life, average surroundings, but she wanted more."

"How's she doing now?"

"She's happy. Married a guy in the northeast section. Mercedes, big house...what a view!"

"You've been there?" asked Frank a little puzzled.

"Yeah, when I pick up the kids." Pete looked away for a moment. "It bothers me that some other man is involved in my childrens' lives, but that's all part of divorce. You gotta put the hostility behind you if your kids are gonna turn out all right. Divorce—not what God intended." Pete downed another beer.

"We're calling it a day, aren't we?" inquired Frank as he ordered another pitcher of beer.

"Looks that way, doesn't it?"

"There goes Edward back over the bridge," noted Frank. "Can't miss that custom paint job."

It was Edward. He was approaching the obelisk glass structure which towered higher than any other building in Fort Lauderdale. Edward was in a panic. He was late for a very important meeting with a very influential man, Joel Meyers.

Meyers was rich. He owned almost twenty-five percent of Fort Lauderdale's undeveloped real estate including two office buildings and a marina. He and his wife were the impetus behind many charitable community affairs and donated heavily to political campaigns. Because of his generosity, he was the recipient of many humanitarian awards. He was the frequent guest of politicians both in South Florida and Washington. They were loved by all except for the Internal Revenue Service who knew Joel Meyers' alter ego.

The year he built a wing to a children's hospital in South Florida, philanthropist Joel Meyers was the subject of an intense criminal investigation. The IRS had learned, from its well developed, but very secretive network, that Meyers was involved in kickback schemes with real estate developers from Florida to his home state of New Jersey. During the latter part of 1975, someone in the tight-lipped organization leaked parts of the investigation to the newspaper. The story made the front page and a supervisory criminal investigator lost his job.

The investigation appeared to have come to a halt with that disclosure since a grand jury never convened and no indictments were ever handed down. To the newspaper and public, the case was a dead issue. But to CI, the investigation was very much alive!

Edward Kemtz straightened his tie and glanced in the hallway mirror one last time before entering Meyers' commodious office.

"May I help you?" inquired the secretary.

"Yes, I'm here to see Mr. Meyers."

"Are you Mr. Kemtz?"

"Yes."

"Please go in, he's expecting you."

Edward entered the office. Meyers was standing, gazing out the glass wall which faced the western sky. He looked even more rotund against the huge wall-sized window. The sun glistened off his bald head.

"Sorry I'm late, Mr. Meyers—traffic you know." Edward was nervous. He didn't want to blow the opportunity of a lifetime. Meyers was reticent.

"Everyday I watch these people struggle home—like little ants, running around frantically day in and day out. How do they do it? Stupid fools." Meyers stared out the window a few seconds longer and turned around. Gold wire glasses hugged his bulldog-looking face and his body dripped of gold chains and diamonds. He was a slob, but a wealthy slob which was why Edward tolerated his presence. "Have a seat." Meyers pointed to a plush, blue velvet chair. Edward hesitated. "Please, be comfortable. You're about to free yourself from being an ant." Edward sat down and just stared at the arrogant man. "Would you care for a drink?"

"No...thank you. Let's get on with it," replied Edward in a firm voice.

"I like a businessman. So, we'll do business. Do you have the figures?" Edward opened his worn leather case and removed nine computer printed accounts. Each 5" x 8" paper assembly package represented a separate tax period assessed against the corporation owned by Meyers.

"Here they are," stated Edward as he handed the figures to him. "They include interest and penalty through today."

"Two point two million dollars," whispered Joel Meyers, grinning as he shook his head.

"And here's what I can do for you." Edward passed Meyers a sheet of paper with his computations showing the reductions and savings. The grand total came to over a million and a half in savings for Meyers who sat back in his tall leather chair and smiled. Edward glanced at his watch several times.

"Never be impatient when conducting business—mistakes are made." Meyers reached into his trouser pocket. "Take this key. It'll open the locker at the "Y". You've got the number. There's fifty thousand dollars for you."

"The agreement was two hundred and fifty thousand dollars!"

"The final installment will arrive when my letter of adjustment arrives. When can I expect it?"

"Within sixty days. I'll need a corporate check for the difference before any adjustment can be made." Meyers pulled out a check and made it payable to the Internal Revenue Service. The amount was $700,000.

"We'll be in touch," remarked Meyers. Edward secured the check and half smiled at the secretary as he left. Joel Meyers spun his chair around and once again studied the tiny ants marching homeward.

9

In a small, leased room two floors below Joel Meyers' office three criminal investigators with the IRS turned their elaborate recording devices off upon hearing Edward Kemtz's departure. Desperate to gather as much evidence against Meyers, they convinced a federal judge to authorize a wiretap of Meyers' phones and "bug" his office. Unexpectedly, the special agents netted one of their own—Edward Kemtz. The agents called their supervisor and advised him of the discovery. The office quickly responded by sending seven agents armed with 35mm cameras and telescopic lenses to the "Y". The agents' only concern during this stakeout was concealment during the picture taking since Edward knew them.

The agents arrived at the "Y" in a dark blue van which had mirror coated glass designed for one-way viewing. Edward arrived ten minutes later and entered the building with only a key which he turned constantly in his fingers. The agents' van was filled with the sounds of camera motors turning and clicking. Edward located the locker and opened it. A black athletic bag was inside. His right leg began to shake uncontrollably since he felt certain everyone in the place knew what was going on. He glanced inside the bag and saw the stacks of currency all neat and bundled. His heart pounded and a lump formed in his throat. He broke out in a cold sweat thinking about what he was doing and the caliber of people he was dealing with. People who would not blink an eye at doing bodily harm to him. Especially to someone who was about to double-cross Joel Meyers.

Without any further delay he exited the building and headed toward his car. Excited agents clicked a dozen pictures in less than thirty seconds. They followed him to Century Bank were Edward's first deposit was made.

Once again, a dozen pictures were snapped of Edward going in and out of the bank. Pictures which would be placed on display like an art gallery showing to a federal grand jury. The agents followed Edward home and then proceeded to their lab where the film would be developed and all of the evidence put together for the grand jury presentation. The agents would be requesting another wiretap. This time to tune in on Edward Kemtz's life.

Once inside his residence, Edward placed a call.

"Art?"

"Yes," replied Arthur Cook.

"It's Edward. I've got fifty thousand dollars. I'll get the two hundred thousand when the adjustments take."

"Good, good. Meyers will be true to his word. You can pay me my share out of the fifty you picked up."

"Okay," replied Edward.

"There's going to be a lot more where that came from, believe me. We'll talk later."

Arthur Cook was a manager of a group of revenue agents with the Examination Division of the IRS. Revenue agents were responsible for conducting field audits on large corporations and individuals who had high incomes.

Edward first met Art in the Newark District where both of them started their careers with the IRS. While the two worked in separate and completely different functions with the Service, Art thought their similar humble backgrounds gave them a unique bond.

Joel Meyers had given Art money, lots of money during the past three years in exchange for favorable audits which included refunds from bogus tax shelters for him and his closest associates.

When Art learned of Edward's return to the field and his overall unhappiness of upper management, he immediately seized what he believed to be an excellent opportunity to recruit Edward into this team. Art knew of the large corporate liabilities which had been assessed against Meyers' many corporations prior to his involvement. These accounts had been tied up in litigation and had finally made their way to the Collection Division. Art also knew these million dollar plus liabilities represented a limitless source of opportunities to get rich. An untapped gold mine in bribes and at last he had found a miner! As far as Art and Meyers were concerned, Edward was "in."

***

Murdock checked into Ernie's motel as requested by Palmetto. A large deck overlooked Florida Bay and a partial view of the ocean could be seen from the front picture window. Murdock walked out onto the deck and saw Ernie and Palmetto sitting at a table near the bay. A small fire danced around an aluminum pot. A large brown trash can had been filled with ice cubes which looked more like diamonds as the last of daylight illuminated them. Ernie gave a wave when he saw Murdock. Moments later they were all digging into the diamonds and pulling out the coldest drinks any of them had had in quite some time.

"Where's Beetle and Cricket?" asked Murdock.

"Rounding up some crabs," replied Palmetto with a slight grin. Whenever the South Miami revenue officers traveled to the Keys they would have several "powwows" as they referred to them. It gave them a chance to coordinate their efforts on various cases prior to going out on complicated seizures. It also gave them an outlet.

The sound of an 18-horse marine engine grew closer and closer. The three of them focused on two dark shapes sitting in a sixteen-foot V-hull boat, uttering obscenities because the main entrees had somehow slipped out of their container and were now crawling about the aluminum boat. Several moments passed by before the duo could corral the escapees—well, almost all of them. What the two hadn't noticed was that the largest of the stone crabs had found a nice dark corner and was about to seek revenge. The crab lifted its heavy, shell-armored claw and latched onto Beetle's worn boat shoe. His scream was deafening as the shoe went flying into the air and two of the largest crab claws he had ever seen went swimming to the bottom of the bay.

"If you two are through playing with tonight's dinner, I've got some boiling water I'd like to dip mine in," shouted Palmetto.

That night, over succulent crab and beer chilled to a frosty 36 degrees, they discussed what role each would play during the intricate seizure of the Dr. Franklin's household goods. Palmetto would pick up the Writ of Entry tomorrow while in Miami. He'd also coordinate with CI. The Criminal Investigators would be taken on seizures as a precautionary measure whenever the revenue officer believed the probability for violence was significant. Revenue officers are assaulted more times than any other official in the IRS, more than any other federal occupation. Five hundred assaults were reported this particular year. Many wondered how revenue officers could last thirty years until they could retire.

The five spent most of the evening around the campfire discussing cases, drinking beer, toasting marshmallows and swapping stories. Beetle and Cricket had the most memorable seizure for the day—a pair of parrots valued at $2,000. The birds would be stored in their hotel room until they were sold or redeemed. The only problem was that the birds' vocabulary were limited to: *You wanna apple?*, *You wanna beer?*, *Hello*!, and a few obscenities, which were repeated at various times throughout the night.

By 10:00 p.m., the five decided it was time for bed. Palmetto, Beetle, Ernie and Murdock would tie up a few loose ends tomorrow morning and head home for the weekend. Cricket, having no one to go home to, decided to peruse the islands for the weekend. Cricket was always the last to leave the campfire. He had consumed his usual two dozen beers and began dousing the flames by urinating on the fire. His arc reached seven feet with accuracy. After dousing the flames, he smiled and nodded in contentment. Sparks flew high into the air and seemed to mingle with a wave of twinkling stars that formed the Milky Way.

A commotion by the shoreline caught his attention. A lady in a V-cut dress was standing alone in knee deep water. He swayed and staggered his way toward her looking around to see who she was with, but no one was there. He wasn't certain if she was a figment of his imagination. When he opened his eyes, the lovely woman was still there. As he approached her, she turned and gave him a smile, but did not speak. Her silence enthralled him. The tightly fitted cotton gown and her long, dark hair were dripping wet. A beam of moonlight spotlighted the woman, giving her an ethereal glow and revealing her flawless figure. Cricket thought he must be hallucinating. The magnificent woman, again without a word, dipped into the warm, black ink of Florida Bay.

"You come here often?" asked Cricket still not certain if he was talking to an hallucination.

"No, I'm here tonight because you're here." She let the water saturate her cotton dress. She was awesome, he thought. "Isn't the night tranquil?" Her voice was melodic.

"Yes...yes, very tranquil," he replied in a drunken stupor. He was in awe of her beauty and wouldn't have given the quietness of the night a second thought if not for her. "What are you doing here?"

"I'm here for you." She sounded sincere.

"Me?"

"Yes, you."

"You always swim in your dress?"

"Not always," explained the young woman. She appeared to be in her mid-twenties. Again she flashed Cricket an inviting smile as she squeezed her hair straight back to remove the excess water. Cricket felt an unusual warmth wrapped around his body as if he had been covered in a blanket. His eyes followed her perfect figure.

"Come...take a dip with me. It's relaxing," lured the Lady in White. Was she real? Cricket didn't know and didn't much care. The beer was kicking in and he figured that he had about fifteen more minutes of consciousness. He quickly slipped off his shoes. She was stunning! He hoped that if she was a dream, he wouldn't awake from the illusion until he had completely satisfied his lust.

The woman playfully giggled at his facial expression. Cricket dropped his jeans and exposed his desire. This time the Lady in White gasped.

"I want you, but we cannot be together in that way." Embarrassed by the moment, he quickly pulled his jeans up. "Come to me." Cricket followed her instructions. He tiptoed through the rocky shoreline to her and into the steamy Florida water. He went to embrace her, but she retreated. She knew his thoughts. "Not in that way. Come, sit quietly with me." Cricket collapsed into the ink and then sat erect. She laughed. "Isn't this wonderful?" She leaned back and dipped her entire body again. "I haven't been in these waters since..." she stopped in mid-sentence. "...well, it's been awhile." An incredibly warm and satisfying feeling overwhelmed him as he sat with her. He was having a dialogue with her without speaking. He would think of a question to ask her and she would respond out loud. How could that be, he thought, or was this the result of the booze. A goose-bump-like sensation covered him. His body tingled. What was she doing to him? His legs were shaking. The woman smiled. He finally made his way over to the shoreline and passed out. His experience with the Lady in White and the two dozen beers was more than he could handle.

The heat from the morning sun bonded the viscous vomit and sand to Cricket's body. His eyes were irritated from the beach sand which lined the inside of his eyelids. A pressure squeezed his sponge-like brain. His arms trembled and could barely support him as he struggled to sit up. Screaming gulls sent daggers ripping through the sponge. His tongue felt as though it had been wrapped in burlap along with his mouth and throat.

"Here." A familiar voice emanated from behind him. Beetle was carrying the necessary first aid to get Cricket back on his feet. Beetle passed a large glass of tomato juice and four extra strength pain relievers to his ailing coworker. After downing the medicine, Cricket stuck his arm up signaling Beetle he was ready for his bath. Beetle helped him to the shoreline and gave him a bar of soap. Beetle and Cricket knew the routine all too well. Cricket lathered his body and clothing and rinsed both in the saltwater bath. He squinted and moved his head slowly looking for the Lady in

White. She was not there.

"Met this woman last night...incredible! Just beautiful."

"Why don't you try laying off the brew for awhile," commented Beetle who was concerned about his friend who was more like family to him.

"There was a woman. She was too real for it to be my imagination this time. Said she would be my escort."

"Escort? You going to a party or something?" Beetle played along.

"Not a party...but somewhere." Cricket rubbed his temples.

"Lay off the brew."

"Suppose you're right. This has got to stop, but what a sensation." Cricket, with the help of his friend, rose out of the warm saltwater and dried off.

It was 9:00 a.m. when the others finished breakfast. Palmetto had already put two hours of work in trying to line up everyone that might be needed for next week's seizure of Dr. Franklin's goods.

"Got everyone we'll need except for the movers. They can't make it until Tuesday morning. They're coming in from Miami Monday night so we'll seize early Tuesday morning. Is that okay with everyone?" Everyone nodded in agreement except for Cricket who had found a picnic table and decided to stretch out in the warmth of the morning sun.

"Monday evening I'll be back in Key West. This'll give me a little time in Fort Lauderdale to check on a couple of cases of mine," remarked Murdock. He was anxious to see if any new information had arrived on the Farmer case.

"We'll all meet at your hotel for dinner Monday night and go over this case one more time. Someone from CI will be here, too. See you then," added Palmetto.

***

Alena's father called another telephone number where she might be, but to no avail. Alena was gone. He regretted his words with her two weeks earlier and hoped he could find her. He needed to apologize. He loved her with every ounce in him and he agonized over the fact that there was nothing he could do, but hope she would call him. He raised Alena by himself after her mother left a week before Alena's twelfth birthday. Alena was devastated and he did everything humanly possible to be a loving, caring father. He never remarried or even had a relationship owing to the pain he suffered from his wife's suicide.

Where was Alena, he thought, and how could he help her if she wouldn't keep away from the Cartel's financial attorney. The only thing he was certain of was that Ward was going down and, if Alena didn't keep her distance, she might be indicted as well. He spent the rest of the evening trying to strategize how he could continue to stall a federal investigation by the IRS, FBI and DEA.

10

The weekend with his wife and children passed too quickly and Murdock found himself back at work sooner than he wanted Monday morning. He slipped into the Fort Lauderdale office early before heading out to Key West. He concealed himself from Davenport by sitting in the rear of the office behind a bright red cloth divider and read his mail. Unfortunately, Davenport was also in early.

"Murdock!" shouted Davenport from within the glass cage. Murdock ignored him. He couldn't have seen him.

"Murdock!" He was more definitive this time. "Get in here." Murdock entered the office holding about eight inches worth of incoming mail which had been piling up for him.

"Have a seat. Must I remind you where you're supposed to be?"

"Thought I'd stop in and check on a couple of my large dollar cases before heading out. I'll be going in a minute." Large dollar cases were defined as having a minimum tax delinquency of $250,000.

"You're not working on Julia's case are you?" Murdock looked at him without comment. "...because if you are I'll have your butt! Understand?" The veins in Davenport's neck were protruding. It was time to go.

"May I leave?"

"Yeah, you can leave." Murdock started to exit his office when he noticed Davenport drinking from a Styrofoam cup.

"What happened to your coffee cup?" He knew good and well Frank had turned it into a planter.

"What do you know about it?" Davenport's blood pressure was rising.

"Know about what?" The phone rang. Davenport covered the receiver.

"Get out of here and get back to the Keys!" Into the phone he said, "Good morning, chief. Things couldn't be better," expressed Davenport in such a cheery voice that made him seem warm and personable. Murdock left the glass cage and was greeted to his surprised by happy coworkers. Murdock's presence brought a feeling of order to the hectic and, at times, confusing office. Davenport despised this most of all about Murdock.

"Some tan you have. Must be tough duty down there," quipped Julia as she turned the corner. Murdock grinned.

"So where's Frank?"

"He's out fishing with Pete."

"How's Pete doing?"

"We met him for lunch yesterday. He needs time." Murdock acknowledged the statement with a nod. He then spotted Lawrence walking over from the mail cabinet with an arm full of paperwork.

"Morning Lawrence."

"This place sucks," mumbled Lawrence as he passed Murdock without acknowledging him.

"A constant," responded Murdock. "Got some information on the Farmer case for you. Let's go in here." Murdock entered the conference room and spread the case out.

"Melissa filed for divorce," stated Julia.

"When did she do that?" Murdock was a little surprised.

"Friday."

"How's he taking it?"

"It's hard to tell. You'd probably know if you saw him."

"Tell 'em I'll call him."

Murdock began listing the information. The first item was from the post office. The Miami Shores listing for Sea Unlimited was marked “No Good.” A change of address for the corporation had been made in early 1979. The new address was a post office box in South Miami.

“We’ll find out who made the change and what the physical address is,” commented Julia. The next item was a response from Florida Power and Light Company. FPL indicated that the utility to the Largo house was transferred by Farmer to Sea Unlimited in care of Phillip Ward.

“So Ward is Sea Unlimited?” asked Murdock.

“He’s definitely an active player in it,” remarked Julia.

“Any returns come in yet on the officers or corporation?”

“Hank sent something to your motel last week. These came in Thursday.” Julia passed two personal income tax returns belonging to Warbington and Ward. Martinez hadn’t filed.

“This is what I wanted.” The two men listed their home address as being the Miami Shores P.O. Box of Sea Unlimited. Warbington’s occupation was listed as “investor” and Ward was listed as an attorney. Murdock studied the attached Schedule K which listed a partnership of Ward’s. A new name appeared: Alena Muller, partner. Her name was on the 1977 and 1978 return, but not on Ward’s 1979 return. The name puzzled Murdock.

“The name Alena Muller sound familiar?” Julia hesitated.

“Not at all.”

“Where’s Warbington’s seventy-nine and eighty returns?”

“Remember he died in seventy-seven,” replied Julia.

“That’s right.” Murdock rubbed his chin in thought.

“Here’s something that might interest you.” She passed him Sea Unlimited’s corporate income tax return, bank statement and cancelled checks which had been photocopied from microfilm. Ten corporate checks were paper clipped together. Murdock spread the checks on the table. Some were issued to Sea Unlimited from Farmer, Ward, Martinez and a Thomas Farley while others were made payable to DUU, Inc. from Sea Unlimited. The checks totaled over four million dollars from March ‘79 to June ‘80.

“Some big bucks. Any idea who Thomas Farley is?”

“He’s the sole officer of DUU, Inc.”

"So he's making healthy deposits into Sea Unlimited's account and then Sea Unlimited is turning around and making deposits into his corporate account."

"Guess who's the registered agent?"

"Ward?"

"Right."

"Did you order Farley's return?"

"Yes, I did...the Atlanta Service Center told me that his seventy-nine and eighty returns were filed in Austin. They'll send them, but get this, prior to seventy-eight Farley doesn't exist."

"They don't have any record of Farley filing prior to seventy-eight? Where's he been?"

"Who knows?" replied Julia.

"Run his name through all the locator services and call me tonight." Locator services referred to all the various databases, federal and state, the IRS has access to via office computers.

"Will do. I haven't received anything from Customs or the Coast Guard on any yachts in Farmer's or Sea Unlimited's name. Any word from the neighbor in Key Largo?"

"No. Hope he hasn't forgotten. Maybe I'll call him." Murdock gathered the documents into a neat pile, "I better hit the road before Davenport finds out I'm still here."

"Thanks again. This case is turning into a full-time job. I've only got seventy-three other cases waiting for me." Murdock just grinned knowing his work was just gathering dust, too, while he was on detail to the Keys. Murdock stuffed his brief case and began his long, but relaxing trek into paradise mulling over the information he had just reviewed and the name Alena Muller.

***

Murdock arrived at the old, but elegant Key West Hotel by late afternoon. He stopped at the Largo house. The neighborhood was quiet. The house looked undisturbed. There were no signs that anyone had entered the house since the last time he had checked. Murdock also picked up the returns Hank had sent him at the motel.

While checking into the hotel, the hoard of insects he worked with entered the lobby. Ernie was with them and surprisingly, he fit in.

"Just in time for sunset, Murdock," shouted Palmetto.

"I'd like to but the ride wore me out. I'll see you guys later."

"All right, but you're gonna miss a great sunset," replied Palmetto who was wearing a straw sombrero that had a chin-strap. Ernie and Beetle were carrying the cooler with iced down beer. Cricket's hand was on Beetle's shoulder for stability as he downed another beer and staggered out with the hoard.

"Mr. Murdock, this arrived for you." The clerk at the registration desk handed him a large brown government envelope. The upper left corner of the package bore the name "Palmetto." Murdock grinned wondering what it contained.

"Thanks." He made his way up the stairs and into the room. He immediately opened the French doors. He could see the dock, which had at least a hundred sun worshippers lining the railings. The ocean was as lazy as the afternoon. The breeze had an unseasonably cool feeling as the air circulated throughout his room chasing the musty odor.

Murdock opened the package. Two summonses addressed to the telephone companies in South Florida and New York City were inside. The first summons requested all the telephone numbers being dialed from the Largo house over the past four months. The list provided the number, names and the time and date the calls were made. Seven numbers were listed with five being called towards the latter part of each month. This information corresponded with the monthly gathering. Four of the numbers were South Florida exchanges while the fifth was a New York City number. One of the numbers belonged to Alena Muller and she had been called throughout the month in addition to the end of the month call. Murdock knew she was a one-time law partner with Phillip Ward. Murdock surmised that she had probably resigned from the partnership sometime in '78 since her name did not appear on the 1979 partnership return. Somehow she was connected to this case but how?

Murdock recognized another name on the summons, "J. Farmer." The telephone company listed Farmer at a Fort Lauderdale address that Murdock didn't know about. The second summons in Palmetto's package was issued by a revenue officer in New York City. When casework outside a revenue officer's district is needed, they send a "Courtesy Investigation" to the district where the information was located. Since Palmetto knew a group manager in New York City the request was handled expeditiously. Otherwise, it would have taken months to retrieve the information, if he were lucky. The New York number belonged to an Abel Sanchez.

Murdock continued his examination of the returns jotting down notes and questions that arose. Warbington and Ward listed income interest from the National Bank of Miami. Warbington, according to an information document attached to the return, was on of the Board of Directors with the bank until his alleged demise in 1977. Murdock knew he was onto something. He could feel it. He just didn't know how the pieces fit together...yet. While in the midst of a mountain of paperwork on his bed, Julia called. Murdock glanced at his travel clock—it was 5:46 p.m.

"Bill, I've got something. I've been trying to get hold of you for a while."

"I took my time. So what's up?"

"Got an address on Farley. He's in Hollywood-By-The-Sea."

"Nice area. Anything else?"

"I ran his date of birth through Fort Lauderdale PD. Same address was listed but the information was established on their files in January 1980."

"How old is he?"

"Fifty-six."

"Did he just start driving maybe?" asked Murdock.

"Kind of difficult to believe isn't it?"

"I guess. What do you think?"

"Well, I checked his social security number and we didn't have any data on it so I checked with a friend of mine in the FBI and you'll never believe what came up."

"I give up, what?"

"Farley is listed with the FBI as a protected witness."

"Really?"

"There isn't any other information on him so whatever we can develop is all we'll know about him."

"If he's part of the protected witness program then Farley isn't his real name," stated Murdock.

"It's a fictitious name."

"Wonder who he really is?" Murdock was puzzled. "He's still involved in something, but this time it's his new identity doing it."

"Palmetto gave me some information on the people who are getting calls from the Largo house. Could you check out a name for me?"

"Sure, but what's a Palmetto?" inquired Julia unaware of the revenue officer's alter ego.

"That's Jake Democko's nickname. You know him?"

"I know the name. From what I hear he's really good. Why the nickname?"

"Everyone in the South Miami office has one. It's like some kind of subculture...strange. Anyway, the name I need checked out is Abel Sanchez." Murdock spelled the name. He's got a New York City address. The telephone company has Farmer listed at Twenty Palm Drive, in Lauderdale."

"It's rental property. His mother owns it," explained Julia. "I talked to the neighbors. He's seldom there."

"He's seldom anywhere. He's got to be somewhere!" said Murdock. "Alena Muller's name comes up too. She was a law partner of Ward's until seventy-eight. She lives in Coconut Grove."

"I talked to CI about Sea Unlimited," mentioned Julia.

"You didn't tell them who we think the corporation is connected to did you?"

"No, I remember the hard time Davenport gave you. CI doesn't have anything on Sea Unlimited. The corporation is clean as far as they're concerned."

"Anything else?"

"That's it for now."

"Thanks, Julia. Catch ya later." Murdock jotted down the information Julia had given him and placed it in a separate pile when he heard the muffled applause of a hundred people bidding farewell to the descending sun. Murdock walked out onto the veranda and gazed out as he leaned against the railing. He succumbed to the breezy, salt air and stretched out on the heavily padded recliner. Moments later he drifted to sleep listening to the repetitive waves and to the streets of Key West come alive.

***

Murdock was startled by the resonant knocking on the solid oak door to his room.

"Who is it?"

"Ernie. It's six."

"AM or PM?"

"AM."

"I'll meet you downstairs." Murdock, drugged by the Key West air, had slept through his alarm clock. In a matter of minutes he was dressed and eating breakfast with the others.

"Bill, I'd like you to meet Ross Cohen with CI. He'll be with us on the seizure," explained Palmetto. "He helped us with the aerial surveillance." Cohen was a special agent with Criminal Investigation. "The locksmith and movers are meeting us at seven in front of the main entrance."

"I notified the Sheriff's Department. They'll be on standby if we need them," interjected Cohen. "My car radio is on their frequency. The doctor shouldn't have any handguns in the house, but after serving the Writ of Entry, Jake and I will do a search first." Special agents with CI were in charge of security only. The revenue officer controlled the seizure activity.

"We'll tell you when to come in," explained Palmetto. "Here's a roll of stick-it notes for everyone." He passed out a roll of fluorescent orange, circular stickers the size of a nickel. Each item in the house would be labeled and recorded in an effort to maintain accountability from time of seizure to day of sale.

"Speaking of rolls..." interrupted Beetle, "...would ya mind passing me the biscuits." Palmetto distributed a sketch of the doctor's house detailing the interior. Each room was lettered and had the name of the revenue officer who was responsible for that particular inventory. The officer would mark and inventory each and every item in the room with the mover. This was quite a time consuming process. Along with the sketching, each participant was given a copy of the action plan that gave explicit instructions for just about anything that might occur. Palmetto had made hundreds of seizures and encountered just about every type of situation.

"I checked with the Sheriff's Department and Island Security. He doesn't have a police record and no mention of any violence," explained Agent Cohen. "I plan to move about the house and stay with the doctor."

"Boys, the doctor is on medication for heart ailments. As tempting as it may be, let's not hide the pills on him," reminded Palmetto. "Any questions?"

"Just one," responded Beetle. "Would you mind passing me the rolls?"

At 6:49 a.m. they departed the hotel in three cars. The eastern sky was barely illuminated when they arrived at the security booth. Three 18-wheeled moving trucks were parked alongside the road. The evergreen color of the trucks hid them in the morning darkness.

"Good morning," greeted the captain of Island Security. "You ready to go in?"

"Yeah. Let me brief the movers." Palmetto explained to the movers the legality of what would take place and that safety was of the utmost importance. The movers were introduced to everyone, especially Special Agent Cohen who would be the only armed IRS personnel at the house should something go wrong.

"We're ready," announced Palmetto. The vibration of the movers' well-tuned Kenworth engines gave everyone's feet a tingling sensation. Sleeping pelicans, prematurely awakened by the rumbling engines, took to the air like a squadron of fighter jets in attack formation.

The security patrol escorted the vehicles through the silent, dormant island to the doctor's Mediterranean-style abode. Palmetto exited his rental car and depressed the speaker button on the gate several times prior to getting a response.

"Who's there?" stated a somewhat groggy voice.

"Jake Democko with the IRS. Is this Dr. Franklin?"

"Who else?"

"I'm here to collect two hundred and two thousand dollars."

"I don't owe it. I told you that before now get out of here," shouted the doctor.

"I double checked the assessments with the Examination Division. They're correct. Matter of fact, Appeals upheld our position when you went to them. Remember?"

"Goodbye!" shouted the doctor.

"Since you refuse to pay the amount, I have paperwork to give you."

"Then leave it in the mailbox. I'll have my tax attorney call you."

"You should've had him call before this. Please unlock the gate."

"Go away!"

"Last chance before we let ourselves in."

"It's locked to keep people like you out!"

"Have it your way."

Palmetto signaled to the locksmith, which gave him the go ahead to unlock the gate. The frail, elderly locksmith studied the gate lock for half a minute and disappeared into his van. He emerged with an intricate looking tool which he inserted into the lock. With a few twists and jerks, the gate door swung open allowing the entourage of IRS agents free access to the mini mansion. Special Agent Cohen was video taping their actions for the case documentation should the doctor allege any wrongdoing by the IRS.

The commotion awoke the doctor's electronic security cameras. Palmetto pressed the speaker button near the door.

"How did you get in? If you damaged my gate, I'll sue you! I'm calling the cops."

"We already did. Please open the door. I have to personally serve you with this paperwork."

"Go away!" Palmetto again motioned to the locksmith who pulled out a large drill and bore the center of the doorknob. The doctor's screaming vibrated the glass above the door. Seconds later the door was opened by Agent Cohen. The doctor was standing with his hands on his hips and mouth open. He was wrapped in a silk, monogrammed robe. His hair was snarled and teased into what resembled a bird's nest.

"I'm suing! As God is my witness, I'm suing! Give me what you have and leave!" Perhaps it was the early morning hours that clouded the doctor's mind, but he still did not realize what was about to happen. He slipped his glasses on as Palmetto handed him the first of three documents. The first one outlined what kinds of taxes that were owed, for which period and indicated how much was due. Palmetto requested the doctor read this form.

"So I can't pay it!" shouted the doctor. Special Agent Cohen's camera zoomed in on the conversation. Palmetto then handed him the second document labeled "Notice of Seizure."

"What could you possibly seize from me? The house and cars are not mine." The doctor gave a hearty laugh thinking he had been clever by having his belongings in someone else's name.

"I believe the very center of the paper makes reference to seizing the entire contents of the house except, of course, your underwear and a few other personal belongings we deem as necessary to you."

"You can't do that. I won't let you." Palmetto presented the doctor with the third and final document. It was the Writ of Entry authorizing Palmetto and the others to use necessary force to gain entry to effect seizure of personal belongings. It was signed by a federal magistrate.

"You think I'm going to listen to another jackass of a judge?"

"This is Special Agent Cohen with the IRS. He's here to help us anyway he can. Let's not make this any more difficult than it already is. We're coming in."

The doctor opened the door and stood aside. He began his first in a series of verbal assaults and protests. The noise awoke his wife who immediately went to her husband's side.

"What is the meaning of this?" asked the graceful looking woman.

"We're seizing the contents of this house for nonpayment of taxes. Your husband has the documents."

"But everything isn't his," responded the wife after a cursory review of the documents.

"We have a year old statement in the file made by your husband." Palmetto passed the document to her. It stated that the furniture was his. The wife looked at her husband in disbelief.

"I thought everything was in my name?" asked the doctor's wife.

"Don't say anything. Do you hear me?" shouted the doctor.

"My children are visiting us. Can't this be done some other time?" asked the wife in desperation.

"How many are here and what are their ages ma'am," asked Palmetto.

"There's three. Twenty-five to thirty-nine."

"We'll give them some time to get dressed before we go into the bedrooms. I'm sorry they're here."

"The first thing we want to do is to confiscate all the guns if there are any," stated Agent Cohen. Cohen and Palmetto followed the doctor up the spiral staircase into the master bedroom. There, a nine-millimeter and a .380 pistol were relinquished.

"Any others?" The doctor hesitated and then produced enough handguns, rifles, knives and swords to completely fill a banquet table. The mere possession of any one of the handguns violated his parole. His tax evasion conviction cost him five years in a federal penitentiary in Atlanta. However, due to his health and profession, he only served fourteen months. He was still a convicted felon who had some of his basic rights taken away such as owning a handgun.

"If he gives us a difficult time can we contact his parole officer on the handgun violation?" asked Palmetto.

"Maybe, but they probably won't do anything. We're lucky he served any time," replied Cohen.

"Why?"

"After he was convicted he was supposed to report to prison. He never showed and the court did absolutely nothing about it until we forced the issue."

"I don't get it," stated Palmetto.

"The judge who sentenced him was going through a divorce himself and wasn't thinking straight. He was unfit for the bench."

"Typical."

"We spent almost two years on that investigation, hundreds of thousands of dollars, got a conviction and the doctor almost walked away from it all."

It was 7:45 a.m. when the other revenue officers filed in and went to their respective positions. The doctor's family was running about in shock. The doctor continued shouting obscenities at everyone, even the movers. The daughters, embarrassed and hurt for their father, joined in the yelling, making it difficult for the revenue officers and movers to hear each other.

"Please don't do this to my father. He's a sick man. Please don't let this happen," pleaded the oldest daughter in tears to Murdock. "Don't you care about anything...you creep!" cried the daughter. Murdock asked the family to meet with him in the kitchen.

"If you want to remain here, you're gonna have to stop this. The yelling and screaming isn't helping your father." The eldest daughter was a beautiful brunette with green eyes and fair skin.

"Why is this happening? I've never heard of something like this," she said, still in tears.

"Instead of filing and paying his taxes like most of us, he chose to live this lifestyle, pay for your private education, weddings, cars, houses and whatever else he bought for you. My question is why aren't you trying to help him financially now?" Just then the doctor entered the kitchen holding onto his chest.

"You can't talk to them like that. They have nothing to do with this."

"If you go into another rage we're going to make all of you leave," explained Murdock.

"No one leaves my house until I say!" exclaimed the doctor. Murdock, recognizing the father's embarrassment having his children witness this, took him aside.

"Listen, this could be a lot worse. If you get everyone excited again Special Agent Cohen will place you under arrest. I'm not going to put up with this confusion, wondering what you're going to do next! Now, if you really care about your family let them know you're okay and things are going to work out for you." The doctor nodded in agreement. He knew what this was doing to his family.

He slowly walked over to the stairway and sat down. He watched as a part of his life passed by him piece by piece. The rest of his family gathered around him and watched.

"Bingo!" yelled Cricket from the kitchen.

"Whatcha got?" asked Palmetto. Cricket opened the freezer and pulled out two bundles of U.S. currency—about twenty thousand dollars worth. "Nice work, Cricket."

The doctor's wife overheard the conversation. "It's not ours, it belongs to the corporation and I need it for business today."

"You need twenty thousand dollars for business today? Not today." Cricket made up a receipt and gave it to the doctor. The wife rubbed her eyes with both hands and wondered how much more she could take.

"Doctor Franklin. We would like you to open your safe now," demanded Palmetto.

"What safe?"

"The safe you installed a while back. The locksmith downstairs is with the safe company who sold it to you."

"I'm not going to help you ruin me."

"You're gonna pay for their work if you don't open it." The doctor shrugged his shoulders. The safe was located in a loft overlooking a spectacular view of a marina and the ocean.

"You can't drill my safe."

"Better read the writ again." He turned to the locksmith, "Go ahead. I'll be back." Palmetto left and entered the room labeled "C" and found Murdock sticking notes on packed boxes. There was a small fortune in paintings.

"Bill, you mind coming with me for a few minutes? We're about to open the safe. I need a witness."

"Yeah. This room is an oven."

"I keep turning the air on and they keep turning it off."

The two entered the loft. "Almost got it...a few more minutes," explained the locksmith. Beetle entered the loft holding a lady's ring.

"Look what I've got." Beetle held what looked to be a two-carat diamond ring.

"That's mine. I just dropped it."

Beetle quickly shoved the treasure into his tight pockets.

"Show me proof it's yours and I'll return it."

"Like what?" sneered the eldest daughter.

"A receipt."

"I don't have a receipt. I have a receipt for the TV downstairs. I gave it to them as a gift. May I have that?"

"If you gave it to them then it's not yours."

"Are you taking everything?"

"We're leaving the pillows, mattresses, appliances and eating utensils," declared Palmetto.

She uttered profanity at him.

"Knew that was coming."

Cricket was in the room labeled "A", the master bedroom. The youngest daughter, a twenty-five year old beauty was pleading with Cricket to let her keep the TV. When he refused she initiated a different approach. She unbuttoned the top few buttons of her blouse and stretched out on the bed. The pressure applied from the mattress pushed and shaped her into a seductive position, teasing him. She continued her pleading from this position, but to no avail. While he liked what he saw, his sense of duty prevailed over his lust.

"Done," stated the locksmith. Palmetto and Murdock anxiously approached the gray wall safe. Palmetto opened the door and began removing the valuable contents as Murdock recorded them.

"One fourteen-carat gold man's watch, brand name 'Rolex' with glass-like stones in assorted sizes; one package of personal papers and two five thousand dollar CDs." Murdock quickly recorded the information on a seizure form which would be turned over to the doctor. Palmetto removed the valuables and placed them in the trunk of his car for safekeeping.

The cool morning sun had risen quickly in the Caribbean sky turning the house and moving trucks into ovens. Sweat drenched everyone. Murdock sat with the others in the loft enjoying the view and the fast food Beetle had picked up.

"Where's Ernie? Haven't seen him all morning," asked Murdock.

"Cricket, go check on him and tell him we've got his lunch," instructed Palmetto. Moments later the two returned carrying four white canvas bags.

"Come on up, your foods getting cold," yelled Palmetto. Ernie struggled up the staircase and dropped the bags in the center of the table.

"What do we have here?" Palmetto was excited. He knew they were moneybags. Ernie untied one of the bags and turned it over letting the silver dollars dated in the 1800s and gold Krugerrands flood the table. Palmetto stood up almost breathless.

"Where did you find these?"

"They were in the crawl space above the downstairs hall closet."

"Outstanding job, Ernie. You've earned your pay today. Now, can I interest anyone in a little poker?" Palmetto pulled a deck of cards he always carried out of his back pocket. The others began stacking and evenly dividing the coins among them.

"The movers take an hour for lunch. Not much else we can do until then," said Palmetto. "Five cards, one-eyed Jacks wild." Palmetto dealt the cards as the five revenue officers played using the seized money. The family members were downstairs with Agent Cohen and not allowed to go upstairs.

When the lunch hour was almost over Palmetto leaned over to Beetle and whispered, "It's time." Beetle rose and took the keys to the rental car.

"Where's he going?" asked Ernie.

"Take care of some unfinished business—you'll see." Murdock leaned back in his chair and wondered what they were up to now. Beetle proceeded off the island in search of a telephone. Two miles outside the island community he found one and called *The Reporter.*

"Hello. My name isn't important but I was driving by Dr. Franklin's house on Palm Island and there's all kinds of police cars, moving vans and what looked like detectives and federal agents. Know anything about it? What do you mean you're not interested in it?" Beetle hung up on them. Beetle fished in his tight pockets for another dime.

"W-T-K-W, I was driving through Palm Island. There's all kinds of commotion going on at Eleven Paradise Drive. What's going on?

You don't know? There's moving vans, police and what looks like federal agents. Looks like something big is going down. They're taking all the furniture out and I saw some seizure notices. You sure you don't know anything about it? My name? Oh, just a concerned citizen. Goodbye."

Beetle quickly returned to the house and nodded to Palmetto who was looking down from the second story. Palmetto smiled and went back to counting the items the movers were ready to load. Minutes later a van from the local TV station pulled up in front of the gate. A cameraman and reporter exited the white vehicle which was prominently marked with the station's blue logo. They immediately began filming through the forest of tropical trees, being careful not to set foot on the doctor's private property. If they did, he would have the right to quash the airing of the news piece.

"Oh no, it's the news! Mother, they must have called them. You're slime. Isn't it humiliating enough having this done? Was this necessary?"

"A concerned citizen must have called. News like this travels fast," replied Palmetto.

The eldest daughter called the station to see if there was anything they could do to prevent the airing of the incident.

"They want to speak to whoever is in charge." Palmetto promptly walked down the stairs and to the phone.

"Jake Democko." The station questioned him. He explained that IRS seizures are usually as a last resort to collect the tax. That the agency issues several notices in most cases prior to taking distraint actions. The station knew the doctor. They had covered the story several years ago when he was sentenced for tax evasion. Palmetto answered their questions and then gave them the name and number of the IRS's Public Affairs officer in Fort Lauderdale who could give them the specifics since all items were cleared through the disclosure office first.

"Why did you tell them that?" yelled the eldest daughter. "Why?"

"You gave me the phone. I answered their questions. Let's not forget why we're here," irritated Palmetto raised his voice.

"We're not going to be able to go anywhere in this community thanks to you," she continued.

"No, thanks to your father's blatant disrespect for our tax laws," replied Palmetto. Palmetto had no sympathy for the family. The doctor knew what he was doing and the family reaped the benefits. Palmetto also knew the doctor's children, if they chose to do so, could easily satisfy the tax due. His superficial background investigation revealed the children had made some wise investments with the money they received over the years from their father. But the children refused to help him. The Collection Division of the IRS was doing what no one else could do—and that was to administer justice.

The remainder of the afternoon was uneventful. The children went home and the wife went to the boutique she owned and operated. The doctor? Well, the doctor spent the rest of the day in the kitchen with his head resting in his arms realizing he was finally paying for the error of his ways. By 5:40 p.m. the entire two-story house was empty for the first time in 35 years. Special Agent Cohen was busy filming the empty rooms. The videotape would show the condition the house had been left in after the seizure. Experience had taught Palmetto that the taxpayers, on occasion, return and commit acts of destruction against the property and then try to blame it on the IRS. The film was his insurance.

When Palmetto was satisfied that everything he wanted was packed and removed, he pulled out a wad of bills and paid the lead mover $50 extra and thanked him for doing two days' worth of work in one. He turned to the revenue officers who were perched on the staircase.

"Another job well done without incident thanks to you guys. Dinner and drinks on me tonight."

"Got any aspirin?" asked Cricket.

"I need some, too," murmured Murdock.

"Let's head back to the hotel and load up on some aspirin and catch the last of the news," explained Palmetto.

"Hey, let's go to Holiday Isle," said Cricket. "I'll drive."

"That's a distance from here, Crick," replied Beetle who was sprawled out on the floor with his head being propped up by the bottom step of the staircase. "Let's go somewhere closer."

"I'd love to join you, but I've got an anniversary tomorrow," stated Agent Cohen. "One final shot for the record." Cohen turned the video camera on them as he departed. The five of them waved at the camera very much like the Beverly Hillbillies might have done.

"Let's go," remarked Murdock struggling to get up. They all left the barren house. By 7:10 they met in the lounge at the Pier House for the remainder of the news. Palmetto hoped that they received coverage and that the publicity would be favorable. Cricket had convinced everyone to go with him after the news for drinks and dinner. The place he described enticed them.

The news aired about the seizure. They listened carefully to determine how the news perceived them; as heroes or villains. The small group was silent as they trained their eyes on the TV hanging from the ceiling. The newswoman mentioned the doctor's background and prior encounters with the Justice Department and IRS. She mentioned that while seizure was the last consideration, the IRS used enforcement action when necessary. She closed by saying that if you're dodging the IRS, think twice. The news story had made it as far north as Fort Lauderdale and surrounding areas. The impact on voluntary compliance would be great. The group of revenue officers cheered and toasted each other after hearing the favorable report. The TV camera had zoomed in on the movers loading the furniture and then on Beetle who was desperately tugging on his underwear which had been wedged in his big cheeks. The crowd at the lounge erupted in laughter. Beetle lowered his head and slipped on his sunglasses.

After the news they honored Cricket's suggestion and drove to Holiday Isle tired and dirty. The three-story, nautical building had two lounges and different types of music from two of the levels. People were shoulder to shoulder singing and carrying on. It looked like one big happy family reunion. Women outnumbered the men two to one. The kind of odds Cricket enjoyed. Murdock, being the tallest, worked his way to the counter. A stream of long neck beers formed as he asked the patrons behind him to pass the bottles to the motley group in the rear. Murdock struggled through the crowd. The group followed Murdock to one of the outside decks that overlooked the ocean. The luminescent glow from a string of colored lights captured the coconut trees as their petiole lightly brushed the evening sky. A dark orange-red dome was afloat on the ocean surface not far from the horizon. Ernie cleaned his glasses and studied the object. The dome grew brighter and changed colors.

"Incredible isn't it?" commented Murdock.

"What is it?" asked Ernie.

"What do you think it is?" asked Beetle still tugging a little at his wedged underwear.

"Some kind of floating stage," he replied.

"You're close," responded Cricket as he downed his beers.

"Keep watching," uttered Murdock. Ernie finished his soda as he witnessed the metamorphosis before them. Slowly, the object began to grow larger and brighter.

"That's remarkable. I didn't know the moon could look like that," replied Ernie. The sight mesmerized him.

"I had the same feelings the first time I saw it down here," said Cricket.

Festivities in the next building overshadowed the lounge. A voice, projected over a PA system, introduced several people as candidates. Crowds of people were climbing the concrete stairs to the second story. Several women donned one piece bathing suits with banners draped over them.

"Sounds like a political rally," observed Ernie. "Let's check it out." They merged into the pedestrian traffic and climbed the steps.

"And who are you voting for?" asked a bathing suit beauty at the top of the stairs. She glanced at Murdock and gave a big smile. Murdock glanced at the name on the banner she was wearing.

"Why Taylor, of course!"

"That's right." She placed her arms around Murdock's neck and gave him a big kiss. A round of applause and cheering accompanied the embrace. Murdock grinned and entered a large room. A crowd of people listened to the candidates' rhetoric. Each of them made promises of what they would do if elected Mayor of Islamorada.

"There isn't any mayoral seat here," stated Murdock. He turned and asked someone. He learned the island holds a mock election in which the residents run for mayor. At the end of the three-day event a bash is held and the winner is announced.

Tables of food including the largest filet of smoked sailfish anyone had ever seen lined the wall. The five were told to help themselves and without hesitation, joined the line and piled the food high, especially the sailfish. They took their turn through the line and exited the rear sliding glass door onto a balcony. The results of the mock mayoral race were heard.

"Ernie..." asserted Palmetto. "...we're gonna hook you up with a woman tonight for doing such a fine job today." This wasn't an easy task especially with Ernie's black Buddy Holly-styled glasses. Murdock thought this might be a good time to leave and call Beth. After going through two different operators the long distance call was made.

"Beth, it's me. How are you guys doing?"

"Oh Bill, I've been trying to reach you all day." Beth was in a panic and sounded as though she had been crying.

"Are the children all right?"

"It's Julia." Beth hesitated.

"What's wrong?" asked Murdock raising his voice. Beth started crying. Murdock's body went weak and his stomach tightened. "Beth, please tell me what's wrong."

"Julia was getting out of her car and someone hit her..." she paused. "...and then drove off."

"How bad is she hurt?" Beth was silent.

"They took her to the hospital—she died this morning."

"Are you sure it was Julia?" Beth tried to answer through her tears.

"Yes. I'm sorry, Bill."

"I can't believe it. There must be some kind of mistake...I just talked to her the other night. Beth, are you certain?"

"I called the office. It was Julia."

"Her son is only ten. Who's gonna look after him?"

"Julia's sister has him...I tried to call you...I left messages." Murdock was silent.

"When did it happen?"

"About nine o'clock."

"I just can't believe it!" shouted Murdock.

"I know. Are you gonna be all right, honey?"

"She was such a caring person...I just don't get it!" continued Murdock oblivious to his wife's question.

"Are you going to be all right?" she asked more forcefully.

"No...yeah, I'll be okay."

"The funeral's tomorrow at two."

"I'll be home by noon. I love you Beth."

"I love you, too. I'm sorry."

"I know...just can't believe it," shouted Murdock angrily.

Murdock wept. He looked out over the ocean, but found no relief this time. There were no answers waiting for him. He said a prayer about her son's well being. What would the son do without her? He walked along the ocean shore. Numbness seized his body. He felt as though his soul had left him. An out of body experience, creating the sensation that he was drifting with the moon through the night. It was as if he were in a dream...a nightmare.

11

It was the second Wednesday in November 1980, when Julia was buried. The day was characteristic of South Florida's version of autumn. The resplendent sun was high in the icy blue sky and a few autumn-colored leaves were mixed in with the vivid green background. A chilly sixty-degree blanket of air covered the area. This was the kind of afternoon people should have been gathering for some festivities; instead, sixty friends, coworkers and relatives paid their last respects under the mammoth limbs of a two hundred year old ficus tree which would forever shield Julia.

Murdock reminisced about the good times the two of them had working together as the pastor concluded the eulogy. Julia's son wrapped himself around his aunt's arm, rested his head against her side and cried. He touched the coffin not wanting to let go. Murdock held his son tightly and closed his eyes as he prayed for the little boy.

Murdock was consoling the relatives when a slender, stately-looking man dressed very conservatively approached him.

"Excuse me, are you Bill Murdock?" Murdock paused and gave the soft-spoken man a once over.

"Yes, and you're...?"

"Mike Durham with the FBI. I was a friend of Julia's. Terrible thing to happen." Murdock nodded. "I know this isn't the time or place to discuss business, but it's urgent. Can we go over to my car?" asked the agent.

"I'll be with you in a minute." Murdock turned to his wife and explained where he was going. Beth nodded and continued talking to Julia's sister as Durham escorted Murdock over to his silver Caprice. Durham opened the trunk and removed a brown file marked in faded red ink, *Confidential.* "Before we go any further I'd like to see some identification?"

"Certainly." After producing credentials the two sat in his car. "I understand that you're interested in the name Abel Sanchez."

"I asked Julia to check him out since the name surfaced during one of our investigations," interrupted Murdock.

"We think it's Abel Nieto. Anyone in his path is in extreme danger." Murdock looked over at him.

"Like Julia?"

"Maybe. Nieto has numerous aliases and probably twice as many disguises. Except for a few rare appearances, he's been underground since bombing a yacht off Long Island the Christmas of seventy-five."

"Anyone on it?"

"A foreign diplomat and his family. The boat belonged to a senator." Durham extracted two black and white photographs from the file and passed them to Murdock. The pictures were taken at night of Nieto.

"He doesn't look like much of a threat," expressed Murdock.

"No, but he's lethal," assured the agent. "During the past couple of years intelligence indicated that he's gone solo...cut the Rosario Cartel out. He's a key figure in these cocaine wars going on in Miami and South America." Murdock studied the pictures.

"I haven't seen him," explained Murdock.

"I hope you never do. He's brutal. He enjoys torturing and mutilating his victims. The people dealing with him are in for a surprise. When he's through conducting business he'll execute them. That's his MO. I've seen some of his handy work."

"So, what now?"

"Thanks to the address you gave us, DEA has the apartment under surveillance...it belongs to his mother. Quite frankly, we're a little embarrassed you found him." Murdock looked up.

"I'll tell you what I know, but I'd like some information from you."

"What is it?" asked Durham.

"The name Thomas Farley ring a bell?"

"Yes. He's with the Protected Witness Program."

"Who is he and how did he help you?"

"I knew you'd ask about him." The agent hesitated. "Farley's former ID was Douglas Warbington. You know the name?"

"He's connected to our investigation," replied Murdock. "Our records indicate he died in '77. We also know he was gong to be indicted for bank fraud in Houston. What did he do for you?"

"With his assistance, DEA has infiltrated the Rosario Cartel. Our agents are still undercover," explained Durham.

"We know a house in Key Largo was illegally transferred to a corporation he headed called Sea Unlimited. Ever hear the name?" asked Murdock.

"Never."

"Investors forked over four million dollars to Sea Unlimited who then made some healthy deposits into their account. What about DUU, Inc?" asked Murdock.

"It belongs to him. Stands for "DW" or Douglas Warbington."

"He's still involved in a lot of dirt," remarked Murdock.

"We know, but what we're gaining from him about the drug network, connections and who's involved is worth it."

"So, it's okay for Warbington to go on doing whatever he wants since he gave you some information?"

"You're missing my point. Let me finish. When we're through, it will be the biggest drug bust in history. Key politicians, judges, bankers and other prominent businessmen will be indicted." There was silence. Murdock looked away. "Did you know that no major drug figure has ever been indicated in South Florida?" asked Durham.

"No, I didn't."

"When one of the lower ranking figures is busted, his sentence is so light that it encourages people to get a piece of the action. So, Warbington is a small price to pay when compared to what our return will be."

"I see where you're coming from. It just doesn't sit well with me."

"It bothers me too, but that's the price we gotta pay."

"I wondered why my office gave me such a difficult time with this case," stated Murdock.

"What do you mean?"

"They asked me to back off the investigation."

"The IRS doesn't know anything about this. It's such a clandestine operation only a few know. What did you find that they told you to stop?" asked Durham as he wiped his sunglasses.

"I'm trying to make a rather simple assessment against the officers of Sea Unlimited for accepting the transfer of property from another taxpayer. Would your office be working with our criminal investigators on this?"

"No. Who are the people involved?"

"John Farmer, Phillip Ward, Ramon Martinez and Warbington."

"I don't know the others you mentioned. Your office isn't telling you to back off because of our investigation. Something else is going on."

"Well, I'm gonna find out what it is."

"How'd you come across Nieto's name?"

"It showed up on a printout we summoned from the telephone company."

"But how did you know what number to summons?" Durham was trying to figure out what they overlooked.

"We found a deed conveying property in Key Largo to Sea Unlimited for less than what it's worth."

"What's wrong with that?"

"Not a thing unless you owe Uncle Sam. Then, it's illegal."

"Why?"

" 'Cause the property is being placed beyond the reach of the government."

"So you summoned the telephone company records on the house?"

"That's right."

"Any problem getting the judge to go along with it?" asked

Durham.

"What judge? We don't have to appear before one," replied Murdock.

"How about when you go to make the assessment?"

"Nope."

"Once you get the assessment, what happens next?" continued Durham's questioning.

"Seize and sell the house."

"Will you go before a judge then?"

"No."

"We can't do anything without discussing it with some judge. That's remarkable!"

"You have to remember that I'm dealing primarily with civil matters as opposed to criminal proceedings and we're the only division that brings in the bucks, so they give us a lot of latitude."

"I'd say they do. I didn't realize how much authority you have. More than we do."

Durham removed the last picture from the worn, but organized file.

"He's with DEA. His name is Rico." Murdock inspected the photograph. The agent had long, straight hair which went well with his dark olive complexion and circular glasses. "He's been tracking Nieto for quite some time. When Julia turned the name into our office we alerted Rico."

"Let me give you a number where I can be reached," advised Murdock.

"No need to. He already knows where you're staying."

"How does he know that?"

"I don't know, but trust me, he knows. I've only met him once. He always knew where I was. An enigma. I'm not real sure about him. Personally, I think he's been under too long. Whatever he discusses with you, let me know immediately." Durham passed him a telephone number. "That's all I've got, Bill."

"One more thing," interjected Murdock. "Have you talked to Davenport?"

"Who is he?"

"My manager," replied Murdock wondering how many fuses

he'd blow over this one.

"Don't worry. Your National Office has been notified that there may be an exchange of information. No one else will know." Without approval from Washington, IRS employees cannot share their information with anyone, not even another government agency like the FBI.

"Why can't Rico get any information from you?"

"That's not his style. He wants to hear from the source and not third hand. Suppose that's one reason he's still alive."

"How involved will I be in this case?"

"Just keep me posted on any developments. That number I gave you is my voice mail."

"I'd like a letter from my National Office instructing me to cooperate."

"You'll have it in the morning."

"Send it to this address." Murdock handed him a calling card with the Key West office address on it.

"Is that it?" Murdock nodded his head.

"Thank you," stated Durham. "One more thing, don't let Rico know we met or that you're briefing me." Durham hesitated. "Again, I'm not sure about his motives. Besides, he'll think I'm trying to take charge." Durham looked out over the crowd. "I'm sorry 'bout Julia. I'll find out if Nieto was involved." Murdock nodded again and exited the vehicle. He joined his wife and daughter who were talking to Frank, Pete and Ernie.

"This is hard to believe," mourned Pete. "We just talked yesterday. Look around, it's like nothing ever happened. What's wrong with the place?" Frank placed his hand on Pete's shoulder.

"I asked that a lot when I was a cop...I never found the answer. I just stopped asking the question and moved away."

Edward Kemtz arrived in his sparkling BMW. He was late, but at least he showed, thought the others.

"Davenport gave us the rest of the day off. You guys wanna come over to my apartment?" asked Murdock.

"We have the day off?" asked Frank still in shock.

"Suppose he's human after all," replied Pete.

"Wonder if he realizes that his completed case investigations are gonna be a little short this month," commented Frank. His acrimony was unrelenting when it came to Davenport. Frank looked over at Pete and then back at Murdock. "We'd love to come over."

"Ernie, what about you?"

"I'd like to, but my father's sick. I'm all he's got. Pretty pathetic, huh?" he remarked, pushing his glasses back up his nose.

"I'd say he's pretty fortunate. Hope he's gonna be all right."

"It's just the flu, but at his age nothing is easy anymore. I'll see you back in the Keys. Thanks for the invite."

The three spent the remainder of the afternoon sitting on a neighbor's sailboat sharing memories of Julia.

Murdock looked at Pete, "You going back to work?" Pete looked away for a moment.

"No. I've got another four months of sick leave I'm going to ride out, but, it's just not worth it."

"How are you doing, really?" asked Murdock.

"All right." Pete hesitated. "I know it wasn't the auction that killed him. I mean, Coolidge was a mess long before I met him. But...I just can't stop thinking about it. My kids, my life in general, and...I dunno...when he had the gun to my head..." His words choked. Barely audible, he continued. "Now this is gonna sound hokey...when he pumped the shotgun, I saw...something...an angel." Murdock and Frank listened intently. "The brightest light I've ever seen...I really can't describe it." He looked down. "She didn't say a thing, but I understood her. No matter what happened to me, she'd be there for me." His voice crackled again and his eyes teared. Murdock placed his hand on Pete's shoulder. Pete regained his composure. "When I didn't die, I came up with some new priorities," joked Pete. Murdock and Frank smiled with him. "And the IRS ain't one of them."

"Been thinking about what you'll do?" asked Frank.

"Yeah, but I'm not coming up with anything except trying to get closer to God. He saved me..." His eyes teared again and his voice lowered. "...and I don't even know why."

They finished the afternoon remembering Julia and realized that something was very differrent despite the afternoon's appearance.

12

Murdock finished his breakfast at Gilbert's in Jewfish Creek when a sleek, black Porsche slowly slithered into the long gravel driveway. Murdock made it a practice to check every dark-colored Porsche he encountered. Perhaps this was the elusive John Farmer.

A tall, slim man wearing a light-colored sport shirt and baggy grey pants, which were gathered in front by a tight belt, exited a black Porsche. His blond wiry hair was at least two months overdue for a cut. The man entered the restaurant while Murdock proceeded to walk past the car to get a glimpse of the license plate number. He turned and the plates matched! Of all the times he needed Ernie with him, *this* was it. IRS regulations required that at least two employees be present when a seizure is made. Murdock reluctantly called the Key West Hotel knowing Ernie had not arrived this early on a Monday morning. Palmetto and Beetle were out, so that left Cricket.

"Hello," growled a very groggy voice.

"Cricket, it's Bill Murdock. I need your help. Can you meet me in Key Largo?"

"Hello," replied the disoriented Cricket.

"Cricket! It's Murdock. Can you hear me?"

"Oh, Bill...not feeling so well. We were..." Just then Murdock heard the deep roar of vomit exploding. The inebriated revenue officer sent last night's dinner of squid and raw oysters with a bottle of the restaurant's cheapest wine onto the rotor of his telephone and down the nightstand.

"Cricket!" yelled Murdock as he quickly hung up. "Sheriff's Department, please."

"Sheriff's Department," answered a deep voice.

"My name is Bill Murdock. I'm a revenue officer with the IRS. I need assistance at Jewfish Creek Bar and Grill. Do you have a unit available?"

"What kind of assistance?"

"I'm confiscating a car and I need someone standing by."

"I'll have him swing by. It'll be about twenty minutes, though."

"Thanks, I'll be waiting in front." Murdock hoped that if the car did leave the Bar and Grill that it was going to the Key Largo house. Murdock placed a call to the number Durham had given him. A recorder activated and Murdock advised him that the black Porsche was in Largo.

John Farmer finished his breakfast and left. Murdock decided against detaining Farmer since he couldn't seize the car. If Farmer wanted to leave, Murdock couldn't stop him since this was a civil matter. Farmer proceeded south on US 1 into Key Largo and hopefully, Murdock thought, to the house.

Almost to the minute, a deputy sheriff arrived. Murdock flagged him down as the car pulled into the parking lot. A short, stocky deputy with a shaved head wearing a green "Smokey the Bear" hat and aviator sunglasses exited the sedan.

"You the IRS?" His southern accent was thick as the syrup the deputy had grown up on.

"That's me, Bill Murdock." He displayed his credentials.

"Sorry it took so long. A lobster fisherman caught a man robbing his traps. He's lucky he's still alive."

"The car I want to confiscate left, but I think I know where it's at." Murdock explained the situation and reviewed the paperwork with the deputy. He wanted him to have a clear understanding of what was about to happen and his role in it.

"Where's the court order?" asked the deputy.

"Don't need one."

"I knew you boys could do a lot, but this is somethin'. I'd sure like to be able to pick up things without a judge's permission."

Murdock cautioned the deputy that anything could happen during the seizure, especially in this case. The two proceeded to the Key Largo house. The Porsche had been backed into the driveway all the way to the spiral staircase. Murdock parked along the street as did the sheriff's deputy.

"Would you call Island Wrecker Service. Here's the number." Murdock passed the deputy a card.

"They'll be here in ten minutes," replied the deputy as he wiped his brow. The temperature was already 91 degrees and daylight had just arrived.

"The car looks different to me," expressed Murdock.

"Plates check out?"

"Yeah."

"Match the VIN if you want to be sure," explained the deputy. Murdock checked the lengthy vehicle identification number. It matched. But why did it appear to look different, thought Murdock.

"I'm serving the paperwork." The deputy followed closely behind him with one hand resting on his .357 revolver. The holster was unsnapped. Murdock knocked on the door and the thin man from the restaurant peered through the venetian blinds and then cracked the door open.

"Mr. Farmer?" asked Murdock not absolutely certain.

"What do you want?"

"I'm Revenue Officer Murdock with IRS and this is Deputy Huckaby. I'm here to collect fifty-five thousand dollars owed to the Internal Revenue Service from your corporation. Also, another fifteen thousand dollars from your income tax. Will that be paid by check or money order?"

"I need t-time," stuttered the man as he turned lily white. "How much time can I have?"

"None. We've tried to work something out with you before but you didn't follow through. These taxes are a couple of years old. How much can you pay right now?"

"I can't pay anything right now. Give me some more time and I'll be able to pay everything...in...thirty days."

"Where's the money coming from?" inquired Murdock. He wanted to know so that he could serve a Notice of Levy on Farmer's client, compelling the person to pay the IRS rather than Farmer. This would ensure that the IRS received the money rather than chance it with Farmer.

"What difference does it make so long as you get it?"

"I'd like to know because I really don't think you've got anything coming in."

"Listen, I'll be able to raise the money," explained Farmer who offered no other information.

"I've got to ask you some questions about the corporation. May we come in?"

"N-No."

Murdock spent the next fifteen minutes probing Farmer for information about his cash register company.

"Tell me about Sea Unlimited." Farmer turned lily white and began stammering again.

"I...d-d-don't know what...what you're ta-talking about."

"I know you transferred this house to them, why?" Farmer offered no comment. "Who is Phillip Ward?"

"I...I have to go," replied Farmer. Like a hawk, the deputy watched Farmer's hand. He had a gunfighter stance and a look like he wanted Farmer to draw.

"I'm seizing your car. Please read this."

"I just ne-need a l-little time. By the end of the mon-month I'll have it. Please don't take m-m-my car."

"I'm taking the car, but I won't try to sell it until the first week in December. If you pay your taxes, you'll get the car back."

"Y-you don't understand. You can't t-take my car." Farmer's voice crackled.

"If you can't raise the money then I'll sell it at public auction."

"Isn't there some agreement we c-can make?"

"Not this time. You had your opportunity when you got the last installment agreement. We need the money, now."

Farmer lowered his head and rubbed both hands through his

hair. Murdock signaled the driver. The lowboy trailer was carefully backed into the driveway.

"May I have the keys?"

"You don't know wh-what you're doing. I gotta have my car."

"The keys, please." Farmer didn't budge. "If I don't get the keys, we'll have the ignition changed and billed to your account."

Farmer passed the single key to him and placed his trembling hands in his pockets and looked out with a blank stare.

"You can reach me at this number. In exactly eleven days we'll sell the car. Here's the sale notice. Where can I reach you?"

"Here...I guess." Farmer began pacing. His mind was tuned into something even more pressing than the IRS.

"Why did you transfer the house to Sea Unlimited when you needed it for your business?"

"I have my r-reasons."

"Help me and maybe I can help you." Farmer laughed. It was a nervous kind of laugh.

"Right, right...y-you can help me. No one is going to be able to help me if you take my car."

"Why?"

"N-Never mind. I have nothing to say."

"If you change your mind, call." Murdock turned and started to walk away. "One more thing..." continued Murdock. "I'll have to seize this house if you don't come up with the taxes."

"That's n-not right," complained Farmer.

"What's not right?"

"That you can do this."

"Mr. Farmer, what's not right is that you embezzled funds from your employees and then, instead of making your tax deposits like most businesses do, you put the money back into your business or...whatever. *That's* what isn't right. I hope you can raise the money."

Murdock told the wrecker driver that the car had to be stored inside and asked if Island Wrecker could take it to Miami. Murdock would have a better crowd in Miami than Key Largo.

"I've arrested people who weren't as nervous as that," remarked the deputy. "I'd say something a whole lot worse than the IRS is bothering that boy."

"I'm gonna find out what that is," replied Murdock. "Well, thanks for the help and if you know anyone interested in a Porsche, let me know."

"Glad I could help you."

Murdock proceeded to his room, roughed out the paperwork for the sale and telephoned the advertisement into the newspaper which was a legal requirement. He had to advertise in the newspaper with the greatest circulation and would post the sale notices in at least three public places. While checking into the motel, another package was handed to him by the clerk. This one was from Revenue Officer Hank Goffman in the Fort Lauderdale office. Thomas Farley's income tax return was enclosed. Murdock compared the Farley signature with the signature on Douglas Warbington's returns and there were similarities. Murdock thought about the deal Warbington received for passing information to the FBI. Murdock reviewed Farley's return, but there was no new information.

After roughing out the paperwork, Murdock called Palmetto. "How are things going?"

"Okay," replied Palmetto. "We just finished inventorying toilet paper and plungers. Must have been five thousand cartons of the stuff. What's up?"

"Need another favor. Can you get someone to type a sale notice and place an ad in Miami?"

"Sure can. What are ya selling?"

"Seized a Porsche 911 in mint condition."

"Nice car. Which taxpayer?"

"One of Julia's cases I'm helping her with. I'd like to sell it as soon as possible." Murdock spent the next few minutes listing all the particulars so that Palmetto could get the advertisement published.

"Something bothers me about the car," said Murdock, deep in thought.

"What?"

"I'm not sure, but the car seems different to me. I spotted it this morning in Jewfish Creek coming in. When I finally caught up with it 'bout an hour later it looked different."

"Sure you tagged the right one?" There's a lot of them here."

"Yeah, everything matched."

"So don't worry about it, it's yours!" reassured Palmetto.

"Suppose so. Let me know when the sale notice is posted," informed Murdock. "I owe you." Murdock organized and placed the file back into his briefcase. He grabbed his deep sea fishing rod and tackle box and finished the afternoon sitting on a seawall that edged a section of Florida Bay. His thoughts kept centering on the Porsche.

The scenery looked as though it could have been a postcard. Old wooden sailboats not much larger than eighteen feet huddled together. Smoke from several small grills formed a column rising in the air. The boat owners' conversation carried across the water.

Murdock fished for another hour and then, like a lightening bolt striking him, he knew what was different about the car. He threw his tackle into the rear of the convertible and the tiny car sputtered away.

"Ernie, can you meet me at Island Wrecker?"

"Sure. What time tomorrow?"

"Now."

"Now?"

"Now!"

"All right. You sound a little excited," observed Ernie. "What's going on?"

"I'll tell you when you get there."

Murdock raced over to the storage facility and was greeted by two of the most ferocious Dobermans he had ever encountered. They salivated at the prospect of sinking their large yellow fangs into Murdock's hindquarters. A small grey speaker box was mounted to a pole near the entrance. Murdock mashed the button.

"Who's there?"

"Bill Murdock with IRS. I've got to check something on the Porsche." Without a word, a man in his early thirties stepped outside and held a silver cylindrical object to his mouth. The dogs stopped barking and instantly returned to the man and sat motionless by his side. After praising the dogs the silver tube was raised to his lips again and the animals disappeared behind the facility.

"Drive in." Murdock hesitated. Visions of Wee Willie's devil dog failing to yield to his master's voice were still fresh in his mind. "Drive in. They won't return unless I call 'em." Murdock proceeded into the compound.

"Bay C." The man pointed to the left. "Why all the attention?"

"What attention?"

"You know, with others coming in to check on it."

"What others?" Murdock's voiced raised.

"Two men showed up. There was one at four-thirty and the other about an hour ago. Said they worked with you."

"Don't suppose you got their names?" asked Murdock.

"No, I remember seeing your name on that warning sticker so when they mentioned you, I thought it was okay. Any problem?"

"Someone should've contacted me." Murdock looked to the left and then the right of a long, well lit corridor.

"That way," instructed the man again.

"Another revenue officer is gonna get here in about twenty minutes. His name is Ernie Shelton. Let him know where I am."

"I'll tell 'em. Oh, make sure you don't leave the building without telling me. The dogs...you know...only have one mission in life." Murdock nodded and proceeded to the car. It was parked under a flickering fluorescent light. The car's beauty was breathtaking. It's flawless body gleamed in the strobe light. Murdock went directly to the rear spoiler which stabilized the vehicle at high speeds. Someone had removed the spoiler and placed it on the pavement beside the car. Murdock inspected the hollow fiberglass spoiler. He then searched the interior of the vehicle.

"So what is it?" asked someone entering the stall. Murdock was startled.

"It's the whale tail, Ernie."

"Whale tail?"

"This part right here," explained Murdock as he pointed to the spoiler which, with a little imagination, had the appearance of a whale's tail.

"So what about it?"

"This morning the car didn't have one. When I seized it with the deputy..." Ernie interrupted.

"You seized with a deputy? Hope Davenport doesn't hear about it."

"He won't unless someone tells him." Murdock paused. "Actually, I don't care anymore. When I saw the car this morning, it didn't have a tail. When I seized it, it did!"

"Are they removable?"

"Not supposed to be."

"I don't get the significance of it," pondered Ernie.

"Think about it. Why would someone want a removable spoiler?"

"I don't know, why?"

"Hidden storage," replied Murdock.

"Not much space for storage," stated Ernie squatting and looking at the spoiler.

"Depends on the cargo."

"Drugs?" asked Ernie. Murdock hesitated.

"I think so. Farmer was scared out of his wits when I mentioned taking the car...and now this. I think it's drugs."

"Who though?"

"The guy up front says two men checked the car out at different times today."

"Who were they?"

"He didn't get any names. One of 'em got whatever was in the tail."

"Let's get some descriptions," motioned Ernie.

Murdock and Ernie took descriptions of the two men who had examined the Porsche.

"You recognize them?" asked Ernie.

"The guy at four-thirty could've been Farmer or anyone else tall and slim wearing a hat and sunglasses. The man at seven sounds like an undercover DEA agent I saw a picture of."

"Why didn't he identify himself as an agent then?"

"I don't know. The FBI told me to watch him."

"Bill, listen to yourself," Ernie was emphatic. "DEA, FBI...you're getting in over your head on this case. Davenport will hand it to you. You've got people sneaking around a car you shouldn't have seized. How much deeper can you get?" Ernie looked away.

"I really don't know what to do about all of this," replied Murdock.

"Just level with Davenport. It's the best thing," pleaded Ernie. He was genuinely concerned about Murdock.

"I'll find a way to explain it. Just wish I'd been here sooner to check out the tail."

"If drugs were in the tail and the first visitor wasn't the owner, I guess you know you're in trouble again," pleaded Ernie.

"How do you figure?"

"If the drugs didn't belong to the first man and he got 'em, the second one will be looking for you. You may not be able to get out of this now."

"I gotta make a phone call." Murdock used Island Wrecker's phone. "Beetle, can you make an anonymous call for me?"

"Sure, I'd love to...it's been a while. Whatcha got?" inquired Beetle who was always willing to go beyond the call of duty.

"Call DEA in Fort Lauderdale. Tell 'em that there's cocaine being stored in the garage located at fifteen-fifteen Ocean Circle, Lighthouse Point."

"Is it?"

"Just a hunch, but I think so. Julia told me that the Porsche is at the house a couple of days each month. I think the car is used to deliver drugs using the whale tail as storage. I could be wrong."

"That's probable cause enough for me to call. Whose house?"

"She's an elderly woman...mother of one of Julia's taxpayers. She's in her eighties. I'm sure she has no idea what's going on."

"I'll pass it on to them."

Murdock placed another call to Frank.

"Hey, Frank."

"On vacation and ya still thinkin' of me. What a guy." Murdock grinned hearing his partner's sarcasm.

"If I'm right, they'll be a termination assessment tonight against someone in Fort Lauderdale." IRS makes what they call a "Termination Assessment" against people caught by the police with large amounts of unexplainable cash on hand. The sizable amounts drug smugglers typically possess. The police then call a criminal investigator who calls a revenue officer, who then calls a revenue agent with the Examination Division. Then, they all meet at the scene, count the cash and figure what the tax on the cash would have been if it had been properly reported on an income tax return. The person's tax year is immediately terminated by making an assessment. The revenue officer would then seize the money and apply it to the newly created tax assessment. This is one method the IRS uses to deal with the drug world.

"What's going on?" asked Frank. Murdock filled him in. "Hope you're wrong. We don't need anymore excitement around here."

Murdock returned to the Porsche as Ernie was tucking a thin, diary-type book into his rear pocket. He found the book in the rear of the vehicle, underneath the carpet. Some pages had been torn and the few that remained had peculiar symbols and numbering system. A code, he thought. This intrigued him especially in light of his computer background.

"Ernie, thanks for the help. Nothing else we can do here."

"Be careful," cautioned Ernie. "Think about your family because Davenport would love to get rid of you."

"It's gonna be okay but...thanks."

After giving instructions to the man at the facility, Murdock and Ernie went home. As Murdock left the area he watched Ernie drive in the opposite direction when another set of headlights appeared in the rear view mirror. Murdock turned and slowly drove down a side street. The wide automobile behind him negotiated the turn and followed. Murdock reached into his glove compartment and retrieved a dark blue, 9-mm pistol and two clips. Enough firepower to take on a small army. He kept it in his right hand and again turned down a narrow street lined with vegetation. The sounds of mating tomcats echoing throughout the alley sounded like a dozen babies crying. He gripped the pistol tighter as the crying became louder and louder.

His eyes darted from the rear view mirror to the street in front of him and then back to the mirror until the stalking vehicle was captured in the mirror once again. Murdock quickly turned the corner and backed into another alley. As he turned his lights out, a huge yellow and black spotted tomcat came flying out of nowhere, pouncing on the hood of his car. His heart pounded. The cat hissed and displayed a series of motions. Sweat was pouring down Murdock's brow. He poked the cat once with the nozzle of his pistol, and was tempted to pull the trigger. The cat fled and the sound of crying babies carried sending a chill over his body as he waited under the fronds of small coconut trees.

Moments later a dark, late-model sedan crept past the alley. Murdock ran to the end of the alley and caught the first letter of the Florida license plate as the car turned the corner. Sweat filled his eyes. He backtracked and went to his motel room. As he entered the apartment he glanced over his shoulder and on the south side of the highway, parked in the shadow of a building, was the dark sedan. Murdock peered through the venetian blinds and studied the driver. With his handgun tucked in his jeans, he left his room and circled the block on foot in an effort to approach the car from behind. He turned the first corner. The street was empty and silent as if nothing was ever there. The hot, humid air clung to him making breathing difficult.

When he returned to his apartment he splashed cold water on his face and lay quietly on the bed fully clothed, gun glued to his palm and to his side. His head was throbbing. In the darkness surrounding him, he sifted through the labyrinth of thoughts. The ringing of the phone sent a shock wave through his body. He hesitated for a few moments and collected his thoughts.

"Hello."

"This is Rico," whispered the DEA agent in a low, monotone.

"How do you know where I am?" Rico didn't respond to his question.

"So what are you working on?" Murdock didn't know what to say. He knew he didn't want to confide in him especially since he fit the description of the second person visiting the Porsche. Murdock also thought it could have been Rico who had followed him.

"Communicate with only me from this point," said the agent. "...and only share what you know with me."

"Why only you?"

"It's how we stay alive in this game."

"Game?" The word didn't seem to fit, thought Murdock.

"You must know who the players are, the rules...then you'll be okay."

"You're not making any sense to me."

"I will...in time," replied Rico. "Just do as I say."

"Why were you at the Porsche this evening?" Murdock was tired of this double talk. "...and why did you follow me?"

"Excellent Murdock. I see you're still sharp. Sharp people...they live longer. I lifted prints off the car and I didn't follow you." Murdock didn't understand Rico.

"How did you know I seized the car and where it was stored?"

"I listened to your conversation with Farmer at the house when you seized the car."

"I don't believe you."

"You no longer have much of a choice."

"Why?"

"A defector from the Rosario Drug Cartel...his name is Nieto...he knows you seized the Porsche and may have the contents it was carrying. You don't think he's interested in you now?" There was silence. "Are you armed?"

"Why do you want to know?"

"Because you're too close."

"I'm armed. How do you know Nieto is here?"

"Farmer's body was fished out of the canal behind his house an hour ago. He drowned, but not before his eyes and tongue were removed. It's Nieto's signature...he *is* here and I'm not losing him this time." Rico sounded obsessed.

"I don't know what you've got in mind, but I can't get involved in this anymore. I'll lose my job."

"When you seized the Porsche you became involved. The contents are missing and Nieto will do anything to get it back."

"Was it drugs?" asked Murdock.

"Yes. Pharmaceutical quality cocaine worth a fortune."

"How do I know you didn't take it...you were there," asked Murdock desperately seeking the truth.

"You don't, but trust your instincts and believe what I tell you. I relied on you once, so now it's my turn to repay the deed."

"When did I ever help you?"

"I was part of Operation Phoenix." There was silence again between them. Murdock took an oath prior to ending his tour of duty in Vietnam that he would never talk about this highly clandestine military assignment. Only a few, at the time, knew about it. Murdock surmised Rico must have been part of the operation.

"What can I do for you?" asked Murdock.

"Say nothing to anyone...and trust me. I'll be in touch." Before Murdock could utter another word, Rico was gone.

Operation Phoenix involved trained expert assassins during the Vietnam conflict. A secretive venture of the military involving two, four-man teams who reported to, and received directives from, a small office in the Pentagon. Their sole purpose for existence was to penetrate the VC and create chaos anyway they could. This chaos usually came in the form of assassinations of key government figures. Rico had been an impressive member of the team. One of Murdock's missions was to secure safe passage into Cambodia for Rico and the other assassins on his team. Ten miles into the Cambodian jungles Murdock's squad encountered a unique type of bamboo-spiked booby trap. The razor sharp poisoned blades sprung, killing four of his six men. Rico learned of the sacrifice Murdock's squad made for him and was now honored to be in a position to help Murdock.

Murdock wondered if a fortune in cocaine could tempt Rico. Five seconds after hanging up, the hotel operator called. "A message from Palmetto came in this afternoon. He said to check the recording. Doesn't make any sense to me. What's a Palmetto?"

"It's a long story, thanks." He dialed the Key West number. It was Farmer's voice on the machine. He was erratic in thought, speech and hysterical. The message read:

"You shouldn't have taken the car! I don't understand it...why! The IRS said it was okay, but not you...now this! He's gonna get me for this...I know he's mad but I didn't do it!"

The phone went dead. The message didn't make any sense.

Murdock left word for Palmetto to send him the tape. While he didn't understand it, he knew those were probably Farmer's last words before his gruesome demise. Murdock called home.

"Beth, it's me. How are you guys?"

"We're fine. The kids just went to sleep asking for you. When are you coming home?"

"Another few weeks and it should be over." Murdock was silent. He wasn't sure how his wife was going to take this next request. "Beth, do you think you could stay with your parents until I get home?"

"What's the matter?" replied Beth somewhat alarmed.

"Nothing. It's difficult for me to concentrate on work when I know you're alone so much. Could you do it for me?"

"What's the matter? You're scaring me, Bill. What's wrong?" Years of marriage were showing. She knew something was up.

"Don't worry, everything is fine. Just spend some time over at your parents. I'll tell you everything later."

"All right, they'd like us around. Are you sure you don't want to tell me something?"

"Later. But I'm fine, okay?"

"All right," Beth was hesitant. "I'll leave tomorrow, but call me every night, do you hear me?"

"I promise...I'll do it." Murdock forced a laugh to try to ease his wife's concern.

Murdock fell asleep, still clothed and gun at his side. As Murdock slept, Rico was filing the tape-recorded phone conversation Murdock had just had with his wife.

13

Edward Kemtz found it difficult to swallow as he pulled into the circular driveway made of imported Italian stone. This would be his second face-to-face encounter with Joel Meyers. The absence of streetlights allowed the twinkling stars to appear even bolder, sparkling like diamonds against a black velvet cloth. Edward followed a path of small, dimly lit amber lights to the rear of the house where he was to board Meyers' multi-million dollar yacht. The ship was sleek and loaded with a million dollars worth of electronic equipment. Lights in the forward cabin illuminated the emerald-green water. Captain Nemo would have been impressed, he thought. As Edward approached the floating monstrosity, a muscular man in his mid-fifties greeted him. By the bulge under his left arm, he was well armed.

"Mr. Kemtz?"

"Yes."

"Please board and wait here," instructed the guard. Edward looked about him and saw a side of the opulent city unknown to most people. Even the finger canals that permeated the area were heavily patrolled by a private security agency. Beautifully landscaped yards with lighted pools and yachts edged the waterways. Most of the houses had thick vegetation, adding to the privacy. A few minutes passed before the guard reappeared.

"Mr. Meyers will see you now." The cabin door was opened and Edward was allowed to pass. Gleaming mahogany wood lined the interior walls. Laughter could be heard from the quarters below.

"Go downstairs," instructed the guard once again. He looked over at the guard's expressionless face. His heart began beating faster and faster.

The spiral staircase opened into a large office lined with books. Meyers sat on a royal-blue sofa flanked by the prettiest woman he had ever seen. The sheer lingerie revealed her youth.

"Come in, come in. Have a seat." Edward sat down across from Meyers and set his leather portfolio beside him.

"I have the letter," responded Edward.

"Not yet, let's enjoy a drink together. We have plenty of time for that. Nina, get Mr. Kemtz a drink. What will it be?"

"I'll pass...got some other things to do."

"I don't conduct business aboard this ship until we've had a drink," responded Meyers adamantly.

"Scotch on the rocks." Nina stood up and her sheer outfit exposed her dramatic curves. Meyers observed Edward watching the woman.

"Lovely, isn't she," remarked Meyers as he gave her backside a gentle rub. "Would you like her?"

"Do you want the letter or don't you?" revealed Edward trying to get the meeting on track so he could get out. The letter revealed that the IRS would abate $248,000 of a $600,000 tax increase.

"Are you always in such a hurry?"

"Business is business," replied Edward anxious to leave.

"You've got to learn to balance business with pleasure. It certainly has helped me over the years." Meyers laughed.

"I'm sure it has and when I've got more money in my pocket, I'll take things a little slower...but for now, I'd like to conduct some business." Nina entered the room. Her wavy, brown hair gracefully cascaded down her satin-like skin to her lower back. She was truly a work of art.

Nina handed Edward his drink and promptly took her place beside her master. She leaned over the end table, placed a platinum straw to her nose and inhaled one of three rows of white powder which had been organized on a six-inch square mirror. The remaining two rows of the powdery substance waited to be sniffed into Meyers' large proboscis. He moved closer to her.

"She's got a nice touch," remarked Meyers smiling and sipped his brandy. Nina then pivoted her body around in front of Meyers. He continued his conversation ignoring Nina. Edward was disgusted, but the woman's methodical movements compelled him to watch. She was mesmerizing. Moments later Meyers stopped talking, and he concentrated on Nina. A moment later he was quiet.

"If your show is over, I'll give you the letter..." commented Edward too nervous to be aroused by her actions. "...if not, I'm leaving."

"All right, all right!" laughed Meyers as he squeezed Nina and instructed her to leave. "She's a sweetie. When I found her she was making a thousand dollars a night."

Edward passed a letter that had been written on IRS stationery. The shiny head of Meyers reflected the humid November night as he slipped his gold rimmed glasses on his chubby bulldog face.

"A man of your word I see, and so am I. This is for...how shall I say...your efforts." Meyers passed a blue canvas pouch to him which contained the final cash installment.

"It's all there. Our business is done. Tell Art it's been a pleasure...as always." Edward nodded. Once again the Criminal Investigation Division permanently recorded the conversation. Microphones at the yacht had been used this time with the permission of a federal judge.

As Edward rose from his chair the muscles in his neck and back tightened. His heart pounded so hard it hurt. He wondered if Meyers was even going to let him leave. His eyes focused straight ahead as his mind concentrated on what the guard on deck might do.

"Kemtz!" shouted Meyers. Edward stopped cold. He didn't move as he contemplated what would happen next. "Be sure to tell Art it's been a pleasure." Edward nodded and without a word he exited the cabin. The guard was now at the ship's bow. He breathed a sigh of relief when his feet hit the ground.

Edward negotiated the heavy traffic on his way to a secluded field near Port Everglades where Art Cook was waiting. Edward located Art's decrepit Chevrolet next to a large stack of lumber ready for shipment and got in. A warm, forceful rain started and bludgeoned the car making the conversation between the two very difficult.

Art laughed, "Easiest money you ever made, kid. And all of it's tax free, too!" He laughed again—not as hardy this time.

"Who else in Lauderdale worked with you?" asked Edward.

"Why are you asking?" replied Art suspecting something was amiss. His eyes penetrated Edward. There was an uncomfortable silence between them.

"Just curious as to why it took you so long to share the wealth. I could've been making this kind of money years ago." Art was reticent. His stone-cold face looked ancient. Art finally smiled.

"Kid, you had me worried there for a second. Thought you might be working the other side. I've been able to do most of the work myself until now. I don't know anything about what Collection does."

"You've helped Meyers before?"

"I've helped that phony get rich." Edward looked down. "Kid, I've done a lot of good for the company during my thirty-two years. The money has been my compensation for putting up with the crazy assignments. I've moved whenever and wherever they needed me, disrupted my family and personal life to accommodate the jerks and for what? They've passed me over for jobs to let less qualified people move ahead. Those fools...but, that's all over now."

"Doesn't look like the money was spent on you." Art smiled.

"It wasn't. My children's education, family vacations...things no one could ever take away. I thought if I were caught at least my efforts wouldn't have been in vain. They can't take my kids' education away or the memories can they?"

"What about the embarrassment to your family if you were caught? You had to have thought about that."

"I've been careful. This is my last favor anyway." Edward looked over in surprise. "If I were caught now, it's too late for 'em. I'd still win." Art gave a slight laugh. "Here, take it." Art handed his portion of the cash to Edward. "Take it!"

"Why?"

"I won't be needing it and, quite frankly, I've had my share. This was Meyers last favor from me. That's why I introduced you to him. It's your turn to make a fortune. Meyers and I go back many years."

"Why can't you use the money?"

"My tests came back positive last week. I'll be dead in a couple of months—I've got the big 'C'." Art was quiet and looked down. "The cancer is in my brain...it's inoperable." The revelation stunned Edward. "They wouldn't prosecute me now. I'd drop dead before the grand jury could ever hear testimony." Arts hacking cough returned. "Edward, we come from the same neighborhood. I knew your family. Take the money and do something meaningful with your life. Don't waste it here...no one cares...but you know that." Edward listened and lowered his head this time.

"Clear your conscience and look at it as bonus money." Art placed his hand on Edward's shoulder. "We'll not talk again. Enjoy your life, kid...enjoy!"

Edward exited the vehicle with the money pouch in hand. The tepid rain immediately drenched his body. As Art backed up, flashing blue lights converged on his car. Edward turned around and three men wielding guns and badges confronted him as well.

"Criminal Investigations, IRS. Up against the wood pile." As his Miranda rights were being read another agent began a methodical search of his person. A third agent held a gun two feet from his head. The rain was unrelenting.

"He's wired!" yelled an agent.

"What do ya mean he's wired?" yelled another agent as rain filled the crown of his hat.

"I mean he's wired!"

"Who is he working for?" shouted the third agent.

"Yeah, who are you working for?" shouted an agent through the deafening rain. Before Edward could respond, three other cars emitting blue strobe lights from the grill pulled into the vacant lot. A man got out of the car.

"Who's in charge of this mess?" No one responded to the barrel-chested man wearing suspenders. He cupped his hands around his mouth and shouted through the rain again.

"Over here," replied an agent standing by Edward. The man proceeded toward the voice.

"Ed, what's going on? Who are these people and why are you handcuffed?"

"They claim to be with CI."

"Is that so," growled the man as he squeezed water from his handle bar mustache.

"I'm the special agent in charge here," identified a woman holding a badge with *Criminal Investigator* embossed on a gold shield. "...and you are?"

"Inspector Stepp, IRS. What's going on here?" The inspector looked around at the crowd of agents and blue lights while the rain pounded them.

"That's what we want to know."

"Edward, here, has been working with us on a bribe case. Has been all along," replied Stepp. "...now it's your turn."

"We've been taping and photographing this man ever since he walked into Joel Meyers' office."

"Well, you can take the handcuffs off of him now. We'll talk about this tomorrow in my office. Oh, one more thing. We'll take the gentleman over there, too." Edward and Inspector Stepp climbed into the car alone.

"I didn't mind helping you on this case, but it just occurred to me you tried to set me up." Stepp looked straight ahead without a word. "I thought it was odd getting cases on Joel Meyers' corporations when I'm not even assigned that area. You knew Art was taking bribes from Meyers and that Art and I were friends so you had some of his corporate accounts assigned to me. I drive a nice car and you thought I was in on it too, didn't ya?" Still no word out of Stepp. "When you found out I wasn't in on it you asked me to help." Edward's voice grew louder and louder as the facts became clearer. "You're too much."

"You know it's our job!" responded Stepp. "...to police the organization. You know that." Edward was reticent. "There'll be a nice letter of commendation from the Commissioner for you."

"Stick the letter!" Edward opened the door and unwillingly played tug-of-war with the wind and rain.

***

Beetle rolled over in bed and turned the light on. He fumbled through a stack of papers until he located a telephone number he had scratched on a small, crumpled piece of paper. After misdialing the number a couple of times he finally got through.

"Drug Enforcement," replied the lone agent at the Fort Lauderdale Federal Building.

"I can't tell you who I am..." replied Beetle. The agent immediately activated the tape recorder. "...but, there's a large quantity of white powder you boys refer to as cocaine being stored at fifteen-fifteen Ocean Circle, Lighthouse Point, Florida. It's in the garage," explained Beetle disguising his voice.

"How do you know?"

"I just know."

"I need your name."

"Now, does that really matter?"

"Is anyone there now and are they armed?"

"Don't know."

"Just for the record, why are you telling us?"

"Thought you might like to know. One more thing, the house belongs to a Mrs. Farmer. She has nothing to do with it. Have a good night." Beetle turned the light out, rolled back over and went to sleep knowing the agents were going to act on the tip.

At 2:01 a.m. two carloads of DEA agents cut their engines and allowed their sedans to coast to a stop one block from the Lighthouse Point address. Armed with sawed off, double-barreled shotguns, Uzi's, and 9 millimeter pistols, the agents approached the garage from different angles. A light inside the long aluminum structure illuminated the surrounding area. Two Spanish-speaking men were talking and laughing when the butt of an agent's gun smashed the rear window. The two men reached for their Uzi's and fired a burst that ripped the aluminum wall in half. A third Latin male hid in the corner, motionless. Two agents simultaneously entered the front entrance, one squatting while the other agent stood erect. Their adrenaline was flowing and their fingers were locked around the triggers. The agents entered firing their guns and didn't stop until their weapons were emptied.

The two men were left lying on the floor, their chests exploded and fried. Dogs howled as the sleepy affluent neighborhood awoke to flashing blue lights and cocoa dust in the air. When the cloud settled, Agent Duncan and his men began searching the garage.

"Hate the smell of burned flesh. It stays with me," snarled Duncan as he fanned the smoke from his face.

"Got another one over here." The third man was squatting in the corner, trembling, speechless as urine dropped from his crotch, forming a puddle on the chalky pavement.

"Get up!" ordered one of the agents as he placed the muzzle of his small, but powerful 9-millimeter to the third man's skull and pulled him up by his hair. Another agent began his methodical search.

"Just a wallet."

"Who is he?" inquired Duncan.

"Ramon Martinez. You know him?"

"No. Read him his rights and get 'em out of here." The agent read Martinez his rights in English then in Spanish.

"Got a mountain of coke, a suitcase full of cash and enough modified guns and silencers to supply a battalion," declared another agent obviously pleased with the catch.

"Appears we got a few of the Cocaine Cowboys. Everyone knows the routine...let's do it!" ordered Duncan. The surrounding area was taped off while the Alcohol, Tobacco and Firearms, local PD, an ambulance and IRS were notified. The three IRS employees who were contacted were well-versed in these situations. They have to be since the court scrutinizes their actions when the defendant sues. And they *always* sue. The three would immediately terminate the person's tax year and assess tax based on the estimated street value of the drugs found. Since there is no such thing as credit in the drug world, the IRS presumes the person had cash to buy them. The revenue agent would make the computations and the revenue officer would seize the money.

By dawn, the elaborate computations were completed and the money seized. Murdock's hunch paid off. The revenue officer and criminal investigator proceeded to the bank and exchanged the money for a cashier's check. A federal tax lien would be filed by the revenue officer against Ramon Martinez and the other two men in the amount of $378,000. The Notice of Federal Tax Lien would alert the public that the IRS had an interest in any property belonging to the three men.

Frank returned to the office with check in hand by 9:30 a.m.

"Fill me in," barked Davenport. Frank explained what had transpired during the past five hours. "Good, good. I told DEA we wanted to be there when they started interrogating Martinez."

"Who's gonna work with me on this?" asked Frank knowing the investigation into the assets would take days to locate and seize.

"Murdock will be in today and use the one trainee you didn't manage to run off. You still have 'em don't you?"

"I didn't know Bill was returning."

"He is now," replied Davenport with a smirk. "This is as good a time as any to inform all of you. Gather, around." The revenue officers formed a semi-circle in front of Davenport. "We've got some budget problems. I've been informed to reduce our field time in half to save money. We'll have to decide which investigations are really important and shelve the rest."

"What about the computer hook-up to the State we've been waiting on?" asked Hank Goffman.

"It's been scrapped."

Lawrence uttered fowl language.

"Hold on to your pencils since they may become a scarce item."

"Why don't you just put up a 'Closed' sign," remarked Frank.

"Non-critical employees are being furloughed," continued Davenport.

"Besides Lawrence, who's non-critical?" asked Frank.

"I don't know yet."

"So *we* could be laid off?"

"Could be," replied Davenport.

"Why the furlough?"

"Congress hasn't approved the budget. All details and training have been cut."

"If we were a company in private industry we'd have to file bankruptcy," remarked Frank. Several nodded.

Lawrence cussed a little louder this time.

"That's enough, Lawrence," growled Davenport. "There's more. Next week a revenue representative for the IRS in Australia will be joining us for a while. It's part of his Americanization process."

"What's that?"

"He's been overseas with OIO for about ten years or so. Washington is reacquainting him with our procedures." OIO stands for Office of International Operations.

"He's in for an education all right," quipped Frank.

"Tell him to bring his own pencils cause I'm not sharing mine. Nope, I'm not sharing any with that..." Lawrence uttered more obscenities oblivious to Davenport's caution.

"That's it, Lawrence, in my office...now! That profanity finally got you!"

"We don't even have enough money to fund our field work but they've got enough for this kangaroo thumper to hop over here," continued the vulgar officer.

"In my office!" Davenport's metamorphoses was occurring. "That's it for now."

"I don't understand how they can do this," stated Becky Williams. Hank Goffman overheard her.

"Listen, you shouldn't be here anyway." She turned toward Hank in disbelief. Becky hadn't filed a union complaint in 72 hours and she was long overdue.

"Are my ears deceiving me or did Hank really say that?" she inquired looking for witnesses.

"Becky, women are the downfall of the IRS," continued Hank.

"Explain that!" Becky pulled out a small pad ready to record Hank's every word.

"We didn't have Kleenex boxes cluttering the desks until women started working. You should be home watching Oprah, playing tennis or just jumping in a pool on hot days like today." The others began to laugh as they watched Becky eagerly record his statement and look for witnesses. Hank turned and shrugged his shoulders.

Lawrence exited Davenport's office head down and looking dejected after receiving a ten-minute counseling session. He returned to his desk and incessantly mumbled.

"Frank! Get in here!" yelled Davenport from his glass cage.

"What can I do for ya boss?"

"I'm getting calls from division concerning a certain telephone call you made in response to this memorandum." Davenport handed Frank the memo. "Remember this one?"

"Sure do. National Office thanked me for my input."

"What exactly did you tell them?"

"Just that the program they were about to implement sucked and that they should always solicit the field's response prior to starting something new. Ya getting a lot of compliments?"

"Not exactly." Davenport's blood pressure began to perk again. "Why would you tell them such a thing?"

"The memo requested a response, so I called them," replied Frank still proud of what he had done while acting as group manager.

"The memo's addressed to the Regional Commissioner. They wanted the Regional Commissioner to respond, not Frank Laccetti, acting group manager!"

"Look here..." Frank pointed to the last sentence on the page. "It reads, '...or a member of your staff may respond,' that's when I called."

"But I don't have any staff and you're not a member of the Regional Commissioner's staff! Now get out of here." Frank limped out of his office and back to his desk as Davenport began writing his response as to why the phone call had occurred.

Murdock entered the office and was surrounded by his coworkers, happy he had returned and glad they could shift some cases his way. The commotion caught Davenport's attention.

"Care to join me?"

"Tell 'em to kiss it, you just got here," mumbled Lawrence.

"Be right there." Murdock entered the sterile office devoid of pictures, plants or any other personal items.

"I understand you seized a Porsche on that case of Julia's."

"That's right, I protected the government's interest. We'll be getting $20,000 for it which is $20,000 more than if I hadn't seized." Murdock sat down in the brown swivel chair.

"That's not the point. You failed to follow my instructions on this case and that's gonna cost you."

"Does it matter that I'm collecting money we wouldn't have gotten? I thought *that* was the point!" Davenport tapped his pencil as he turned it end over end and nodded his head in frustration.

"If you want me to stop doing my job on this case, put it in writing. You willing to do that?" asked Murdock certain of Davenport's answer. Davenport was silent. "I didn't think so. Isn't it a little unusual that you're not giving me written instructions on this case, especially when the government's interest isn't being protected and there's big bucks involved?" Davenport's silence continued. "What's going on? Why the secrecy?" Still no comment from Davenport. Murdock stood up. "Why can't a routine assessment be made against the sole officer of a defunct corporation? We make these assessments everyday, but we can't on this one. Instead, the file gets lost. Pretty unusual wouldn't you say, Richard?"

"Files get lost...it happens."

"On this kind of money and in the middle of an assessment? Come on." The two were silent. Murdock turned suddenly. "Why were Julia and I asked to stop the investigation?"

"Not your concern, Murdock. Management dictates where the resources will be placed, not you." Davenport leaned back in his chair, hands folded on his abdomen.

"Did you know Criminal Investigation stopped the Fort Lauderdale detective because of the sensitivity of the case? Richard, what's keeping us from doing our jobs?"

"I don't know!" yelled Davenport as he sat erect in his chair. "The Director didn't tell us anything."

"The Director? Is he behind whatever this is?"

"Forget I said that. I don't know what's going on!"

"I believe you, Richard, but it sounds like you oughta know. I'm going to unravel this case—I'm just wondering where your name will surface and how it'll affect your retirement. How many more months do you have?"

"Don't you threaten me! Get out of here!" barked Davenport.

"I'm leaving, but it seems to me you're going out on a limb, all alone, and you don't even know why. I'll even bet you don't have anything in writing requesting the investigation be stopped. Think about it." Murdock returned to his desk when Frank caught him.

"Hey Bill, coffee?" Murdock nodded. "How'd ya know about the termination assessment before anyone else did?"

"I'll tell you later."

"Hank made a quick check of motor vehicles and the courthouse. So far he's found a Maserati and a house near Pier Sixty-six worth about four hundred and fifty thousand dollars. Uncle is gonna get his money on this one. Hank thinks there's a Lear Jet, too."

"Good work. Who's that lady in the gloves?" inquired Murdock. A woman at the front counter assisting walk-in taxpayers was wearing a bright green pair of rubber cleaning gloves and a surgical mask as she sifted through a voluminous stack of Form 1040 returns.

"She transferred from California. Allergic to ink," replied Frank.

"You're not serious." Frank laughed.

"I am." The two sipped their coffee on a rear balcony of the Federal Building watching Fort Lauderdale's rush hour traffic come to a halt as a man dressed in a Superman costume walked into traffic greeting people.

"How long has he been around?" asked Murdock.

" 'Bout the same time you left. A few of us thought it might be you." Murdock grinned.

"Not yet."

"Melissa filed for divorce." Murdock looked at him in disbelief.

"I'm sorry. Any chance of reconciliation?"

"Only if I leave for New York."

"She won't come back?"

"Nope."

"You going up there?"

"I don't know. I like the job and I love it here."

"Don't think about it too hard. You'll make the right decision."

"So how did you know about the termination assessment going down and Martinez being there?"

"Martinez?" asked Murdock.

"He was picked up during the raid at Lighthouse Point you called me about." Frank looked a little puzzled.

"Ramon Martinez?"

"Yeah."

"Where is he now?"

"Either with DEA or CI."

"Gotta go. I'll talk to you later." Murdock raced to the third floor. After presenting his badge he was allowed access into DEA.

"You here to see Martinez?"

"If it's convenient," replied Murdock. Police emblems from several departments adorned the walls of the agency.

"Now is as good as any. Can't get the scumbag to stop laughing. I should have fried him back there. Maybe you can get something out of him. He did mention the IRS would get him out." Agent Duncan escorted Murdock to the holding cell.

"You a two bit cop?" asked Martinez. His accent clearly revealed his Latin extraction.

"No, IRS. I'd like to ask you a few questions and then I'll leave you alone."

"What?! You ain't gonna leave me alone. You'll get me out of here, now! I'm Ramon Martinez!" he stood up and clutched the cell bars.

"Why would I want to do that?"

"Our understanding, you know!" Murdock was expressionless. "...Phillip Ward!" exclaimed Martinez. He turned to Duncan. "You don't know what you have here," continued Martinez.

"What do you mean?" asked Murdock.

"DEA may have dealt with a lot of people in my line of work, but none as sophisticated as I am."

"I want to ask you some questions," barked Duncan.

"And I want guarantees!" Martinez fired back.

"Such as?"

"First, no prosecution and you return the money you confiscated. I have to deliver it within forty-eight hours or I am dead. But..." Martinez hesitated. He was erratic in thought and speech. "...that's not my biggest concern."

"What is?"

"That my family is protected. I have enough money to have someone take care of them. The money is tucked away. You couldn't even find it." Martinez laughed.

"What's the deal with the IRS?" asked Duncan.

"He knows, ask him." Martinez looked over at Murdock.

"Are you referring to Sea Unlimited?"

"Of course I am! What else would I be..." Martinez stopped in mid sentence again. "You don't know, do you?"

"I know about the corporation, Ward and Warbington." Murdock tried to play along hoping he'd provide the missing pieces to the puzzle. Martinez stared at Murdock through his black, beady eyes.

"You don't know about our arrangement, I can tell. I'm not going to talk to some IRS flunky. Send me the big boys. You hear me! THE BIG BOYS!" shouted Martinez.

"No one is gonna rescue you. They don't want you around anymore," bluffed Murdock. "You're a liability." Martinez laughed hysterically again.

"You're lying, you don't know what's going on. Go on, get out of here." His accent, thick as the humidity, annoyed Duncan.

"They wanted you dead. Who do you think tipped off DEA this morning?" Martinez stopped laughing. "They didn't expect you to make it through the raid either." Martinez listened to Murdock. He made sense. "We're the only ones who can help you now. The others are tired of you...you're a risk."

Agent Duncan turned from the cage. "He wasn't concerned about anything this morning. I read him the riot act and told 'em about all those animals waiting to pop his can in prison. He just laughed."

"He thinks someone is gonna get him out of this," responded

Murdock.

"I'd say so. Who knows who he has in his pocket. What's the IRS gonna do?"

"We'll seize and sell everything he owns until the assessments are paid. So far, it looks like we'll get our money. Maybe that'll shut him up." Murdock turned to Martinez. "Tell me about the deal the IRS gave you." Martinez looked as though he had something to say and was going to say it when he burst into his maniacal laughter. Murdock shrugged his shoulders and gave Duncan his calling card. Upon returning to the office, he began sorting his mail which had piled high owing to his detail to the Keys. Davenport then received a call from the Chief of Criminal Investigation.

"The termination assessment made this morning should not have been made," whispered the Chief of CI.

"It's our operating procedure," explained Davenport to the Chief.

"Why wasn't I notified?"

"Couldn't reach you," replied Davenport a little perturbed the Chief chose to contact him directly rather than go through his Chief of Collection. CI had no organizational authority over the Collection Division.

"Ramon Martinez was arrested because of your people."

"So," responded Davenport.

"He's part of the package deal. Since the assessment was made we'll have to let it stand. Just don't seize anything else...yet."

"When can we seize?"

"I'll notify you."

"I just can't keep our investigation on hold indefinitely. I need a reason for the delay...something in writing preferably through channels," requested Davenport remembering Murdock's caution.

"You heard what the Director said. This case has the highest priority and security. Do you want the Director to personally call you?"

"No, that's okay. I'll wait for further instructions."

"One last item, what has the DEA been told?" asked the Chief.

"I thought this was an interdepartmental effort," replied Davenport.

We'll, it's not. What do they know?"

"I don't know. Martinez is in their custody, but he isn't talking."

"All right. Just remember the security needed in this case. If you have any questions call Carmichael."

Davenport massaged his temples as Murdock's words came back to him and the sudden change in tone was unsettling.

***

"Frank. Take a look at this and tell me what you think." Murdock passed a brown file to him. "It's a copy of Julia's case and everything I've done."

"Bill, call on zero-three," interrupted the secretary. "It's the DEA...says it's important."

"Hey, Murdock, Martinez has taken a liking to ya. Wants to talk, but to you only," reported Agent Duncan.

"Why the sudden change of heart?"

"He called someone and, whoever it was, pissed him off. I think you've got his attention. Can you come up?"

"On my way." Murdock was again ignoring Davenport's counsel. A few minutes later Murdock was in the DEA's office.

"For some reason, the ol' boy wants to talk to us," said Duncan as he lit his pipe. The cherry-scented tobacco permeated the office. Murdock and Duncan proceeded to the cage. Martinez was standing with his back to them, staring out a distant window.

"You look like an honest man so I'll talk to you," stated Martinez, his back still to them. His greasy black hair came to a sharp point in the middle of his neck. Murdock pulled a chair up to the bars. "But before I talk I need assurances."

"The best we can do is explain to the judge the assistance and information you've given to us. If it's significant the judge will listen and probably go our way. So what do you want in exchange?"

"Not much. I want out of here by tonight. No jail time and a new life somewhere far away for me and my family—maybe overseas. When they don't get their money, they'll kill all of us."

"You better have something good," declared Duncan.

"So what do you know?" asked Murdock. Martinez began his

maniacal laughter. Murdock and Duncan looked at each other in amazement.

"He doesn't have anything. He's just another scabby dirtbag," commented Duncan. Martinez stopped his laughing.

"I've got the information, but not for you two."

"Why did you call me?" asked Murdock.

"I trust you. Arrange a grand jury and I'll tell it to everyone at the same time."

"I'll tell you how it works," reported Duncan. "You give us a clue as to what you've got. If it's good, we'll get with the U.S. Attorney and he'll cut the deal."

"It's good all right?" laughed Martinez, "...it's good."

"So give us a clue."

"All I'll tell you right now is that it involves some big boys in the IRS, some federal judges and I'll fill you in on our offshore money laundering business."

"Are they involved in the drugs and guns we found this morning?" asked Duncan.

"The judge is."

"What about the IRS?" asked Murdock.

"No, not exactly..." Martinez hesitated. "...but we're all untouchable because of them."

"Why do you think that?"

"I'll save my reason for the grand jury."

"Can you substantiate your story?" asked Duncan.

"Yes."

"And you're prepared to tell it all to a grand jury?"

"Only if I get what I've asked for. And what I want right now is to get out of here."

"It'll take a little time to make the arrangements."

"Just be quick about it. Small spaces make me sick and you wouldn't want that." Martinez could not take his eyes off the single window which offered him the only relief from the constricting iron walls.

The Internal Revenue Service touches each of our lives whether we like it or not...

Shadows of IRS is the first novel ever to provide the reader with an exclusive look inside the *real* Internal Revenue Service from someone deep within the agency. This is an organization that Senator Roth has called, **...“*the most secretive bureaucracy in the U.S. Government”....***

Why Wait? . . . Order Now!

Have this exciting novel gift wrapped (at no extra charge) for a friend or family member. Simply call Book Clearing House, M-F, 8:00-4:30 p.m., or visit our impressive website at

www.americasuptown.com

and order via secure lines—either way, it’ll arrive within 72 hours!

If you have a question for the author, or a comment you would like to make to us, please write americasuptown@aol.com. Thanks.

Now . . . back to the story!

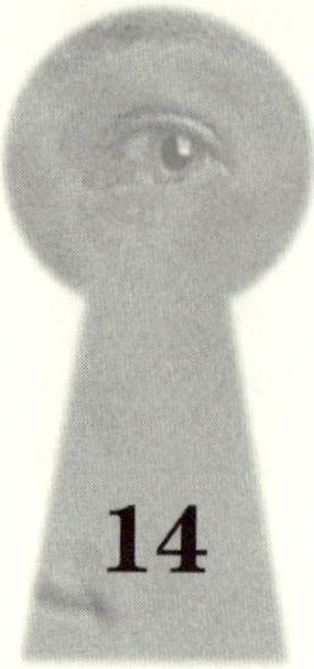

14

Something peculiar caught Beetle's attention as his eyes etched the gentle, frosty-white shoreline gazing out from the balcony. He scrambled for his glasses and focused on the object for several seconds.

"Oh no!" He ran downstairs almost breaking his neck. The body of his Indian coworker was lying face down, with limbs fully extended. Several small crabs were clinging to his shirt. Beetle kneeled beside him and rolled Cricket over. Beach sand came pouring out of his mouth, eyelids puffy, red and sealed shut. An empty bottle of Tennessee whiskey was by his side. Had he been there all night?

"Oh, please no!" Beetle immediately made the sign of the cross and prayed for his friend's soul. He frantically felt for a heartbeat, but none was found. "God, you don't want this lost soul, yet," mumbled Beetle as he looked around for help. Surprisingly, one of Cricket's swollen eyes opened and looked around. Cricket tried to speak. His sand-coated tongue muffled the words.

"You're alive!" shouted Beetle who was convinced his friend had passed on to the happy Indian hunting ground. "What is it?" he asked unable to decipher Cricket's words. He kneeled closely beside him and placed his ear close to Cricket's mouth.

"I said...I was with the Lady in White last night."

"You...you," Beetle stammered. "You were with the Lady in White again!" repeated Beetle in disbelief. "You ass! Here I am thinking your ugly butt is dead and you're just drunk again. I oughta bury you right here and now you hallucinating drunk!" Cricket threw one arm in the air signaling Beetle he was ready to be pulled into a sitting position.

Beetle quickly returned with Cricket's first aid. After downing the juice he washed the sandy vomit and crabs off him. The two then struggled back to his room.

"So what happened this time?"

"She came to my room and warned me."

"The Lady in White?"

"Yeah."

"You were drunk."

"That was later. When she first got here I wasn't."

"Warned you about what?" asked Beetle confused.

"I dunno, I passed out."

"Does the mystery lady have a name?"

"Well, of course she does," replied Cricket who appeared insulted over his friend's palpable disbelief.

"Well?"

"Well what?" asked Cricket.

"Well, what's her name?"

"I forget."

"All right, try this one, where is she now?"

"Don't know."

"A little louder," requested Beetle.

"I said, I don't know!"

"Where is she from?" Cricket shrugged his shoulders.

"But she's real!" Beetle shook his head.

"I'm telling you, you better cut the booze out or I'm gonna find ya dead somewhere."

They opened the door to his room and found it in shambles. Drawers had been pulled out, clothes dumped everywhere and the furniture turned over.

"What happened?"

"I don't know."

"Now why doesn't that surprise me?"

"I don't have anything. What would they be looking for?"

"I'll contact the manager."

Beetle called Palmetto about the incident and to request the day off. Palmetto reluctantly granted time off to the duo since they usually wound up in more trouble.

"Palmetto wants you to think about what you and Ernie have in common," relayed Beetle. Cricket was quick to respond.

"Trust me, nothing."

"Someone ransacked his room last night, too."

"You're shucking my corn," replied Cricket.

"No, he went out for dinner and when he returned his room looked like this."

"They knew just when to hit. Can't think of anything," commented Cricket.

"All right, meet you down by the pool in a couple of hours."

Moments after noon a plain white sedan rolled up to the seedy-looking motel Ernie was staying at. Two men dressed in dark suits and sunglasses approached Ernie and identified themselves as IRS inspectors. Ernie had been expecting them. An hour and a half later the inspectors left with the information Ernie had passed to them. Ernie then called the Fort Lauderdale office.

"Let me speak to Bill."

"Murdock," yelled the secretary.

"Bill, it's Ernie. I have some important info."

"I'm listening," replied Murdock.

"Cricket's and my room were broken into."

"What did they get?"

"Nothing. I'm not sure what they were looking for, but it has something to do with the Porsche you seized."

"What makes you say that?"

"The three of us were at the Porsche the other night. It's the only common denominator. You might be next."

"That night someone followed me back to the room and left. I couldn't get the plate number. You think they're looking for their drugs?"

"I don't think it's drugs they're after," responded Ernie.

"What then?"

"I don't know, but would you look in someone's clothes for a trunk full of cocaine? Half the pockets in my clothes were torn out."

"That doesn't make sense."

"That's what Inspection said," replied Ernie.

"Inspection?"

"It's for your own good, before you're in over your head," replied Ernie, satisfied he had done the right thing.

"What exactly did you tell them?" asked Murdock in a stern voice.

"Everything I know."

"Ernie! You shouldn't have," replied Murdock infuriated.

"It's for your own good. I'm just trying to help you."

"This isn't helping me. Davenport is ready to lay into me and all I need is an inspection report going to him. Listen, don't do anymore good deeds for me, understand!"

"You'll thank me later," replied Ernie, still convinced that he had done the right thing.

"I don't think so. No more, okay?"

"Goodbye," replied Ernie, clearly annoyed.

***

Alena Muller parked her automobile in the carport of the Key Largo house, unaware of the violence Farmer had sustained a few nights earlier. Key Largo was her sanctuary. It was a place of solitude away from the confusion of Miami. Tonight she would confront Ward about his rendezvous and her intent. She had a solemn look as she climbed the stairs, anxiously anticipating her words with Ward. As she opened the door everything was as they had left it, but she sensed something was wrong.

"Phillip," she shouted. Where was he? In all of their secret liaisons he had never been late. How unusual she thought since Ward was annoyingly punctual. Perhaps he was at the grocery store. But the house was closed up and the air conditioning was off.

She called his house, but there was no answer. Fifteen minutes passed without a word, so she called him at his condo in Miami. She was surprised when he answered.

"Why aren't you here?" asked Alena.

"You're in Largo?" His tone made her nervous.

"Where else? What's the matter?"

"Get out of there. Get out now and come to the condo."

"Why?"

"Just listen and get out, now!"

"Okay, but you're scaring me. You're not making any sense, but I'll leave."

An hour later she was at the Brickel Avenue condominium overlooking the Miami skyline. The two embraced.

"What's going on?" asked Alena still clutching him.

"Farmer is dead...murdered."

"When? How?"

"A couple of nights ago in Largo."

"You've got to stop what you're doing. I told you it would get out of hand. It could've been you!" she cried. "I saw photographs of you with the Colombians." She pulled away and walked toward the terrace. "I want our child to have a father." She paused. "If you love me you'll get out of this now."

"It's all right..."

"No! It's not!" interrupted Alena. "It's *not* all right! What must I say to you?!"

"A few more meetings and I'm done. We'll travel..."

Alena interrupted him again, "How can I get through to you? I don't care about the money or anything else except you and our baby. I want to get married and raise your children. What good will the money be if you're dead or in prison? Please, Phillip, please get out now! I've got this terrible feeling," she pleaded.

"Nothing is gonna happen to me. Another meeting and I'm done." Ward finished pouring the wine into chilled glasses.

"You're not listening! You didn't hear a word I said. For once in your life listen to what I'm saying! You have to stop this, now!" she yelled emphatically. Ward flashed a look of surprise. Alena had never raised her voice at him. He paused long enough for her words to sink in. She was alarmed and, for the first time, he felt it.

"Who took the pictures?"

"I don't know. My father wouldn't say, but they're watching you." Alena started crying as she walked out onto the veranda.

"I swear it's going to be all right." Ward placed his arms around her from behind. "Believe me, okay?" Alena was silent while she watched the sun set behind Miami.

"Phillip, I love you...but I'm leaving South Florida for good." Ward turned her around in disbelief.

"Why?"

"Because you just don't get it." She paused. "I have to get my life together."

"Where would you go?" He was hurt by what Alena had said.

"Does it really matter to you?"

"Of course it matters!" Ward released his hold on her and walked into the living room. He kept his back to her. "Who do you think this is for?" he shouted.

"It's not for me, Phillip," she declared as she turned and looked at him. "It never was." He started a slow pace. She looked back over the city and inhaled, then slowly exhaled. She needed strength for what she was about to say to him. Alena turned and faced Ward. "Go ahead and chase your money..." she hesitated. "...I'm leaving next week for Rhode Island. If you love me as much as you say you do, you'll be there." She walked to the door. Ward stood with his back to her again and waited a moment before responding.

"I'll be there, Alena...because I love you."

Alena opened the door, stopped without turning toward him, "I pray you're there—goodbye, Phillip."

15

The sweltering mid-morning sun turned the high security cell at the Broward County Jail into a sauna. Ramon Martinez had been transferred there the night before awaiting his appearance before a federal grand jury. Beads of sweat took turns streaking down his slick face and onto the drenched pillow. Without windows to soothe him, the quietness of the morning was alarming.

Moments later the clanging of a cell gate echoed throughout the halls followed by the clicking of heels. Not guard shoes, thought Martinez, but the sound of expensive leather shoes clicking louder and louder. Martinez sat erect on the edge of his cot. His heart raced.

"Ramon Martinez," announced a man in a green uniform. "Follow me." The man with the expensive shoes stood behind the guard and smiled. Not a friendly smile.

"Who is he?" asked Martinez.

"Just do as you're told," replied the guard.

"Where are we going?"

"You're a free man," said the guard.

"Has the grand jury convened?"

"No, not yet."

"I was supposed to stay here until I testified."

"Change of plans. We didn't see a need to keep you here until then."

"Why was I told I would have to stay?" No one commented. Martinez slowed his pace. The guard waved his hand and nodded to another guard who opened a final gate to the rear entrance of the facility. As he exited, the guard escorted him to a dark-blue, 1980 Oldsmobile. A rear door opened—Martinez got in and the car crept slowly away. He turned and the black hole of a sawed off shotgun greeted him. The man in the front seat held the gun on him while a third man in the back seat prepared a large syringe.

"I haven't talked to anyone. I'm making plans to leave the country and never return."

"Well, you got half of it right," replied the man with the gun. The others laughed.

"Give him your arm."

"You don't have to do this. I'm not saying anything! Let me leave. You can put me on a flight. I'll leave right now," pleaded Martinez. He reached for the door but it was locked. He knew that was it. The drive down Andrews Avenue would be his last look at life. "I have a wife and children to take care of."

"Maybe we'll pay them a visit when we're done with you." The men laughed again. Martinez struggled, determined to break free. He shoved the shotgun as far back and up as he could. His finger inched to the trigger squeezing a blast out of the stubby gun that shook the heavy car and blew a four-inch hole through the roof. Moments later he felt a tingling sensation cover his body. He looked down and a syringe had been shoved so deep and hard that the needle broke as it hit the bone.

"Come on, now, be a good boy about this. You'll pass out before your heart explodes and brains fry." The man with the gun smiled. Seconds later Martinez's eyes rolled back into his skull as his muscles began to uncontrollably contract. Thirty seconds later the convulsions ceased. Ramon Martinez was dead.

Less than four blocks away Davenport was making his way over to Murdock's desk. He placed a memorandum in front of Murdock. He looked up and read the document.

"I told you not to get involved in this." The memorandum was from Inspection. "I'm going to fire you for failing to follow my directives."

"What directives? I never saw anything in writing," explained Murdock. Davenport had a smirk on his face.

"Your time is coming," he replied.

"And you better be careful what you say to me and the tone you use," cautioned Murdock as Davenport turned and left.

"Got a minute?" asked Frank as he adjusted his crutch. "Let's talk about the file."

"I'm surprised you're finished with it," stated Murdock.

"Once I started, I couldn't put it down." The two went into a small conference room.

"I'm not sure, but something tells me you're in deep ca-ca...with everyone."

"Tell me something I don't know," replied Murdock.

"Whoever is behind this probably thinks you have whatever was in the Porsche."

"Why me?"

"Or anyone who was at the car," answered Frank. "If Farmer had what the guy was looking for, Ernie and Cricket's rooms wouldn't have been ransacked and I'll tell ya, he's looking for something other than the drugs."

"What then?" asked Murdock.

"Anything small enough to fit in a pocket, right?" Frank replied.

"Yeah, I thought that was odd that Ernie's pockets had been ripped out." Murdock paused. "Wait a minute, he told me that he found a small diary-type book in the Porsche." His speech quickened.

"What did it say?" asked Frank.

"He didn't understand it...there were numbers and symbols. It didn't make any sense...I never saw it," replied Murdock.

"Sounds like some kind of code. Does Ernie have it, now?"

"I think so."

"Ya might want to lock it up until you figure out who can decipher it. If that's what they want they're not gonna stop looking for it."

"You really think that's it?"

"Maybe."

"What am I gonna do?" asked Murdock as he ran his hands through his brown locks of hair.

"You need to talk to someone about this, now. You're a sitting target for anyone who has it in for you," cautioned Frank.

"The FBI is working the case."

"I wouldn't trust them, especially this character Rico. Where did they dig him up? And Warbington resurfaces as Thomas Farley who's still involved in money laundering, but this time he's got the government's blessing. Smart guy, he must have given the Feds some good stuff."

"Talk to Inspection," encouraged Frank.

"I can't. They'll report to the Director and he'll talk to Davenport."

"So?"

"He gave me specific instructions not to work the case."

"That sounds strange, doesn't it?" asked Frank.

"Well, maybe there is another investigation going on and CI doesn't want me interfering with it. We've been told to delay investigating the civil aspects of this case until CI completes the criminal investigation," stated Murdock trying to figure it out.

"Bill, there isn't a freeze code on this case, just a bunch of restricted files. CI didn't even cut a memo to us like they usually do when there's a criminal investigation taking place." Murdock nodded.

"Don't we always get a memo?" asked Frank.

"Yeah."

"You've got to talk to someone...now!"

"Got anything else?" asked Murdock.

"Wait a minute. I read something a while back about the Treasury IG."

"Inspector General?" asked Murdock. Frank nodded.

"It was an article about how they look into improprieties."

"But who's done anything wrong here except me looking into something I was told not to."

"That's just it, Bill. There's assets available to satisfy the corporate taxes and management is telling you not to touch it and *no one* is putting it in writing. That doesn't sound kosher to me." Frank talked with his hands.

"But what if there is a legitimate...a genuine investigation going on that I'm screwing up, then what?"

"I know a good furniture store you can work for in upstate New York," joked Frank.

"Thanks, I may need it."

"The Treasury IG is in Washington. Talk to them. If they're not the right agency maybe they can tell you who to talk to. After reading everything in this file, something ain't right." Frank handed the brown file back to Murdock. "I'd make another copy of everything. They're good notes." Murdock nodded in agreement.

After gathering all of his notes and locking them in the bottom drawer of his cabinet, Murdock headed upstairs to Criminal Investigation looking for a few answers.

"How are you, Bill?" greeted Marlene.

"Not well. Where's Carmichael?"

"He's not here."

"Who's acting for 'em?"

"No one. All the special agents went fishing. Peace and quiet at last."

"The entire office went fishing?"

"Yeah, they do that every now and then when the weather is nice."

"Now I know what makes them so special," replied Murdock sarcastically. "Anymore talk about what we discussed?"

"Nothing, why?" asked Marlene a little puzzled.

"I'm getting pulled into this mess. Anything at all seem peculiar these days?"

"No, I'd tell you if I thought something was wrong."

"Thanks. Well, see ya later." Murdock turned toward the door.

"Wait!" Marlene hesitated. "The Director calls all the time now."

"What about?"

"I don't know."

"What so unusual about the Director calling?"

"Maybe it's nothing, but he just started calling over the past two weeks...a lot. He sounds irritated over something."

"No idea what?"

"Sorry, Bill."

"I want to look in Carmichael's cabinets and desk."

Marlene looked up quickly pushing her glasses back up. "That's not a good idea," she replied.

"It's important. Something is wrong here and I gotta find out. I won't take anything."

"What are you looking for?"

"I'm not sure. Anything connected to this thing. Trust me, no one will know." Marlene inhaled and exhaled deeply before answering.

"The keys are in my desk. I'm running some paperwork over to the U.S. Attorney's Office. I can't be a part of this. I get too nervous. At least this way I can answer honestly that I didn't know anything about it when they hang you."

Murdock smiled. "Marlene, thanks and no one will find out." Murdock scanned the huge mahogany desktop for clues...messages...anything. He then methodically searched the drawer. "Breath mints, gum, paper clips, more gum, tobacco, pens and a key—key to which cabinet?" mumbled Murdock aloud. A two-drawer file cabinet faced the desk and the key fit. Neatly organized manila folders awaited his perusal. Each one carrying a code name—*Operation Sundown, Operation Greenback, Operation Dome*. The list of code names went on and on. Certain files appeared to be ongoing investigations while others were courtesy investigations in which the Fort Lauderdale District was conducting background investigations for the other IRS districts. Photographs and transcripts filled the folders. Murdock searched, but did not find anything related to his cast of characters.

The bottom drawer contained a few files stamped "Pending." One case, *Operation Liberty,* caught his attention. Inside was an alphabetized listing of names. Hispanic surnames. Murdock glanced down the list. Two names had been lined through while others had several additional names printed below them, slightly indented. He continued his search when his memory grabbed the seventh name, Carlos Rosario. The file stated that he was indicted three years earlier on narcotic trafficking in New York City and then Florida requested extradition so that he could stand trial on several drug-related crimes in Miami, but managed to beat everything. Three names were indented below Rosario's name. The third name was Phillip Ward. Murdock continued scanning the names while listening for the opening of the front door. If he was caught rummaging through the files he knew he would be fired. Along the margin next to Ward's name was a handwritten note, "Suspend investigation—will notify. 12/19/79." After reading what few notes there were, he made a copy and replaced the file.

Just below the credenza was a box labeled, "Shred Material." Murdock's heart sounded like a base drum pounding inside his chest. Sweat began to fill his eyes. Several telephone messages were in the shred material. He quickly transcribed the names and numbers and went back to his office.

Fifteen minutes, which seemed more like an hour, finally passed before he could reach Marlene by phone. "It's me again. What's Operation Liberty?"

"I know about that one," replied Marlene.

"My lips are sealed," whispered Murdock.

"Mine should be too, but I guess it's a little too late for that. They're investigating attorneys who represent drug traffickers. They seem to think there's a lot of unreported income or they're getting repaid in drugs."

"How long has it been going on?"

"About a year now. What's going on, Bill?"

"One of the attorneys listed in the file is connected to the case I can't get anywhere with. He was given a house in Key Largo by one of our taxpayers. I did a little digging and now all kinds of weird things are happening."

"Bill, you never cease to amaze me."

"Why would CI suspend the investigation on one of the attorneys?"

"How do you know it was suspended?"

"There's a handwritten note next to his name to suspend the investigation and then there's a date, hold on—the date is December 19, 1979."

"That's my birthday! Think it has something to do with that?" asked Marlene. Murdock grinned. "I don't know why...maybe higher priority cases." Marlene hesitated a moment. "Bill, the previous director came into the office and met with Carmichael that day."

"You sure?"

"It was my birthday. I joked with Carmichael about inviting him to my party. He was very aloof all day, not himself at all."

"Has the ex-director ever come in before?"

"Never."

"What's his name?"

"Wilson...Al Wilson."

"Any idea what they talked about?"

"No. They talked for about an hour and he left. He didn't look happy and Carmichael's mood didn't get any better."

"Anymore talk about Operation Liberty?"

"Not much after that meeting. It seemed like the enthusiasm died."

"So just before the meeting the operation was active."

"I can't be sure of the exact date, but somewhere in there it stopped," replied Marlene.

"Thanks again and I owe you lunch."

"You owe me more than that!" yelled Marlene as Murdock raced out of the office.

Murdock jotted his notes down. He looked up and Frank was on his way over, hobbling on the crutches. "Forget your leg at home again?" quipped Murdock.

"Nah, Butthead's doing a file review today. Ya know how he feels about my leg being off. Should be a short review." Murdock laughed.

"Leave it to you to find the advantages of losing a leg."

"Yeah, I scoot real close to him and when he asks me about something in the files, I rub my thigh against him. He turns pale, forgets what he was asking and moves on to the next item. Works like a charm." Murdock grinned.

"Later you want to help me research some phone numbers?" asked Murdock. "CI is delaying an investigation on Ward. I'll tell you later, our buddy is coming." Davenport was making his way to Frank.

"Where's the prosthesis?" asked Davenport frowning.

"Had to air it out again. You ready for the file review?" asked Frank waving his stump. Davenport's eyes were glued to it. Murdock turned and lowered his head holding back the laughter. Davenport turned pale.

"Something the matter, Murdock?" asked Davenport.

"No, not at all," laughed Murdock giving up on holding the laughter in.

"Frank, give me your cases and I'll return them to you in the morning."

"But I'd like to give you some input while you review them." Davenport looked down at the stump again.

"That's all right, I'll manage." Frank rolled his eyes as Davenport turned and walked back to his office.

"Better luck next time," quipped Murdock.

The intercom interrupted the cadence of typewriters and printers. "Bill...Frank, Mr. Davenport would like to see both of you." The office erupted in laughter; even Lawrence laughed.

"Hey Frank," whispered Lawrence smiling. "Tell him to get..." Frank cut him off and patted Lawrence's thick curly hair.

"Now, now, simmer down. Everything is gonna be all right. That's a good boy. Don't blow a fuse."

Lawrence exploded.

"Well, well, well," glared Davenport as he looked over his glasses. "Here we are again." Davenport smiled, really smiled. More than the two had ever seen. The cold smile of revenge thought Murdock as he glanced over at Frank.

"Got a call from the Chief, Exam. They have a large assessment coming down and the taxpayer's assets are in the Virgin Islands. St. Thomas to be exact. I want both of you to go and seize what's there."

"This is a plum assignment," replied Murdock. "Why not have OIO do it?" (Office of International Operations.) The IRS has offices all over the world.

"They're short-staffed and need assistance. Besides, I thought you two would enjoy the trip." Davenport smiled again.

"I don't get it," remarked Murdock. "We're the guys who keep you up nights, remember? It doesn't make sense when there's a lot of people here who would love to go."

"Maybe, but I want you out of my hair and what's even better, you'll be under the supervision of OIO." Davenport reached into his desk drawer and extracted two airline tickets. "One for you and here's one for you."

"We leave tomorrow evening?" commented Murdock in disbelief.

"That's right, boys. Better get packing."

"I need more time to take care of some personal things. Not that you care," sneered Murdock.

"You've got the rest of today and most of tomorrow to take care of it. See you later."

"Who's our contact and what are the assets?"

"It's all in here." Davenport passed a briefing document to him and smiled. "See ya around, boys." Davenport left his office with a bounce in his step while Murdock and Frank slowly got up only to find the office peering over partitions, from around corners, in silence.

"Folks, we're going to the Virgin Islands! When you guys start doing the caliber of work we do, maybe you'll get to go, too," shouted Frank. He held his ticket high in the air as if it were a trophy. Everyone cheered except Lawrence.

"You big pile of..." a secretary cut him off. "Now, now Lawrence."

The two cleared off their desks as Lawrence continued his barrage of profanity.

***

Phillip Ward made the final deposit into the Colombians' account as agreed upon. Now he was ready to take the key they had sent and retrieve the cocaine from the trunk of a '75 Pontiac LeMans which was always parked along a side street in Coconut Grove. All was going according to plan. The noon traffic was congested as usual. He turned down a quiet street and there was the car. For the first time he felt a little uncomfortable as he approached the vehicle. The car appeared too isolated. Ward looked around as he gently inserted and then turned the trunk key. The lid popped open. As he slowly lifted the lid he retrieved a duffel bag and took it to an office he rented in a desolate section of the city. Less traffic, he thought. Fewer chances of being interrupted. Once there, he tested the quality of the narcotic and then cut it with other ingredients for further resale.

After an hour and a half, he proceeded to Dinner Key Marina where he met his first customer of the afternoon. The sale transpired without a glitch. Three hours later he was at the Deerfield Beach Pier parking lot and consummated the final transaction of the day. He didn't feel as comfortable with these men. The short time frames he was operating under as a result of Alena's ultimatum did not allow for the usual background checks and security—this was the second deadly sin in the Rosario Drug Cartel.

He pulled his vehicle beside the windowless van and tapped on the driver's side window. Three men exited the rear of the dark van. One looked like he could have easily been recently released from prison. The other two were businessmen. Ward retrieved the duffel bag which held several clear plastic bags containing the white powder. Each bag weighed 2.2 pounds. The convict-looking man watched for cops and plain wrappers or undercover policemen. One of the businessmen tested the quality and gave a nod. The other man passed him an attaché case which Ward opened and scanned. No one spoke as the men climbed back into the vehicle.

The total return on Ward's investment at the end of the day was many times what he had paid. At this rate, he thought, he really could retire. There wasn't much time before Alena would leave so Ward changed his strategy. He decided to call on established Cartel clients—the third deadly sin in the Rosario Drug Cartel and the most fatal—strike three.

16

In the distance, through bloodshot eyes, Cricket could see her getting closer. The Key West surf occasionally slapped him as he struggled to maintain consciousness. He had many questions to ask. The soft moonlight cascaded down revealing her perfection. The white cotton dress was aglow against the sea. His Lady in White had finally returned. He rolled over on his back and after several minutes managed to prop his body up with his elbows. Her long dark hair draped her sensuous shoulders. She knelt beside him, smiled and gently ran her fingers through his thick black hair.

"I knew you'd be here. You're in terrible shape again," she whispered with concern in her voice and expression.

"Your name..." Cricket could barely speak. He had downed a fifth of bourbon during the course of the evening, but luckily, had blown most of it out along with a dinner of deep fried octopus. Tentacles he had regurgitated clung to him.

"Your name...what is your name?"

"Does it really matter?"

"Yes...I think it does," replied Cricket in disjointed sentences. "I have to know if you're real. These days...these days...I'm having problems sorting fact...fiction...real people...they have names. Do you have a name?"

Without a word the Lady in White leaned over and kissed him gently on the forehead. She then placed her hands on his body and paused. "This is not good. The drink is killing you. Your liver will stop functioning soon. I want you to stop. It is not your time." She closed her hand and rubbed her thumb across his forehead back and forth several times very slowly. "The desire you have for alcohol is no more. You are free of that evil." She repeated herself as she continued rubbing his forehead.

"Your name...what is it?" She leaned over and embraced him and sat erect, legs folded.

"When the time is right, I will tell you." She lay beside him in the sand and rested her head on his chest as he stroked her silky hair. He tried to stay awake, but quickly drifted into oblivion and dreamed. He dreamed, as he often did, of his grandparents who raised him in Oklahoma. They were forced to live there along with the remainder of the Sioux Nation in the late 1800s. In addition to inheriting the rugged Sioux look, Cricket acquired his grandfather's proclivity for drink and lots of it. He hired on with the IRS in Tulsa and, because of the promotional opportunities afforded in a larger or super district, as the IRS refers to them, like Fort Lauderdale, he decided to transfer, which paid off. During the first three years in South Florida his salary increased by $12,000. He also enjoyed the companionship of Palmetto and Beetle who were like brothers to him, especially Beetle. There was, however, a certain loneliness created by the separation from his family in Oklahoma. At the rate he was drinking, there was a good chance he'd never live long enough to see them again.

Cricket was an hour and a half overdue and Beetle was worried. Beetle became his blood brother in a ritual performed several years earlier. And like a good brother, he worried when Cricket was out too late. Beetle knew he was drunk somewhere, but where? He also knew he had to find him before the fog rolled in and stayed until mid-morning tomorrow. Beetle began his methodical search of the shoreline just outside the hotel. Ahead he heard laughter. The unmistakable laughter of his brother. As he approached, a faint figure-like fog rose and drifted through the waves and out to sea.

"You okay?"

"Not sure. Did you see her?"

"Who?"

"The Lady in White!"

"I saw something...fog," replied Beetle.

"Fog! Fog!" Cricket's voice crescendos. "Fog don't look that good!"

"Then who is she?"

"I don't know who she is or how she finds me, but she cares about me. Told me to stop drinking." Cricket again faded in and out of consciousness. "Said she'd check in on me...later."

"Did you get her name?"

"You and your names. She said it didn't matter."

"Enough fun for one night. Got to get you back. We've got a big case tomorrow. Can you walk?"

"Don't think so." Cricket threw his arm up into the air.

"Well, don't blow dinner all over me." Beetle reached down and picked him up, positioning him over his left shoulder. With a mighty heave, Beetle managed to carry Cricket. The added weight buried Beetle's feet deep into the cool beach sand as he carefully negotiated his way through the white, blinding fog.

Palmetto, Beetle and Cricket ate breakfast at 6:00 a.m. the next morning. The fog was like thick, puffy cotton blocking the morning sunrise.

"Got a call from the Vice Presidential Task Force in Lauderdale 'bout the arrest of John Korpi," said Palmetto breaking the morning silence.

"Who is he?" asked Beetle as he wolfed down his breakfast.

"He's suspected of running one of the largest pot smuggling rings in the Miami area. A confidential informant notified them that he was unloading his property and getting ready to flee the country.

"So what's our role?" asked Cricket as he struggled to stabilize his five senses.

"He's got some planes and they think they're in the Keys. Supposed to have a powerboat, too. I'll look for that if you two would check out the airports and landing strips."

Beetle and Cricket called the EPIC, or Enforcement Police of the FAA, to assist in locating the aircraft. By noon the craft, a Lockheed JetStar-6, was located in Marathon. The jet was in the possession of a broker who would have priced the craft at $600,000 if it had all of the requisite inspections. But, without that, the jet was worth about $200,000. The jet was seized from the broker using an alter ego levy and lien. Whenever assets are mingled with another entity to the extent that it is difficult to differentiate between the person and the entity an "alter ego" exists in the eyes of the IRS and seizure is made even though the asset is actually in another name. Beetle confronted the broker again.

"Sell any other planes belonging to Korpi?"

"Two in the last month. Three weeks ago I gave him $180,000 cash from one sale and I've got $39,000 in escrow for him."

"We'll take that off your hands," replied Beetle as he served another form to seize the funds. Cricket was motionless as though he had seen the ghost of Geronimo.

"Is your friend all right?" asked the broker as he walked toward the zombie.

"You got a trash can handy?" asked Beetle. "And I wouldn't get too close to him."

"Why, what's the..." the broker's question was answered when Cricket vomited with the force of a shotgun blast. Pieces of pancake scattered across an executive desk and onto the broker's three-piece suit. "Ah!" The broker stood up in shock. Maple syrup mixed with booze stained the light-blue poplin suit.

"Sir, I'm really sorry about that," lamented Beetle. Cricket fell to his knees in front of the desk as he stared at the broker, eyes crossed and rolling back. An odd, deep sound emanated from him.

"Get that possessed moron out of here!"

"He's had a terrible bout with the flu." Beetle grabbed the proceeds from the sale of Korpi's second plane as he attempted to pull Cricket out of the office.

"Ah, right...the flu. How am I gonna get home to change?" The smell filled the room which sent Cricket into another series of blasts, leaving a trail from the desk.

"Have a nice day, sir."

"You idiot!" yelled the broker as he continued standing with his arms up in the air assessing the damage. Beetle poked his head back in the doorway.

"Send us your cleaning bill. We'll take care of it. The address is on the form we gave you. I'm terribly sorry, but you know how the flu can be."

While it was only noon, Cricket's day was done. The two returned to Key West. Cricket was asleep against the window. Beetle looked over and couldn't help feeling concerned for his inebriated friend who was drinking himself to death.

As Beetle pulled into the hotel parking lot Palmetto was on his way out.

"Hey, hold on," shouted Beetle.

"What's up? Did you get it?" Palmetto looked at Cricket. "Not again!" Cricket's face was flush against the car door window pushing his nose one way and lips another. He was trying to go unnoticed as he looked back at Palmetto, but his crossed eyes and drool gave him up. "Was it bad?"

" 'Fraid so. A series of blasts."

"Anyone hit this time?"

"A direct hit on the broker."

"Hope it was after you seized."

"Yeah, we got a plane and thirty-nine thousand."

"Good. Better get him inside. The boy's a disgrace to the Service," complained Palmetto. "Let's clean him up and get 'em to bed. You can help me work on a 'Writ to Enter'."

"You found the boat?"

"It's on the canal between Coquina Drive and Welk Street. Saw enough of the boat to get the registration number. Too many shrubs to get a good look and there's these cats...seems like hundreds of 'em around the place, huh!"

"You don't need a writ for that, do you?"

"Not really, but it's tied to a private dock so I thought I'd get one. Besides, he's got a dozen attorneys working for him."

The two prepared the necessary documents in a matter of minutes and presented them to a visiting magistrate, Mr. O'Connell, on the island. After waiting an hour and a half they finally got to see him.

"I'm not signing this trash!" shouted the 67-year old magistrate. His glasses hugged the end of his nose.

"Why not?" asked Palmetto.

"I just don't like the way you boys do business. You ought to be abolished and half of ya locked up. Besides, you're wearing a Hawaiian shirt and sandals in my office." Palmetto looked down at his feet and wiggled his toes.

"Sir, the U.S. Attorney in Miami authorized this writ. The taxpayer happens to be a drug smuggler. Surely..."

"Nonsense, young man! I decide if this is proper or not in my court, not some punk in Miami. And I say it's not proper or necessary. Why Korpi's got enough cash to satisfy any tax he might owe, and I say *might* because after his tax attorney gets through with your assessments, the IRS will probably owe *him* some money. No! I'm not signing this, not now, not ever. And furthermore, if you *ever* come before me again with any writ in that attire, I'll lock you up for a night or two."

Palmetto and Beetle, without a word, turned to leave.

"One more thing..." The two froze. "Don't you smoke those nasty Cuban cigars in this courtroom, ya hear?" With haste, the two exited.

"Let's find out what his problem is," muttered Beetle. As soon as they returned to their office Beetle called the South Miami field office and requested an extensive search on the magistrate. This would take a few hours, but well worth it if they had something on him. If no open accounts existed then the two would be in violation of IRS procedure and subject to discipline because employees cannot merely browse an account. But, their hunch told them he had tangled personally with the Service.

"Is he always like this?" asked Beetle.

"This was my first with him. I'll bet he's been audited."

"Just hope he hasn't paid it," replied Beetle. "What now?"

"When did we ever let a senile judge get in our way?" sneered Palmetto. Beetle smiled. "The canal is public access. We'll get the Florida Marine Patrol to help us."

The two proceeded to the FMP office where they briefed the lone officer. Without much discussion the three climbed into the 24-foot open patrol boat loaded with electronic gadgets.

"Beautiful boat. Bet it cost a bundle," remarked Beetle as he examined the craft.

"Seventy-five thousand with the electronic equipment. Take a look below." The officer opened a door beneath the control panel and steering wheel. The most impressive collection of weapons lined the compartment: Uzi's, handguns and rifles.

"You're equipped to take on a battalion, aren't ya?"

"If I had to. We've had one shoot 'em up this year. Pretty nasty. The guy's boat blew up. Coke dust went everywhere. We refer to it as the day it snowed in the Keys. Okay, here's the canal you're looking for."

The officer pushed a few buttons on the control panel and the engines whispered as they entered the passage. The silence was disturbing. Several manatees were swimming about as the officer maneuvered around them. The sunlight was blinding as it struck the chrome of the boat's massive engines. The sleek, black cigarette-styled racer appeared ominous just lying there in wait. The blood red letters spelled out the name, *Marauder.* The officer shifted gears and maneuvered the craft with ease alongside another dock one hundred meters away.

"What's up?" asked Palmetto.

"Let's see if we can hear anything going on at this place," replied the officer as he reached into another compartment and pulled out a funnel shaped device with wires attached to a recording system. "Try these on," advised the officer. He passed a set of sponge earphones to Palmetto.

"I've read about this surveillance stuff," commented Beetle.

"Works great." Palmetto listened intently as the tape-to-tape micro reels began turning.

"I didn't know you guys used this kind of equipment," said Beetle.

"It's mine. Bought it through my brother-in-law. It saved my rear end a couple of times already.

"How?" asked Beetle.

"That shoot out I mentioned...came up on this Hatteras that looked out of place. Before I moved in, I tuned it on and heard them talking about the coke they were unloading...'bout five of them. After the boat blew up someone found one of their arms on a bench. Heck of a way to start your day. Without this gadget I would have been fried."

"Sounds like everyone in the Marine Patrol should have one."

"If I'm caught, I'll probably be reprimanded—oh, well. Besides, the equipment makes the slow nights around here a little more tolerable."

"What do ya mean?"

"See the house over there?" asked the officer with a grin as he pointed across the Intracoastal to a small white house on a point.

"Yeah."

"She gets it at midnight every Wednesday and Friday. I can set my watch to it."

"Gets what?"

"A baloney sandwich, of course. What do you think?"

"I think I know why they don't want you to have one of these," smirked Beetle. Palmetto removed the earphones.

"You're in a sweat. What's going on?" asked Beetle.

"There's got to be a dozen people in that pool carrying on," answered Palmetto.

"Give me those earphones," demanded Beetle still intrigued by the officer's story.

"How do you want to handle it?" asked the officer.

"Let's seize the boat and hook it up without going onto private property."

"The seawall is public," replied the officer.

"We'll hook the boat up and I'll serve the papers after we get out of there," interjected Palmetto. "Think we'll have a problem with the fornicators?"

"Don't think so. But, if someone gets out of line I'll lock 'em up."

"Hey Beetle, we're going in."

"What a party. I think I'm ready though."

"Thought you might be," replied the officer. The engines quietly shifted into gear. The patrol passed the boat, circled around and docked in front. The officer immediately turned on the PA system. "Ladies and gentlemen, no need to be alarmed. This is the Florida Marine Patrol and IRS. We are confiscating Mr. Korpi's boat."

Eight couples were partying in the pool and about half of them ducked under the water upon hearing the announcement. Clothing had been spread from one end of the yard to the other. Suddenly, a muscular, balding man with a white beard worn close to his face climbed out of the pool in his birthday suit.

"Look at this guy. He's not even embarrassed," observed Beetle.

"If you looked like that would you be?" quipped Palmetto. The three laughed.

"What's going on here?" asked the bearded man.

"I already explained that to you," replied the officer. "Shouldn't you be serving papers of some sort?" The officer turned to Palmetto who was folding the documents and stuffing them into an envelope addressed to Korpi.

"Here." Palmetto passed him the envelope. The man accepted the papers and proceeded back to the pool and did a cannonball without saying another word. The party continued as if nothing had happened. The back of the house was all glass with coconut trees, shrubs and rocks throughout the pool area. It was a perfect retreat, especially for someone who did not want to be seen coming or going.

Without incident, the powerboat was towed to the FMP office where it would be auctioned.

"How long before the sale?" inquired the officer.

"Couple of months. We've got to give Korpi time to appeal the assessments we made otherwise we'd sell it in about ten days," answered Palmetto as he inventoried the boat.

"I didn't think your assessments could be appealed."

"Oh yeah, especially these kinds of assessments. We seized the boat under what we call a jeopardy situation which means we have knowledge that a taxpayer is moving assets beyond our reach...like selling them, moving them...that kind of thing. His attorney will have an opportunity to appeal this procedure. He'll lose, but he still gets the chance. Thanks again for the help."

"Call me anytime."

When the two arrived at their office a message was on the answering machine.

"Your magistrate seems to owe us $18,000 after an audit nailed him on some tax shelters. He didn't pay the final notice so he's all yours. Oh, one more thing..." reported the voice on the recording, "he only owes $3,500 on his Mercedes. Call me if you need anything else."

The two looked over and smiled. Palmetto prepared two handwritten documents and proceeded back to the courthouse and waited for the magistrate. Twenty minutes later he arrived.

"Mr. O'Connell," boomed Palmetto in a loud voice. The magistrate looked around and appeared disoriented. Palmetto and Beetle approached him as he unlocked his spotless silver automobile.

"Oh, you two again. I said all I had to say this afternoon. No sense begging. Out of my way," he waved his cane.

"Mr. O'Connell, we'd like to leave, but ya see our duty as federal officers of the Internal Revenue Service compels us to issue these documents to you for unpaid taxes totaling $18,243.13 that, by the way, are currently due and owing. Can you pay the monies now?"

"I'm fighting the assessments. This is preposterous." The magistrate looked at both of them.

"So you can't pay it. In that case, we're seizing your car. Here's your copy of the seizure form. Read it. The keys please." Palmetto stuck his hand out.

"I won't give them to you. Get out of my way or I'll..."

"Or you'll what?" asked Beetle.

"We thought you might be a little cranky so we asked a deputy sheriff to come along." Palmetto flagged the officer.

"The keys please."

"No. Get out of my way."

"Come now. Let's play fair..." asserted Palmetto. "...It's our turn."

"I'll have you fired for this."

"For doing our jobs! I don't think so," Palmetto motioned to the tow truck driver who was waiting a half block away. A man with blue work pants hanging down around the cheeks of his protruding buttock climbed out of the truck.

"One last time, would you give me your keys?" The magistrate folded his arms tightly and looked away. The tow truck driver inserted a long silver blade and quickly unlocked the door while the deputy extended his arm, blocking the magistrate.

"Are there any personal items in the car?" The magistrate was speechless. "All right..." Palmetto turned to the driver, "it's yours." Palmetto then turned to O'Connell, "Pay the full amount within ten days if you want your car back or we'll sell it." Palmetto pulled the judge aside. "If you've got a legitimate concern over our writs we'll listen, but don't you ever, *and I mean ever*, jack us around and interfere with our jobs. Korpi is a known drug smuggler and you had a fair hearing on your tax shelters. So don't take it out on us, got it!" The magistrate was silent. "Let's go."

"Wait, how am I going to get to Miami?" asked O'Connell.

"You could walk," smirked Palmetto.

"Or hitch hike," responded Beetle.

"Or catch a bus," added the deputy who had one too many problems with the magistrate.

"I'll have your jobs by tomorrow morning."

They left the magistrate standing in front of the courthouse still in disbelief and still swearing as he looked around.

The sun was setting and the usual cast of characters came out to honor the day. Palmetto and Beetle picked up a bottle of rum and headed to Mallory Square. After living in the Keys and attending the sundown celebration, they had become as much of a fixture on the dock as anyone. Their distinct yelp during the ceremony was a trademark known to the locals. The sun vanished and the two of them carried the warmth of the ceremony with them. When they returned to the hotel they were surprised to see Cricket conscious, able to utter and actually comprehend complete sentences.

"How was sundown?" asked Cricket.

"Ahhoooooo!" yelped Beetle. Hotel guests turned and watched him carefully.

"That good?" replied Cricket who seemed very refreshed and alert. Work papers and summonses were spread across the table.

"Whatcha looking at?" inquired Beetle.

"The telephone numbers Murdock wanted us to summons came in. Take a look." Beetle scanned the names, numbers and the footnotes Cricket had made, which were attached to the back of the summonses from the telephone company.

"Two different phone numbers at the same Coconut Grove address. Alena Muller calls Phillip Ward in Miami throughout the month and then the Largo house calls Muller toward the end of each month."

"Murdock said something about the drug meetings at the Largo house each month, didn't he?" asked Palmetto.

"He said a big group gathers at the end of each month," remembered Cricket.

"So she attends the meetings," replied Beetle.

"If she attends the meetings then she's involved in the drugs, right?" queried Cricket as he looked at the two.

"If it's drugs, I'd have to say...maybe," answered Palmetto.

"What are you getting at?" asked Beetle.

"Okay, now look at this name." Cricket pointed to a name that had been underlined.

"Albert Wilson," declared Beetle aloud.

"Albert Wilson?" asked Palmetto as he looked away in thought.

Beetle smirked, "Name sound familiar?"

"I'm not certain it's him but..." Palmetto looked away again. Beetle and Cricket stared at Palmetto. "The last district director we had was an Albert Wilson," recognized Palmetto. "But...I guess there's a few Al Wilson's floating around..."

"I did a little homework, guess what?" Beetle motioned Cricket to speak up.

"I called Al's number and told him I was the new president of the local CPA chapter. Asked him if he'd say a few words to us about the IRS. Told him I thought it would be an honor if an ex-director of the IRS addressed the group. You know what he said?"

"What?" the two asked in unison.

"He said he'd love to!"

"I can't believe it!" said Beetle.

"And Al Wilson is at the same address with Muller. Take a look." Cricket passed the list to Palmetto.

"Wait a minute," Palmetto hesitated. "She's at 486A not 486. It's probably a garage apartment. Look!" Palmetto pointed to the "A." Cricket glanced at the list. Palmetto continued, "Just because Alena Muller attends the monthly meetings in Largo and lives next to Wilson doesn't mean she and Wilson are involved in drugs."

"But we agreed she's involved in the drugs because she attends the monthly meetings, right?" questioned Cricket.

"We said maybe."

"Okay, maybe. She's got to know what's going on," replied Cricket.

I'll give ya that, but Wilson doesn't have anything to do with it," declared Palmetto sure of himself.

"I knew you'd say that. How 'bout this...Wilson is probably renting to Muller, but I've got him calling Ward twice last month!"

"Let me see," requested Palmetto in disbelief. Cricket retrieved another summons. Palmetto studied it. "Someone, and not necessarily Wilson, called Ward's number. This still doesn't mean he's involved."

"Of course it does, Palmetto. I was with ya till you said that," replied Beetle as he crossed his plump legs and downed another long-necked beer.

"If he's not calling Ward, then Muller is using his phone to call which means one of two things," interrupted Cricket.

"They're either related or they're lovers," responded Palmetto.

"You've got it!" exclaimed Cricket. "Either way he's involved, somehow."

"We'll see."

"Cricket, didn't expect to see you among the living for another twenty-four hours," remarked Beetle.

"Can't explain it. I feel like a different person."

"Wish you looked like a different person," quipped Palmetto.

"I think it's the Lady in White."

"Did you happen to get her name?" Palmetto knew she had to be a hallucination.

"No, but she'll be back...I'll get it," Cricket looked out and followed the horizon north wondering when she would return.

***

Rosario sat patiently listening to all that Miguel had to say. What he heard caused him great heartache.

"How much business is he generating for himself?" asked Rosario. His elbows helped prop his head as he looked down at the table. The last defector had been Nieto which cost the Cartel in many ways since he was still alive. Rosario knew deep down that the Cartel could not tolerate another incident.

"That's not the issue, we..." Rosario slammed his fist hard onto the table startling Miguel.

"I know what the issue is, now *tell* me how much!"

"Not much. We estimate about five million dollars so far." Rosario stood and gazed out his glass penthouse and lit a cigar.

"Are they our contacts or new ones?" Rosario inquired, still assessing Ward's impact, searching for a way around the incident.

"So far as we can tell, new ones." Miguel wanted to inject more of his opinion, but wisely restrained himself. He knew the difficult time Rosario would have arriving at a decision about Ward.

"New ones?" Rosario turned toward Miguel, eyebrows raised. Miguel nodded. "Then he's not hurting us. It's not like he's taking away from the Cartel like that leech Nieto." Rosario continued his gaze, enjoying the silence. "By the way, I'm still waiting for Nieto's head to be presented to me." Nieto was a blemish on an otherwise flawless corporate operation. "I know you're looking for guidance from me, but I need more time to think about this one." He turned and looked at Miguel. It was safe for him to speak.

"I realize how difficult this is for you..."

"Do you?" asked Rosario sternly. His piercing hazel eyes riveted Miguel.

"Yes, but you gave me an awesome responsibility in the Cartel. So, in the role that you gave me, sir, I respectfullly say this, Ward must be dealt with quickly and severely or there will be others."

"Should I decide to listen to you, do we even have a replacement?"

"Yes."

"I must think about this some more." Rosario, standing across from Miguel, placed both hands on the table, leaned over and pointed his cigar at him. “Not a hair on that boy’s head will be touched unless I say. Am I clear, Miguel?”

“Yes, sir.”

“If you get anxious, go find Nieto for me.”

17

The glimmering, silver ocean ended quickly as the plane gently pushed its way along the concrete path in Charlotte Amalie, the thriving capitol of Saint Thomas. Columbus discovered the islands during one of his voyages in the late 1400's and most of the buildings reflect Danish architecture dating back to when they ruled in the 1600's. The area had been a rendezvous for pirates like Captain Kidd and Blackbeard. Most of the pirates were eventually hung for terrorizing the settlers. The U.S. purchased the Virgin Islands in 1917 and, since then, it's pristine beaches have been a haven for the many culturally-diverse tourists who have created a unique flavor for the island.

Murdock and Frank exited the plane. Murdock's stomach tightened—his sixth sense was warning him once again. Someone was watching them. He could feel their eyes on them. Murdock slowly turned and looked back toward the DC-9.

"What is it?" asked Frank noticing Murdock's peculiar behavior. Murdock turned and, without a word, slowly started walking back to the plane bumping into a stream of tourists eager to begin their vacations. "You okay?" Frank stayed with him wondering what he had missed. Murdock was in a trance, focused on someone or something. Frank knew something was wrong. He trusted Murdock's instincts. He was always right when it came to his gut feelings.

"Someone's watching us," responded Murdock in a soft monotone voice.

"There's a lot of people here, Bill." A few more steps and they were approached by a tall, trim black man dressed in a white military uniform that made his skin tone look darker than it was.

"Mr. Murdock with the United States Government?" inquired the man in a distinct British accent.

"And who might you be?" replied Murdock.

"Jona MacQuiddy, at your service," he replied in a deep voice. "I'm your contact point while you're on the island." He smiled, but not a fond smile.

"Someone else was supposed to meet us," replied Murdock

"A personal emergency called him away."

"Have you been briefed on why we're here?" asked Frank.

"The yacht. It's at St. Croix, our next door neighbor."

"We were told it was here," asserted Frank with piercing eyes.

"*Was* is correct. They had to do some diesel work and the best there is lives on St. Croix."

"Who ordered the work?" asked Murdock a little puzzled.

"A boat has been arranged to transport you at sunrise."

"Who ordered the repairs?" Murdock raised his voice. MacQuiddy glared back at Murdock for a moment.

"Your government, of course. The gentleman over there will take you to your quarters. I trust you'll have a pleasant stay. Please, let me know if there is anything I can do for you while you are here." His smile was too reassuring.

A tall, stocky man dressed in a red vest and purple hat with a long pink plume opened the rear door of his '73 Cadillac and stood by. The driver, who looked as though he should have been wearing a football uniform, smiled revealing a gold inlaid star on his lonely front tooth. Murdock looked back and found Jona MacQuiddy staring at them. Without a word the taxi driver whisked them to the Mafolie, a Mediterranean villa of stone placed neatly above the town almost in the clouds.

"Maybe Butthead did us a favor after all," remarked Frank looking out over the area. Red rooftops dotted the bright green hills down to the turquoise-colored harbor. Ships now hugged the shoreline where boats flying pirate flags once docked.

"Maybe, but something ain't right." Murdock looked off into the horizon. Thoughts of how Farmer died surfaced.

"How did he know who I was?"

"Someone gave him a description," replied Frank.

"I guess."

"If you're in doubt, let's call the office." The two went to the lobby and placed a call. After about five minutes of dealing with operators he got through to Lawrence.

"What mess are you fools in?" replied Lawrence.

"How'd ya guess?"

"It figures with you two."

"Call the Honolulu office and check the location of the yacht we're seizing and if anyone ordered engine work." Murdock gave him the number to call. Thirty-five minutes passed before Lawrence called back.

"The boat is at Blue Reef Marina, Saint Thomas, and no one ordered any repairs."

"Maybe the taxpayer paid for it?" asked Murdock.

"I asked and they said he wouldn't have done it. The guy is broke and even if he had the money he knew we were seizing it."

"I guess he wouldn't have dumped money into something he knew he was about to lose," replied Murdock somewhat confused. "Why is the yacht at St. Croix?" asked Murdock.

"No one knows. They think the boat is still at Saint Thomas." Murdock could hear Lawrence shuffling papers. "Did you know that the boat was used to transport heroine. Did you know that?"

"No, no one told me," replied Murdock concerned.

"Guess it wasn't important."

"Thanks and..." Murdock hesitated. "...if something happens over here..."

Lawrence interrupted.

"Like what?"

Murdock paused. "Like...if something happens to us...there's a file I've been working on in the bottom drawer of my cabinet. It's in a brown folder. Give it to someone to investigate other than the

IRS, all right?"

"What's going on, Bill?" asked Lawrence hoping Murdock would level with him.

"I can't say over the telephone. I've probably said too much already."

"You've really step in it this time," observed Lawrence detecting the seriousness of Murdock's tone.

" 'Fraid so."

"You think whoever moved the yacht is involved in your case?"

"I just don't know. Too many weird things have happened."

"Let me know if I can do anything else." There was genuine concern in Lawrence's tone.

"Will do and thanks."

On the way into town Murdock briefed Frank on the information from the Honolulu district office. The two passed a blur of shops and a kaleidoscope of colors as tiny flags zigzagged high above the steep streets. They looked for some island food as they passed picturesque alleys. As they searched for a restaurant, someone back at the villa was picking the door lock to Murdock's room. A silhouette of a small, thin man entered the room and began his methodical search, ripping into pockets and turning everything else upside down.

When the two returned from dinner Murdock was appalled at what he found outside his room. A monkey's head with a small arrow piercing its forehead had been nailed to the door. The head was still warm as blood dripped, streaking the door and forming a puddle. The lower jawbone of the monkey uncontrollably quivered. A hotel employee making his rounds approached them.

"What does this mean? Who would do this?" The employee's eyes widened as he pushed Murdock aside and ran toward the lobby in fright. Murdock ran back to Frank's room.

"What's the matter?" Frank was startled by this sudden interruption.

"Come here!" he was out of breath. "Bring your gun." Frank gripped his .38 Smith and Wesson.

"Where's yours?"

"Inside the room."

"I'm ready," replied Frank reassuring Murdock that if there was trouble, they'd come out okay. Frank hugged the wall as they approached the room. The two inched their way closer and closer thinking their jumping hearts would give them away. Frank signaled for Murdock to stop. Frank studied the head as he went in alone, disappearing into the darkness as Murdock drifted back to Nam.

He and his platoon sergeant were torching quonset huts along the Mekong River, seventy miles north of Phnom Penh. The entire village was ablaze, but the North Vietnamese sympathizers were spared even though Murdock was given orders not to take any prisoners.

It was during the igniting of the eighth hut and the events which followed that would haunt Murdock for the rest of his life. Murdock's flame-thrower had just engulfed the dwelling when the screams of children sent dreadful chills down his spine. The platoon sergeant, without hesitation, ran into the inferno pulling out the first two children as his clothing began to burn. He quickly entered the hut again and disappeared. Murdock ran closer to the hut in time to see his sergeant slowly walk out of the flames like a human torch. It was only when the sergeant fell to his knees, grabbing his head, that he saw a bayonet which had been pushed diagonally through his nostrils and into his brain. Murdock opened his flame-thrower and finished baking the occupants for what they had done.

"Bill." There was no answer. "Bill!" exclaimed Frank a little louder this time. Still no response. Frank returned to the doorway. Murdock quickly turned toward him.

"What?" asked Murdock sounding disoriented.

"You okay?"

"Yeah, I'm fine. What did ya find?"

"Come on in." All the drawers had been emptied and his clothes, especially the pockets, had been ripped out.

"Just like the Keys. What do they want?" shouted Murdock. He walked out of the room, cupped his hands around his mouth. "You spineless coward. Come back...I still have what you want...come back!" he taunted. The only response was the rustling of leaves from an ancient forest centuries old. Frank saw another side to his partner, one he had never seen before.

"You gonna be okay?"

"Yeah, I'm just tired of this. I'm gonna nail those guys, wait and see." Murdock reached into a zipped pocket in his garment bag and found his gun. He tucked it in his jeans.

"Should we go to St. Croix tomorrow?" asked Frank. He already knew the answer.

"Doesn't look good does it? Honolulu can't tell us why the yacht was moved and now this. Someone wants us off the island. How do you feel about it, you're the ex-cop?"

"I think there's two different things going on here. My guess is that the monkey head is a warning...to leave maybe. But whoever is going through our clothes has a different agenda and I don't think he cares where we're at, he wants something. Something he thinks you've got, but not me."

"Something he thinks Ernie and Cricket have, too," continued Murdock. "It didn't take him long to find us. IRS has to be in on it."

"Maybe," replied Frank.

"Well, how else could he find us so fast?"

"Davenport, OIO..." replied Murdock.

"The director had to have known," agreed Frank.

"And anyone else they wanted to tell."

"You feel like calling Davenport?" asked Frank.

"Not really. I think he's in on it," replied Murdock.

"In on what?"

"Whatever it is they don't want us to know," replied Murdock in frustration. He ran his hands through his hair.

"Call him anyway. If he tells us to go, after all this, we'll know he's in on it somehow," replied Frank.

"I don't trust him. But I never thought he'd do something illegal, did you?"

"I don't believe he'd do anything that wasn't written in that manual of his," sneered Frank. Murdock's sixth sense was kicking in again. The night breeze swept the cheerful calypso island music from town to the surrounding areas. The people were coming alive as the two sat in the dark room with the door open. The music's rhythm was disturbed by the ringing of the phone which startled them.

"This is Rico." Murdock was silent.

"How did you know I was here?"

"It's what I do," replied Rico in a low voice.

"Right, how could I forget," responded Murdock sarcastically. "So why are you calling?"

"Nieto is on the island. I'm close to retiring this assignment."

"He's found me—my room's been ransacked just like the Keys and there's a monkey's head nailed to the door."

"Voodoo," replied Rico. "An invitation to the Angel of Death."

"Of course, I should've known and I guess I should know this, but why me?"

"Someone doesn't want you near the yacht. It still has heroine on board...that's why it was moved."

"How do you know it has heroine on board?"

"I know. The boat is booby-trapped, wired with C-4." C-4 was short for Composition Four, a plastic explosive.

"How do you know that?"

"I did it." The revelation surprised Murdock.

"Why?"

"Because there's a fortune in heroine and I'm counting on Nieto being the next one to board."

"*We* were going to be the next ones to board the yacht!" Murdock was understandably upset.

"That's why I'm calling." Murdock felt a moment of uncomfortable silence. "It wasn't Nieto who ransacked your room," continued Rico.

"You said he was here."

"He is, but he wouldn't waste his time with that. Look to someone else. Nieto stalks his targets and when the time is right he confronts them. The time, my friend, has come."

"Got any advice?"

"You're still armed aren't you?"

"Yup."

"You were quite thorough in Nam. Rely on your instincts as you did then and you'll get through the night. But catch the first flight out tomorrow."

"I was supposed to seize that yacht."

"Don't...it's bait."

"How do we know we're not the bait?" Rico was silent.

"You don't, but look within for the answer." Murdock was tired of the esoteric meanings and he was tired of Rico's charades. Murdock began wondering about Rico's intentions. He now understood the depth of Rico's obsession with killing, not capturing, Nieto. Would the obsession cause Rico to view him and Frank, or anyone else, as reasonable expenditures in his quest to kill Nieto?

"Stay with your partner and trust your instincts," replied Rico. Without another word Rico was gone.

Murdock spent the next minutes digesting the conversation and sifting through his gut feelings. Frank didn't have any doubts. His police instincts told him not to trust Rico at all. The two quickly walked back to Frank's room and waited while the blackness of the evening began suffocating the tiny island. Like an artist's signature on dark canvas, a cluster of stars streaked the night and seemed almost within reach.

The two lay still, covered in a thick blanket of humidity. Frank was in his bed and Murdock stretched out on the sofa with his 9mm close to his side. A clock on the end table had suddenly turned into a snare drum, creating a rhythm that kept twisting their nerves into tight strands.

Murdock broke the silence. "I had the same feelings in Nam."

"Bad experience for ya, wasn't it," replied Frank. Murdock had never spoken about Vietnam.

"Yeah, some painful memories are coming back. This night...this night I've lived before."

"What do you mean?"

"I spent the night with my squad deep in the jungle. A night a lot like this one. Hot...humid, sticky. Most of the assignments we traveled by night and slept during the day. But not this night. We were exhausted so we slept for a couple of hours...as deep in the bush as we could." Frank listened. "Didn't even realize we were practically sleeping with ol' Charlie...they were only a few meters away. Our job was to clear the way for assassins. Rico was one of them."

"*This* Rico?"

"Do you believe it?" Murdock gave a chuckle.

"Who were the assassins after?"

"The NLF," Murdock hesitated. "The National Liberation Front. They were top Vietcong leaders."

"Did he get 'em?"

"Some."

"What about your team?"

"Not as lucky. There were six members in my squad and by sunrise only two of us made it through." Frank looked over at Murdock and saw his silhouette. He wanted to ask more questions, but didn't feel comfortable. Murdock continued. "None of us were expected to make it back. We knew it. We were too deep into Laos, too far away for help because we weren't supposed to be there. The mission didn't exist." Murdock hesitated. The sound of the snare drum returned. "Punji sticks."

"What?"

"Punji sticks...ya know what they are?" asked Murdock.

"No."

"Balls of mud filled with razor-sharp pieces of bamboo that spring when you trip a wire." Another thirty seconds passed without a word. "Killed four of 'em...one instantly...the three others weren't so lucky. They had a very slow and painful death. They were family to me and there was nothing that I could do for them." Once more silence fell upon them. "Ya know, there was no way we could win the war. The guerrillas fought in small bands...compact fighting units that specialized in surprise hit and run attacks. They were effective. Same tactics Indians used. Did you know that?"

"No. How'd ya find out Rico was an assassin?"

"He told me. Knew too much about the Operation and what I did. This was top, top secret stuff. I could get locked up talking about this even now. Rico knows all about you, too."

"Give me his number, maybe he can figure out Melissa."

"Better hope she doesn't hear about this one," warned Murdock.

"Knowing her she already does." Murdock grinned. "You don't trust him, do you?" asked Frank.

"I'm not sure. I'd like to."

"You wanna sleep in shifts?" asked Frank.

"I guess. You want me to work the first one?"

"How'd ya guess. Wake me...'bout sunrise," gibed Frank.

"With the smell of biscuits and sausage?" asked Murdock.

"If you were decent you would." Murdock grinned.

"See ya in a couple of hours. Hey, Frank..."

"What?"

"This Nieto's a pro. When he shows we won't have much time to react. He's lethal."

"I'll be ready. Melissa gave me plenty of practice." Frank never forgot his sense of humor. It's what Murdock liked most about him.

Time was stagnant as the island air. Shortly after midnight Murdock heard a noise. The sound a stone would make rolling and then hitting a door. His hand gripped the 9mm.

"Frank." There was no response. "Frank!" he whispered. Still no response. With reptilian movement, Murdock slithered over to where Frank was sleeping. "Get up!" Frank grabbed his revolver.

"I don't smell any sausage." Without another word Frank stretched his arm over a pillow, revolver in hand. Murdock wedged himself between the sofa and coffee table and, without blinking an eye, studied the front window. The two listened to the snare drum as they awaited Nieto's next move.

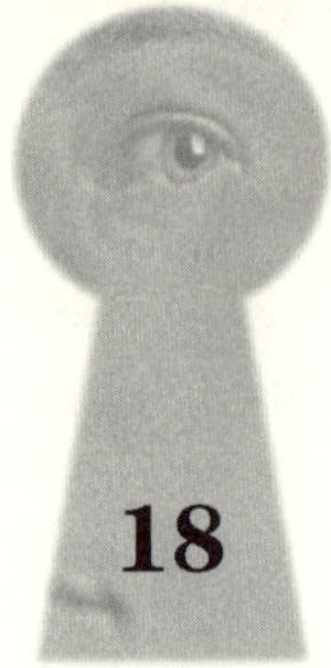

18

A scratching sound emanated from just outside Frank's door. Both had been near catatonic as they continued their frozen stares. The muscles in Frank's hand felt like steel bands steadily contracting around his pistol. The blood had been squeezed from his fingers, turning them into lifeless clamps.

Murdock, relieved at finally being given an opportunity to confront Nieto, did a snake-like crawl toward the window as he attempted to get a glimpse of the elusive, and deadly, Nieto. His 9mm was raised close to his cheekbone. The blue-black metal felt surprisingly cool against his warm skin. As he peered between a small opening in the curtain his eyes followed the dark shape of a slender man. Could this be Nieto? Murdock kept shifting his eyes. First to the right of the outline, then left as he tried to maintain his night vision. After several minutes of straining his eyesight, his stomach tightened even more as he realized what was about to happen. He had completed this same exercise many times while in Nam. Murdock slithered over to Frank while the grey shadow continued his slow methodical movements.

"Is it room service?" jested Frank.

"I think he's wiring the door."

"As in explosives?"

"You got it."

"Maybe if you'd explain that we're just visiting." Frank's humor continued. He was nervous.

"What do you want to do?" asked Murdock.

"We could blast him now," replied Frank.

"What if I'm wrong."

"Wrong? So you do think it could be room service."

Murdock searched for a phone, but couldn't find it. "Let's wait for sunrise and go through the window."

"What if it's not a booby trap and he's gonna blow the room up, now?" inquired Frank.

"I believe it's a trip wire. If I'm wrong, you won't have to worry about selling furniture with your in-laws."

"Bill, I *want* to be a furniture salesman! I've grown inexplicably fond of wood."

The scratching at the door ceased. The two awaited for morning to pierce the black veil that draped the island. Murdock would have a better chance of disarming the explosive in daylight. They waited, mostly in silence, for two hours until the veil was lifted.

Murdock crawled back to the window using his pistol to part the curtains just enough to see out. All was quiet. Using the sturdiest utensils he could find in the kitchen, Murdock began the tedious process of removing the window jalousies, hoping they hadn't been wired as well. After removing four jalousies he carefully put his head through the opening and checked the window. He couldn't see any wires. He then felt below the sill and froze.

"Frank, pull the mattress up and get behind it."

"Can't I help?"

"No! I'm going to try and remove the wire from the explosive. He's done a good job."

Frank angled the mattress against the wall and crawled behind it wondering if his partner could disarm the explosive and, if he couldn't, how much of the room would be destroyed. He felt helpless as he lay there motionless, barely breathing. He wanted to help.

Murdock, with a surgeon's touch, followed the wire across the underside of the outside sill, removing one jalousie at a time as he worked his way across the bottom window. Midway across

Murdock found the source, a round sphere the size of a tennis ball. The devise felt cool and deadly. A dozen years earlier Murdock had worked with the deadly sphere and had killed many people. Perhaps, he thought, this was payback.

Murdock prayed before starting the task. He had to be perfectly still to disarm the explosive. One uncontrolled movement as he removed the detonator would obliterate half of the building, not just the room. His breathing slowed and, at times, stopped. Occasionally, he closed his eyes as he worked. After clearing his eyes he began the difficult task of disarming the bomb. Gently, using the sharpest knife he could find, he made a slicing motion against the first wire. His fingers cramped. At any moment, no matter how careful he was, the volatile material could ignite.

Sweat filled his eyes again. To be successful, he knew his mind had to be cleared of all thoughts. Thoughts of his family were turned away. Voices disappeared. Thoughts of holding enough explosives to almost level the entire building left him.

7:18 a.m. An hour and a half later the detonator had been removed from the incendiary material.

"I think it's okay."

"What do you mean, '*I think?*'" inquired Frank. His voice was muffled. "I really need more assurance than that. Did you know that the most successful furniture salesman last year still had his head attached?"

"It's safe, but do *exactly* as I say," replied Murdock still intense from the ordeal. He knew Frank was more courageous than that. Frank had earned NYPD's Medal of Valor for his heroics.

"All right, here I come if you insist."

Th two packed as quickly as they could and proceeded to the lobby.

"Mr. Murdock? Is everything all right?" inquired the clerk from behind the wooden counter.

"Everything was fine except for the bomb on my door." The clerk's mouth gaped. "It's disarmed, but have the police check it out. We're leaving. I need a taxi to the airport, now!" The clerk panicked.

"Yes, right away," replied the woman in a distinct British accent.

Her hands began to shake. While they waited Murdock called his in-laws and checked in on his family.

"Hi, Beth."

"I've missed you. How is everything?" asked Beth.

"All right. Just got a minute. I want you to stay with your parents until you hear from me, okay?"

"What's the matter, Bill?" Beth's nervousness never left.

"I can't talk right now, just stay with them."

"I will. Please be careful...and we love you."

"I love you guys, too. I'll be okay. Gotta go."

Murdock placed another call to the Fort Lauderdale IRS office. Before Davenport could finish his introduction Murdock interrupted.

"Someone tried to blow our room up last night and the yacht's been moved to St. Croix. Got any ideas?"

"Preposterous!" replied Davenport who was now on his feet pacing. "What has gotten into you? Have you lost your mind?"

"Plastic explosives...military stuff. You better tell me what's going on," shouted Murdock. The few people in the lobby area looked over at him.

"Lower your voice," ordered Davenport.

"Why didn't you tell me the yacht was used to transport heroine?"

"Heroine! Where did you get a notion like that?"

"Oh, come on! Everyone knows what the boat was used for. My room was ransacked, completely turned upside down. I want some answers!" he shouted.

"You better change your tone with me or I'll..." Murdock interrupted.

"I'm leaving the island and when I get back you better have the answers." Murdock hung up abruptly nearly damaging the phone.

"Murdock? Murdock!" shouted Davenport and then immediately called the director's office. This was the first time in his life he had ever called this office.

"This is Richard Davenport."

"Who?"

"Group Manager downstairs."

"Why are you calling me?"

"Just got a call from Murdock and he said someone tried to blow up his room."

"Notify Inspection, I can't do anything about it."

"Why wasn't I told about the yacht?"

"What about it?" asked the director in a stern voice.

"That it was used in heroine trafficking."

"What difference would it have made?"

"I would have requested the DEA."

"Oh, you would've sent them. Who do you think you are? You'll do as you're told or..." The director paused. He didn't have to finish, Davenport knew his power. "You haven't been successful in diverting Murdock's investigation. Maybe we've got the wrong person managing. Don't call me again." The director hung up. The glass walls of Davenport's cage closed in around him. He loosened his tie so that he could breathe and then buried his face in his hands as he rubbed his temples. He realized that he was an expendable pawn at the director's mercy and that retirement was just around the corner. He also knew that procedures were not being followed and that the case Murdock was working on with Julia had been "misplaced."

While Murdock was on the phone, Jona MacQuiddy had been conversing with the same colorful taxi cab driver from yesterday.

"Wonder what he's got to say?" asked Frank. MacQuiddy was on his way over to them.

"Mr. Murdock, leaving us so soon?" The creases in his uniform were razor sharp.

"Immediately."

"Thought you had business to take care of. We've got an island hopper waiting."

"We're going home."

"Without taking the yacht?" Murdock was silent as he stared at the officer.

"You'd best spend your time by making sure I disarmed the C-4 taped to my door."

"C-4?" MacQuiddy appeared to be surprised, but neither of them trusted him. He turned to his two aides who then disappeared.

"I am sorry you could not accomplish your business. We have a taxi waiting for you. Please accept my apology."

Without saying a word the two climbed into the back seat. Jona MacQuiddy again stared as they pulled out of the driveway. The taxi descended from the clouds, down the coiled road. Five minutes later it turned onto a coral shell road big enough for one and a half vehicles. Frank interrupted the long silence.

"I don't remember the airport being this way." Murdock waited for a response.

"This isn't the way to the airport," snarled Frank to the driver. His forceful tone made the cab driver's eyes shift from the road to the rearview mirror. Sweat covered his brow. Frank pulled his .38 revolver and pushed the muzzle into the thick dark folds of the driver's neck.

"Turn around now and take us to the airport."

"Yes, mon...right away," he replied nervously. "Just don't shoot me. I've got a wife and family to raise." His large hands turned the steering wheel.

"Did you ever think we've got family too!" yelled Frank. His fingers tightened around the trigger. The whites of the huge taxicab driver's eyes enlarged.

"Where were you taking us?" asked Murdock.

"To the far side of the island."

"Why?"

"Don't know, mon."

"You better tell us before my friend gets upset again."

"I don't know! The officer paid me to take you...that's all I've been told."

"MacQuiddy, the man in the white uniform gave you the money?"

"Yes, mon. I mean you no harm."

"Faster," instructed Murdock. The taxi's speed created a cloud of white, chalky smoke. "If we don't make it to the airport, you won't either."

A navy-blue Mercedes, with two men in front and Jona MacQuiddy sitting in the rear, entered the coral road. The Mercedes traveled at a high rate of speed unaware that the taxi had turned around. Visibility was now nonexistent as the sunlight reflected off the blinding, thick white road dust.

"Faster," ordered MacQuiddy to his driver.

"Faster," ordered Frank pushing the barrel of his pistol deeper into the folds of skin.

Any faster on the narrow coral road and the drivers would lose control. As they negotiated the bend, the drivers of both vehicles had only a few seconds to respond. The Mercedes emerged from the unsettled cloud while the large hands of the cabdriver began turning the steering wheel. The driver of the Mercedes froze. The front end of MacQuiddy's automobile erupted like a fireball spewing black smoke and flames upward. Each occupant was thrown forward with the drivers of the vehicles absorbing most of the tremendous impact. No one moved as both vehicles came to a rest.

Minutes later.

"Frank...you...all right?" asked Murdock.

"Yeah...my head is splitting, but I don't feel any blood," replied Frank. "You're bleeding," observed Frank. Murdock had a two-inch gash above his right eye with blood trickling from it. He quickly ripped a piece of his shirt, folded it, applied pressure to the wound and then tied it around his head.

"Let's get out of here before this car blows."

"I gotta find my gun." The two looked, but the gun was lost.

"The car is sizzling...we gotta get out of here."

"A little more...I found it." Frank pulled on the revolver, but to no avail. "Ah!" The gun was jammed underneath the driver's seat. The car was sizzling and could explode at any time. Murdock exited the vehicle.

The smell of burning flesh permeated the area. A smell they both recognized from their former lives as a team leader of a special forces squad and as a police officer.

"Frank, now!" He reluctantly gave up. He felt naked without his pistol. The intensity of the heat precluded the two from pulling the driver out. They tried to open the rear door to save MacQuiddy, but it was jammed from the impact. Working together they managed to get all 6'6" of MacQuiddy out through the window and pulled to a safe, shady spot.

"He's still alive," asserted Murdock after checking for a pulse. Moments passed before his eyes opened.

"Where...de others?" asked MacQuiddy.

"They didn't make it," replied Murdock. "Who are you doing this for?" There was silence. "Who paid you?" Still no answer. Murdock placed the muzzle of his 9mm to MacQuiddy's head and cocked the hammer. The clicking of the hammer slowly being pulled back into firing position opened MacQuiddy's eyes and his mouth.

"I don't know who they are."

"But they're from the States?"

"Yes."

"They're with the government?" asked Murdock.

"I don't know that...all I know is that I got a phone call a week ago from a man explaining what he wanted done. That afternoon money was wired to my account. More money was coming once the job was done."

"Why did you go through my room? What are you looking for?" There was a brief silence. Murdock didn't have to wait long nor did he have to say anything else. MacQuiddy's eyes were fixed on the cocked hammer and he knew Murdock was tired and tense.

"We were looking for a small black book. Property in your possession that belongs to the man that called me. If I couldn't find it I was told to...eliminate you." MacQuiddy was silent. Sweat poured down his face.

"We're leaving. If you interfere, I'll kill you," informed Murdock. The two proceeded through the primitive forest en route to the airport.

MacQuiddy staggered back to the car and retrieved his phone. "Close the airport and barricade the routes, they're loose! They killed everyone. Shoot to kill...shoot to kill."

Ten minutes into their journey through the forest a final explosion engulfed the automobiles, entombing the three occupants.

"Can you ride a horse?"

"Eighteen years ago...why?" asked Frank. His question was answered when he looked up and saw the horse stables. "Bill, I can't do this."

"Sure you can. Besides, it's the only way we're gonna make it to the airport in our condition." Several horses were saddled awaiting the arrival of a group of tourists. "Let's go."

"We're just gonna take 'em?"

"Borrow them for a little while. You ready?"

"I guess."

The barn blocked the line of sight from the farmhouse as they gently escorted the two horses from stalls labeled *Moonbeam* and *Laser.* Murdock mounted Moonbeam first.

"You would leave me Laser. I can't lift my leg that high." Laser nudged Frank as if they were lifelong friends.

"Let's go. Someone's coming." With a heave Frank pulled his sore body up and, with lightning speed, Laser followed Moonbeam back into the dark glen.

Murdock yelled back to Frank who was in hot pursuit.

"Watch out for these branches." Twenty minutes later the woods came to an end. One of the barricades had been placed about fifty yards away. "A few more minutes and we're there."

"You sure?" Murdock pointed to the plane rising above the treetops."Then what?" continued Frank. "We can't just waltz into the airport. MacQuiddy's men will probably be there." Frank looked away in thought.

"Got any ideas?" asked Murdock.

"No, but our best chance is now."

"All right, when those guys see us they may shoot, so don't slow down. Ride low and ah, try and stay on the horse, will ya? Let's go!" Murdock strapped Moonbeam who shot like a bolt of lightning with Laser close behind. The men at the roadblock looked, but didn't realize who the riders were until they had passed them. The sound of gunfire made Moonbeam gallop faster. Suddenly, Laser reared up in the air throwing Frank to the ground just before the beautiful horse fell. It's hindquarters were bleeding.

"Bill!" MacQuiddy's men began charging. Murdock turned around gripping Frank's arm almost pulling it out of the socket as he helped Frank up on Moonbeam. The gunfire continued. Moments later they dismounted Moonbeam just outside the airport perimeter.

"Can you run to the hangar over there?"

"I'll try."

They startled a pilot cranking his blue and white Cessna. Its engines were humming. Neither one of them could speak when they approached the pilot. Each onc allowed time for the other to say something, anything. The running made them nauseous. The pilot began to back off. Frank pulled out his badge.

"Get us out of here, now!" The pilot, a man in his late fifties wearing a cowboy hat and boots studied the badge.

"This has got to be worth a free 'get out of audit' card." He hustled into the cockpit. "Guess you boys ain't interested in knowing the airports been ordered closed and I'm flying to Palm Beach."

"Right," replied Murdock still catching his breath.

"Didn't think so." The throttle was pushed forward and the plane was taxiing out when a military vehicle appeared on the runway. The pilot slowed the plane.

"We've got company!" exclaimed the pilot. His mirror sunglasses reflected the blue cloudless sky.

"Get us out of here!"

"I'll try." The car gained on the aircraft, just a few feet away from the tail. "If they hit us we're not going anywhere."

The pilot worked several controls simultaneously. He knew he'd either just make it or just miss takeoff. The car gained distance and was now only six inches away. Murdock chambered a round in his semi-automatic pistol and pumped a few bullets into the grill and hood.

"Never saw a car stop so fast," laughed the pilot as the plane lifted high into the air. Frank fell back into his seat exhausted. "You boys gonna have to help me spot planes since the tower won't respond."

"How soon will you pick up the West Palm Beach tower?" asked Murdock dabbing his wound.

"In a few minutes. Just hope they don't call the States and make up a story about us."

"What if they do? It won't affect you," remarked Frank.

"It will if the Air Force scrambles a couple of their F-14s!"

The two dozed and touchdown quickly awoke them.

"We're there?" questioned Murdock.

"You fell asleep 'bout two minutes after takeoff. I wish you both a lotta luck."

"Thank you. Hey, we didn't even get your name."

"Bubba Andrews."

"Murdock and this is Frank Laccetti. We owe ya, Bubba Andrews." The plane came to a stop just outside the hangar and the two climbed out.

"Hey!" yelled Bubba. They stopped and looked back. "I'll call you if I'm ever audited." Bubba smiled. Murdock gave a thumbs up. The two proceeded to the phone located in the hangar office.

"We use the phone?" The clerk motioned to go ahead.

"Morning, IRS."

"Palmetto."

"Bill?"

"Yeah. Run a check through the phone company. I want to know who called Jona MacQuiddy last Tuesday at his office and home." He gave Palmetto additional information on MacQuiddy.

"Got the numbers?" asked Palmetto.

"No, see what you can do."

"Where are you?"

"West Palm Beach Airport."

"Are you okay?"

"Not really. Can we stay at your place in Lauderdale for a while?"

"Of course. You know where the key is. Can I do anything else?"

"We'll talk tonight... and thanks."

19

Palmetto's vacation houseboat was a floating "A" frame located on the New River not far from downtown Fort Lauderdale. While he resided in south Miami, he maintained the houseboat for weekends in Fort Lauderdale. The tinted glass at both ends gave the 1964 structure a more modern appearance. The deck was covered with small potted shrubs and hanging ferns. At night, the tiny white lights nestled in the plants created a unique ambiance against the backdrop of the city's skyline.

Murdock and Frank had traveled a little more than an hour in their rented car when they arrived at the houseboat. They climbed aboard and entered the living room. The interior was nicely decorated. A wrought iron spiral staircase led to a loft which was used as a bedroom. Looking east, the winding river nestled trawlers, yachts built in the '40s through '70s, and numerous sailboats all worth a fortune. Coconut trees thrived along the river which began at Port Everglades and meandered miles inland. To the west, the Third and Andrews Avenue bridges, Broward County Courthouse and part of the downtown skyline could be viewed.

"What now?" asked Murdock.

"Go to the Treasury Inspector General, they're set up for this kind of stuff." Murdock lifted his head and looked over at Frank.

"You said they were an independent agency, didn't you?"

"Yeah. They're the ones you turn to when you want to blow the whistle."

"Well, it's time." Murdock picked up the phone.

"Who you calling?"

"Marlene in CI. She'll have the number."

"Bill?" she immediately recognized his voice.

"Yeah."

"Don't come near the building." Her voice was tense and low.

"Why?"

"People are here just waiting for you to show. They're saying you broke into grand jury files and botched a four-year long investigation."

"I need the number to the Treasury IG in Washington."

"Can they help you?" She was genuinely concerned about Murdock.

"I hope. I don't know what else to do."

After getting a number from her, Murdock was transferred seven times before getting the Inspector General's office.

"Mr. Rubenstein, my name is Bill Murdock. I'm a revenue officer with the IRS in Fort Lauderdale and...I'm not certain if I've got the right office or not, but...huh..." Murdock hesitated searching for the right descriptive. "...I've stumbled onto what I think is wrongdoing by upper levels of IRS management." Rubenstein took his feet off the corner of the desk and leaned forward in his leather highback chair.

"What kind of malfeasance and is there any evidence?" inquired the resonant voice.

Murdock explained his inability to get a simple assessment against the officers of Sea Unlimited and the sequence of events that followed.

"Your story...I suppose you know it's hard to believe."

"Yeah, but it happened."

"What makes you think management stopped the investigation into Sea Unlimited?"

"No, the investigation into certain drug attorneys stopped. The U.S. Attorney's Office was ready to indict several of 'em and the IRS pulled out, stopped the whole thing after years of work."

"What makes you think it was management?"

"Who else could stop the train so quickly?" My manager told me not to seize the Porsche. It was paid for!"

"Has he ever done that before?"

"Never. If CI has a legitimate investigation going on they give us a memo to cease."

"You didn't get a memo?"

"No memo, nothing except Davenport verbally advising me not to seize."

"Tell me about how you obtained information on 'Operation Liberty' again."

"No one would talk to me even though I had a need-to-know. The opportunity arose, so I reviewed some files that pertained to my investigation."

"Where were the files located?"

"In CI," replied Murdock.

"Did CI turn them over to you?"

"Not exactly."

"What do you mean?"

"They don't know I saw the file."

"So your review was unauthorized."

"I had a need-to-know." There was silence between them. A few more seconds and Murdock continued. "My investigation stalled for no apparent reason and I knew the files in CI would tell me." Murdock could hear Rubenstein's continuous scratching of pencil on paper.

"All right, here's what we'll do. Over the next couple of days summarize what happened. Don't leave anything out. Tim Sylar from my office will be down..." Murdock could hear the rustling of pages. "...Thursday. Have your notes ready. What number can I reach you at?" Murdock didn't say anything. He wanted to trust him, but he didn't.

"Have him meet me in the lobby of his hotel. I'll call you later to find out which hotel."

"You don't trust me, do you?"

"Sir, I don't know you."

"He'll be at the Marriott on Seventeenth Street Causeway."

"Tell him to have a green handkerchief in his hand," requested Murdock.

"Okay. What time?"

"Nine."

"See you then."

"What's up?" asked Frank, anxious to hear the details.

"He's sending someone from his office. We'll meet him at the Causeway Marriott.

"Great!" exclaimed Frank happy an outside agency was getting involved.

"I'm not getting a good feeling about this," remarked Murdock.

"What's the matter? What else did he say to you?"

"It's not what he said, it's what he didn't ask me."

"Don't worry, you did the right thing. In a couple of days you can put this all behind you and let someone else get to the bottom of it."

"I hope you're right," replied Murdock as his stomach tightened. "All this because I seized a car." Murdock stood up and stretched his back.

"A car that distributed coke." continued Frank. "Wonder who they are?"

"They were powerful enough to get IRS to back off." Murdock glanced out the window looking east. The coconut trees along the New River seemed to be socializing as they danced and turned in the breeze. "Who's behind all this?" Murdock continued as he tapped a pen on the kitchen countertop. "Wish I could tell them I don't have what they're looking for."

"Give me the names of everyone who knows about this," requested Frank. A yellow legal pad was in his lap ready to scribble down names. Murdock started the lengthy list of names:

"Rico, Nieto, Ward, Martinez, Farmer...scratch that, he's dead. Warbington, A.K.A. Thomas Farley, Alena Muller and the two men in the car that followed me," Murdock paused.

"Davenport, Carmichael, you, me," responded Frank.

Cricket, Palmetto and Beetle." Murdock hesitated.

"Anyone else?" asked Frank.

"Inspection and Mike Durham." He scribbled the names down.

"Mike Durham?"

"He's the FBI agent who approached me at Julia's funeral. He's the one that told me about Rico and Nieto."

"Right. Is that it?"

"Think so. I'm surprised there's that many," asserted Murdock.

"I can only eliminate five names. Yours, mine, Cricket, Palmetto and Beetle," summarized Frank.

"Add Ernie's name," interrupted Murdock.

"Okay, six that I know aren't involved."

"There's different issues involved," interjected Murdock.

"Go on Columbo."

"Some of the people involved were interested in stopping my earlier assessments against Farmer. Others want the drugs and maybe that book if it means something."

"Good point...we'll make two lists." They studied the names again.

"Davenport and Carmichael are involved in curtailing the investigation. The others are with the drugs and book," mused Murdock.

"All of them interested in the book?" asked Frank. Murdock looked at the list.

"You're right. Rico, Nieto, Martinez, Warbington and the one unknown man at the Porsche should be on the drug list only...well...maybe the book, too." Murdock continued, "Rico is really interested in Nieto. I really don't think he cares about anything else."

"Okay, so we have three lists. Stopping your assessments, drugs and the book. Couldn't the unknown man at the Porsche be interested in the book, too?" asked Frank.

"Sure, but where is this getting us?"

"I don't know, yet. Maybe it won't tell us anything. Where does Alena fit in?"

"I don't know. Let's leave her on the drug list."

"Ward?" asked Frank.

"Drug and book list. He's an attorney and you can bet he knows the people listed in the book."

"Martinez knows the people in the book," asserted Frank.

"He was one of the workers. The people in the book wouldn't have associated with him. Inspection...put them on the list with Davenport and Carmichael. Durham...I don't know. He wanted me to let him know everything Rico and I discussed. He said he'd contact me. I just don't know where he fits in." Frank circled his name.

"Why wouldn't you place Carmichael on the drug list?' asked Frank.

"I'm not sure. I just don't think it's the drugs with him," Murdock hesitated. "I don't know why."

"You said Martinez was gonna talk to the grand jury, did he?"

"I don't know. He did think I knew something because I worked for IRS. Maybe the grand jury will find out," asserted Murdock who still didn't know Martinez was executed. "So what did we learn from this exercise?" asked Murdock.

"We've placed everyone except Mike Durham on a list. He's the unknown," replied Frank.

"The more I think about it, the main thing Durham was interested in was Rico. If you were still a cop in this situation what would you do?" asked Murdock. Frank pondered the question.

"I'd learn more about Durham before I went any further and, if we had more of a lead, the two men who followed you and the one at the ." Murdock nodded in agreement.

Palmetto stopped by the Ft. Lauderdale office before arriving at the houseboat. He wanted to inform Murdock of the latest information.

"There's a crowd in Davenport's office. I think he's gonna have a stroke."

"What did you hear?" asked Murdock.

"I caught a little of it. You're interfering with CI's case and you're not following directives."

"We almost got killed in St. Thomas!" exclaimed Frank.

"How?"

"Someone rigged the door and windows with explosives," replied Frank.

"When that didn't work they chased us. Barely got away in someone's plane," finished Murdock.

"What now?" asked Palmetto.

"He's talking to the Treasury IG in a couple of days. They'll investigate," corroborated Frank sure of what he was saying. "They'll get 'em!"

"I didn't know there was an IG office," remarked Palmetto. "Hope they can help—I've never seen them so intense. The Director was yelling at Davenport and Carmichael."

"Yelling? In Davenport's office?" asked Murdock in disbelief. This was especially surprising since the director never left his palace.

"You should've seen the gang in there. All I could hear was that Davenport, and apparently Carmichael, let something get out of hand. I couldn't get close enough. What can I do?"

"If you could put up with us for a few days. I don't want to go back to the condo."

"No problem. I've got plenty of room. Oh, I almost forgot." Palmetto passed Murdock a list from the phone company. "You wanted a listing of the people who called MacQuiddy." Murdock searched the list as Frank looked over his shoulder.

"Sea Unlimited has business with him. Look at this." The company had phoned MacQuiddy four different times during this particular day.

"Beetle and a Mike Durham called you. They said it was important." Palmetto passed them an ice cold drink as Murdock searched for the telephone numbers in his wallet.

"Beetle?"

"Hey Bill, you're not going to believe this...you sittin' down?"

"Go ahead."

"We got the summoned telephone numbers back on the Largo house. Someone at the end of each month called Alena Muller in Coconut Grove."

"I knew that."

"Well, here's something I bet you didn't figure."

"What's that?"

"Alena Muller lives in a garage apartment above Albert Wilson's house."

"Albert Wilson?"

"Al 'Ex-District Director' Wilson ring a bell?"

"You're kiddin'?" Murdock stood up.

"I wouldn't shuck your corn on this. It's him all right. That's not all. Someone from his house calls Ward and the Largo house."

"He's part of this?!"

"Not sure how, but he can't be totally innocent."

"I just can't believe it." Murdock paced.

"I thought this might make your day. Well, gotta run. Let me know how this turns out."

"I owe you. Hey, keep the summons in a safe place."

"Later," asserted Beetle as he hung up.

"Frank, add another name to your list," stated Murdock.

"Shoot."

"Albert Wilson."

"Our last director?" asked Palmetto.

"You got it. A little before your time, Frank."

"How'd ya get this?" asked Frank as he placed his prosthesis in the corner for the night.

"His number showed up on a list we summoned."

"The end of the month calls fit the drug meetings, but it doesn't mean he made the call," mused Frank.

"But he's got to be connected, right?" asked Murdock. Palmetto listened to the two in their state of excitement. They sounded as though they were engaged in making the closing arguments of a trial. Palmetto pulled several stone crabs from the traps for dinner.

"The IRS wouldn't stop an investigation on a drug attorney so an ex-director could catch part of the action," declared Frank.

"The fact that his telephone is used to call a drug attorney under investigation *and* the Largo house which was, if you remember, fraudulently transferred to a corporation owned by *this* drug attorney, connects him!" insisted Murdock. Frank was in thought.

"We do know his phone is being used," summarized Frank.

"Well that connects him! You're impossible today!"

"What if Alena is making the call from his apartment while he's away?"

"Then I say he's connected. I don't think she's breaking into his house each time to use the phone. She's got a key or he invites her in. Either way, he's connected. He can't be innocent of what's going on." Murdock raised his hands in the air and walked outside in frustration. There was a touch of salt in the warm breeze as it gently caressed his head and tight, aching shoulders. Frank turned to Palmetto.

"What do ya think? Is he connected?" asked Frank using both his hands. He was as frustrated as Murdock.

"His phone?"

"Yep."

"He's in on it somehow. Doesn't mean he's dealing or buying though," replied Palmetto. The water boiled and in dropped the meaty claws. "A few more minutes and you're in for a treat," declared Palmetto.

The sun, in its dying moments, gave birth to an explosion of color as it surrendered to the downtown buildings. Murdock leaned against the railing which outlined the boat. The breezy massage had ended. The three sat at the bow listening to an "oldies" station and eating fresh stone crabs.

"Marlene said Wilson visited CI last December." Murdock was thinking out loud. "Ward and Muller were law partners until about a year ago. Now why would they end the partnership, but continue the relationship?"

"Pursue another career?" injected Palmetto.

"She's still a lawyer!" exclaimed Murdock raising his voice.

"They couldn't work together...kinda like Bill and me." Murdock grinned. The phone rang.

"Bill...for you," called Palmetto.

"Murdock, here."

"Bill, I have some information I know you'll be interested in. Can we meet?"

"When?" Murdock recognized Agent Mike Durham's voice from when they had met at Julia's funeral.

"Now."

"I'm pretty tired, can we do it tomorrow?"

"Could, but it's good stuff...but if you're too tired..."

Murdock interrupted, "What is it?"

"I can't discuss this over the phone...too hot."

"All right, where?"

"I'll be on a catamaran at Bahia Mar, slip number thirty-three."

"I'll be there."

"Good." Palmetto and Frank waited for Murdock to fill them in.

"Where's the meeting?" asked Frank.

"Slip thirty-three at the marina."

"I'll go, too. I'd like to know about him," stated Frank.

"You're beat, I'll meet 'em."

"Just be careful. He's the only one we don't know anything about." Murdock nodded as he left the boat. Palmetto continued the conversation where they left off.

"Someone with influence over her told her to quit."

"Okay, how's this," said Frank as he sat erect. "Maybe Wilson and Muller are lovers. She quit the practice to please the ol' man, but couldn't get Ward off her mind."

"Then Wilson would lead the IRS to Ward just to nail him and get him out of the way," continued Palmetto.

"I like it, but would you stop an investigation if you wanted to nail the guy?" asked Frank. The phone rang.

"It's Rico," whispered Palmetto passing the phone. Frank collected his thoughts before answering.

"Excellent work getting off the island. No one has ever eluded Nieto this long. But his search for you isn't over."

"Where is he?"

"He's here...in Fort Lauderdale...somewhere. It won't be long until he finds you. Now he wants to teach both of you a lesson."

"Is MacQuiddy working with him?"

"Nieto's a loner. MacQuiddy is bought and paid for by the businessmen in your journal."

"So what's on your mind?"

"The final piece of the puzzle."

"I'm listening."

"Alena Muller and Phillip Ward were law partners in Miami up until a year ago. They're still intimate."

"Why did she quit?"

"Her father knew what Ward was and despised him. He knew Ward was under investigation and would go down. He didn't want his daughter to be associated with him or the partnership for fear she'd be disbarred or worse, implicated."

"Operation Liberty was nixed, how come?"

"Not cancelled, delayed to give Muller time and distance from Ward and the business. They didn't want Murdock to continue his investigation on Sea Unlimited, the officers of the corporation, the Porsche or the Largo house since Ward's name would surface. Enough time and distance had not come between them."

"All this to protect his daughter...wait...how did he know Ward was under investigation and how could he delay IRS?"

"Her father is..." Frank interrupted.

"Albert Wilson!" exclaimed Frank before Rico could utter the name. "Unbelievable! What about the names in the journal?"

"Don't know."

"What about the drugs or the journal...who has them?"

"Don't know. The police found Ramon Martinez in the middle of Andrews Avenue."

"Who did it?"

"Anyone's guess," replied Rico.

"He was about to give testimony to the grand jury in exchange for a new identity. He seemed to think the IRS would bail him out. This whole thing seems too far-fetched. I'm having a hard time believing anything myself," expressed Frank.

"That's the way these games are," replied Rico in his low, monotone voice.

"Mike Durham just called. Said he had some information for Bill. Guess he's gonna pass on what you just said."

"Who is he?" asked Rico.

"What do you mean?" asked Frank alarmed.

"I don't know the man."

"He told Bill he's with the FBI in your office!"

"I don't know the man and he's not with the FBI."

"He showed Bill pictures of you and Nieto." Frank's voice was beginning to crescendo.

"There are no known photographs of Nieto," replied Rico with conviction in his voice.

"I don't believe this! Whoever he is, Bill just left to meet 'em."

Frank's skin crawled.

"Where?"

"Bahia Mar, slip thirty-three on a catamaran. Who is he?"

"Stay away from the boat. I'll take care of this." There was a nervous excitement in Rico's voice for the first time.

"Take care of what? Who is he?"

"I have him!"

"Have who, tell me!"

"Nieto!"

20

Traveling east past houses hidden behind thick walls of tropical plants and trees, Murdock negotiated the winding turns toward Highway A1A. His stomach tightened. Durham's call bothered him, but he wasn't certain why. Just past the Sheraton Yankee Clipper, on the left, was the marina. Before exiting his convertible he subconsciously ejected a round into his pistol and placed it behind him, tucked in his jeans.

After several minutes of searching he found slip #25, then #27...#29. The planks of the dock vibrated and squeaked, announcing his arrival. Slip #31—his heart pounded and the adrenaline strengthened him. Slip #33! He cautiously scanned the 34-foot catamaran. The boat's multi-hulls had navy-blue striping which matched the tightly wrapped sails.

"Mike." Murdock's voice carried across the water. There was no response.

"Mike?" An eerie feeling covered Murdock. The slapping of water against the hulls of some of the most expensive luxury boats ever built was the only response. Murdock's eyes traced the catamaran when, all of a sudden, he felt a hand on his right shoulder. He quickly turned his head.

"So glad you could make it," declared Durham. Murdock was still unscrambling his thoughts. The sudden contact was unnerving. “Come on board.” Murdock slowly followed. The two went below deck and into the cabin.

“Have a seat.” Murdock sat on a teak wood chair. The interior was impressive. Polished teak wood lined the inside areas with mirrors and indirect lighting.

“Your boat?”

“A friend’s. Anyone know what happened to the coke?” Durham quickly cut the small talk.

“No.”

“What are you and Rico discussing?”

“We don’t talk much.”

“When you do talk, what’s it about?” Durham stood at the wet bar, his back turned to Murdock. He turned slightly. “Drink?” Durham had an odd look about him. Murdock’s stomach was in a knot as he flashed back to Nam. His hands and feet had been tied for hours, making them puffy and violet in color. One-by-one the American POW’s were tortured to death if they didn’t give the VC useful information. The reward for giving useful data was still death, but it was instant and painless. There were three POWs before him. A few died painlessly and quickly as promised while the screams from others haunted Murdock. The VC officer in charge entered the room and ordered another American out. The officer’s back was turned to Murdock when, unexpectedly, the VC soldier ordered the American to sit down. He then turned slightly and went out of sequence ordering Murdock to get up. The restraints around his hands and feet were cut. Murdock tried to stand but couldn’t, so he crawled to the adjacent room where the POWs lay in a pool of blood. The soldiers who had given new information had their spinal cords severed at the base of the brain stem. To the right, a pile of toes, fingers and ears belonging to the POWs who refused to cooperate.

“Drink?” asked the VC officer holding a glass of water. Murdock refused.

“Drink?” asked Durham again. Murdock abandoned his thoughts of Nam. “When you last talked to Rico what was it about?” Durham was annoyed.

“Nieto.”

"What about him?"

"Nothing much." Murdock didn't like the questions.

"What did he say?" asked Mike more forcefully.

"Only that he was close to Nieto...the closest he's ever been." Durham smiled. "What did you want to tell me?" Durham went to the wet bar again.

"The drugs in the Porsche belong to me. I want them but now it's your time!" Murdock wasn't certain he heard him. His stomach tightened. A second later Durham turned and pointed a pistol with a long, sleek silencer at him. Murdock considered his alternatives. There weren't many. His adrenaline soared. "Hands on your head and don't take them off." Durham approached Murdock and removed the handgun from his pants.

"Who are you?"

"I go by many names. You know me as Durham, your government calls me Nieto." He pulled out a blue nylon rope and tossed it to Murdock.

"Tie your ankles together and then to the chair."

Murdock looked at him and slowly began tying the knots, exploring his options again. He would make his move when Nieto approached him. This, he thought, would be his last opportunity to save his life.

"I'm going to remove your eyes from their sockets. First the right one...then left. Do you understand me?"

"Just like Farmer," remarked Murdock.

"That's right, just like that."

"Why?"

"I lost a substantial amount of money because of you and now you're going to pay for it. Nothing personal."

Nieto turned his back to Murdock and adjusted the silver instrument he would use to scoop his eyes out. Murdock knew he would have just one chance to overcome Nieto. As Nieto made the final adjustments on the instrument, Murdock caught the movement of a shadow just outside the boat. With the stealth and quietness of a panther, Rico entered the cabin, pistol in hand. Murdock started breathing heavy. Rico approached Nieto from behind and pressed the gun to his head. Nieto froze. He knew who it was without looking. Only one person could get this close to him.

"It's been a long time, Rico," noted Nieto who then smiled.

"Six years and now it's time to meet your maker, Nieto. Time to pay for all your misdeeds." Nieto laughed.

"I'll be on a plane to South America before the ink dries on your report." Without another word Rico cocked the hammer of the gun. Murdock's breathing quickened with anticipation. Nieto laughed again.

"What report? Checkmate, my friend," exclaimed Rico.

"You think?" Nieto's flip attitude was nauseating. As he reached for a weapon, a blast sent the front of Nieto's cranium onto the walls of the cabin. Brain matter mixed with blood dripped from the ceiling and walls. Murdock quickly untied his ankles.

"Wipe your fingerprints off everything you touched and leave immediately. You weren't here," instructed Rico. Murdock was speechless. "My work is done and my debt to you is paid. Adios amigo." Without another word the mysterious agent disappeared into the night—Rico was gone.

Murdock followed Rico's instructions. He felt as though he was moving in slow motion. He was stunned even though he had seen this kind of mayhem many times. The vibrating dock planks signaled another visitor approaching. The police, thought Murdock. His heart raced as he tried to figure out what he would do or say. With Rico not there, who would believe him? The squeaky boards got louder until he was certain the visitor was searching the catamaran. Silhouettes lurked just beyond the boat, then boarded and froze. Murdock found his pistol and prepared for a battle.

"Bill?" whispered one of the shadows. Murdock immediately recognized the voice.

"Frank, don't touch anything." Frank and Palmetto made their way to the cabin.

"What happened?" asked Frank disgusted. Palmetto exited immediately.

"I'll tell you at the Rooftop. Let's get out of here. Wipe your prints off the railing," repeated Murdock.

For ten minutes they traveled in silence northbound on A1A until Murdock realized he was going in the wrong direction. He turned around just before Oakland Park Boulevard and back-tracked. Silhouettes of coconut trees slept along the moonlit ocean.

Shortly after arriving at Ernie's, they quickly downed a pitcher of beer as they sat on the rooftop in silence. Palmetto signaled the waitress for another pitcher.

"What happened?" exclaimed Palmetto. His hands were noticeably shaking as he gulped his beer.

"Nieto...Mike Durham was Nieto! I can't believe it. I was in his car at Julia's funeral."

"Rico shot him?" asked Frank.

"Yeah, just before he was gonna carve my eyes out." Palmetto had a difficult time keeping the beer down.

"Rico called just after you left. He said Alena is Wilson's daughter."

"Daughter?"

"He confirmed everything," asserted Frank.

"Guess they stopped Operation Liberty because she'd be linked to Ward," observed Murdock.

"Wilson thought she'd be jailed or disbarred if the connection to Ward was made," remarked Frank. "Their plan was to delay the investigation. Wilson thought the delay might buy her some time and save her from being associated with him."

"What Wilson didn't count on is Alena continuing the relationship with Ward," admonished Murdock.

"He didn't count on her using his phone to keep in touch with a drug attorney under investigation," replied Frank.

"So I couldn't make the assessments or investigate the transfer of the Largo house since Ward was involved."

"You got it!"

"Think the current director, Davenport and Carmichael are in on it?" asked Murdock.

"They delayed the investigation," replied Frank.

"There's a lot of powerful people involved in this and we don't even know who the businessmen in the journal are. How can we ever get clear of this mess?" Murdock was perplexed.

"Bill, your room was never ransacked, right?" asked Palmetto.

Murdock nodded in agreement.

"Then they're still after you. They could be anyone...IRS, bankers, lawyers, Colombians...anyone!" exclaimed Frank.

"When do you meet with the Treasury IG?" asked Frank.

"Tomorrow morning."

"The IG out of Washington?" asked Palmetto a little surprised.

"Yup."

"You're going all the way," remarked Palmetto.

"Not much of a choice."

"At least this will be over tomorrow and we can get on with things," said Frank.

"I hope so Frank...I hope so."

Murdock made a call to his wife and children. He returned as the third pitcher was being drained. The table was covered with baskets of conch fritters. The three were quiet for some time.

"How's Beth taking all of this?" asked Palmetto.

"It's hard on her. I've been gone awhile, but she doesn't complain."

"Wish Melissa was blessed with that virtue," responded Frank. "The woman was born complaining." The diversion in conversation from what they had viewed on the catamaran was relief.

"Things still not any better?" asked Palmetto.

"How can they be with her not here?"

"She with her parents?" asked Palmetto. Frank nodded.

"Guess I'll be getting divorced. It's such a shame."

"Your life isn't over. You'll meet someone. Maybe it's a blessing you don't have any kids with her. It's tough trying to see your children when their mother does everything she can to stop it," interjected Palmetto, desperately trying to focus his thoughts on something other than what had taken place.

"It's rough on you, isn't it?" asked Frank.

"I'm not worried about me, it's the kids that get caught up in this nonsense. It's hard on them. She only thinks about herself...revenge against me for calling it quits. It just doesn't matter to her if the kids are hurt in this or not."

"Can't you get custody?"

"Tried," responded Palmetto as he wiped his brow.

"Well, if Melissa doesn't start calling soon I'm..." Frank didn't finish his statement. He loved her.

"She cares about you, it's the job that scares her," Murdock remarked.

"So that's a reason to leave, because you're scared!" Murdock shrugged his shoulders.

"You've been married a long time," reminded Frank looking at Murdock. "How do ya do it?"

"I'm not sure...keeping your sense of humor helps."

"You ready to call it a night?" asked Palmetto.

"What about your car?"

"I'll get it tomorrow."

Frank and Palmetto struggled down the stairs. A sing-a-long was taking place and, in light of the tense atmosphere they had just come from, the two felt obligated to participate. They climbed up on a table just in time to lead the group in a beer-drinking song. The patrons loved their graphic interpretation of a Jimmy Buffet tune. Murdock stood by the door and laughed along with the crowd knowing that their secret identities as IRS officers were the most humorous part of the skit. As the song ended someone from the audience yelled out, "Hey, Bubba, ain't that the IRS man that took our boat?"

"It sure looks like 'em."

"Let's whoop 'em good."

The two oversized men in overalls struggled through the crowd when Murdock intercepted and eventually convinced them that the two were from Canada just visiting awhile. Murdock grabbed the two revenue officers and ushered them out.

Murdock traveled north on Federal Highway and made a right turn just before the New River Tunnel when car lights caught his eye. The treetops along the winding road formed a canopy. The road offered several turns to test if someone was following. After the third turn Murdock pulled his pistol out and placed it under his right thigh. His belly tightened.

"We're being followed." The two were asleep. "Frank! Wake up!" Murdock nudged him. "We're being followed!"

"I know a couple of ways to lose him," responded Palmetto.

"I don't want to lose him."

"Why?" asked Palmetto. Frank looked befuddled.

"Let's see what he wants." Murdock gunned the car and lost sight of the mysterious follower as he crossed over a small bridge in the Rio Vista community. As soon as he crossed the canal he sped through the jungle-like neighborhood and, without warning, whipped into a circular driveway and back into the middle of the road where he cut the lights. He then left them in the car and hid down the road in some bushes, waiting to greet the uninvited guest.

Twenty seconds later a car, traveling at high speed, topped the bridge. The underbody rubbed the pavement sending a fireworks display everywhere. As the car approached, Frank flashed his bright lights at him. The sound of screeching tires sent dogs barking. Ten feet from impact the car stopped. The smell of burning rubber and smoke permeated the tropical air. Murdock approached the vehicle from behind. A lone man exited the car as Murdock twisted his pistol into the man's temple.

"Put your hands on the hood." Without comment the man obeyed. Frank patted him down and retrieved his wallet. No gun was found. Palmetto looked on from just outside their car.

"He's clean."

"Who is he?" Frank looked at his license,.

"Bill, meet Tomas Concepcion of North Miami Beach."

"Well, Tomas, you're out of your neighborhood, aren't ya?" Murdock spun him around. His silk white shirt was buttoned with his shaggy black hair resting on his shoulders.

"He's 'bout forty miles from home," declared Frank.

"Why are you following us?" asked Murdock still holding his gun to Concepcion's left temple.

"Following you?" replied Concepcion. Murdock cocked the hammer of his gun.

"Who hired you?"

"A small group of businessmen in Fort Lauderdale."

"Why?"

"You have something that belongs to them."

"And what's that?"

"A thin black book. It's theirs and they just want it back."

"We don't have it."

"As I said, they're businessmen. They're willing to pay for its prompt and safe return."

"We don't have the thing. Never did."

"Name your price. They'll pay cash."

"We don't have the book! Frank, is he listening?"

"WE...DON'T...HAVE...IT!" blasted Frank.

"Who does?" Tomas Concepcion looked at Murdock.

Murdock ignored the question. "Who's in the book?"

"I don't know. I'm only to find it."

"We've been through a lot today and we're tired so I'm gonna ask you one more time..." Concepcion answered the question before it was asked.

"I've never met them. I get paid and receive new assignments at a post office box. They like their anonymity."

"I want you to convince them that we don't have it and never did. You understand?"

"Yeah."

"You the one who ransacked our rooms in the Keys and St. Thomas?" asked Frank squinting his eyes.

"I did in the Keys. Another contractor must've been assigned to St. Thomas."

"What do you mean?" asked Murdock.

"The group I work for, they sometimes hire several people to get the job done if it's important."

"So this is important to them," remarked Frank. Concepcion nodded.

"Very."

"Tomas, get out of here and we don't ever want to see you again, got it?"

"Yeah."

"Let's go and get some sleep. We've gotta meet with the IG in the morning."

"Hey," yelled Tomas Concepcion. "For what it's worth, I believe you, but they won't. If the book doesn't show up, they won't stop."

***

"Dad?" she spoke softly into the telephone.

"Are you all right?" Alena hesitated.

"Yes."

"I've missed you so much. I'm sorry..."

"No, Dad, I'm sorry for what I said," interrupted Alena.

"Where are you?"

"With friends."

"Ward is still with the Colombians," added her father. There was silence.

"Doesn't matter anymore. I'm going home in a few days." She sounded resigned to the fact that there was nothing else that she could do.

"You're coming back here?"

"No. Back to Rhode Island. I need a fresh start...away from here."

"Who will you stay with?"

"I'm a big girl, Dad. I'll manage."

"You can stay with the Stang's. They'd love to have you and..."

"Dad," interrupted Alena, but her father didn't hear her.

"...you can help him out with his law firm. I'll make a call..."

"Dad!" He heard her that time and stopped. "I'll manage. Thank you anyway." An awkward but familiar silence grew.

"Do you need some money?"

"No, I'll be fine."

"I love you, honey." There was so much more he wanted to say to her. "Will you get a chance to come by before you leave?"

"I'm not sure. I've got a lot of loose ends to take care of." Alena's tone was noncommittal.

"Oh, sure...I understand." He didn't really. He knew he had just lost his daughter and didn't want the rift to get any wider. His heart ached. "God bless...and...well, you know how to get a hold of me...I love you, Alena."

"I love you, too. Goodbye, Dad."

21

7:30 a.m. The Atlantic Ocean waited for the luxury sailboats to gain passage from the 17th Street Causeway bridge-tender. Murdock and Frank were having breakfast at Pier 66's Pelican Restaurant which offered a view of the causeway and Intracoastal.

"I still can't comprehend the money that's here," remarked Frank gazing at the boats, each costing over a million dollars.

"Maybe we ought to start an RCP on the owners," he continued. RCP is a Returns Compliance Project which a local IRS office can initiate at any time to determine the level of tax law compliance in a given area or industry—be it sailboat owners, general/subcontractors, antique dealers, luxury car owners, etc.

"Thinking about the meeting?" asked Frank realizing his partner wasn't listening.

"Yeah."

"What are you worried about?"

"It's just that I don't know them. I'm gonna tell a perfect stranger everything that's happened. I don't know, it just doesn't sit well with me."

"You've got to trust *someone*, Bill. There's no one in the district you can turn to for help so there ain't much of a choice."

The two finished and looked out over the Intracoastal. The driftboats, loaded with eager fishermen, were just cranking their diesel engines.

"What if this guy has a different agenda?"

"We'll go to someone else until they listen. Your brother still works for the Herald doesn't he?" Murdock looked at him realizing the seriousness of that statement.

"Frank, you haven't been around long, but the IRS doesn't take too kindly to employees showing their dirty linens. This IG is bad enough, but a newspaper!"

"They're dirty and they know that you know they are. You've got to be first to blow the whistle."

"I am with this IG meeting." The two were silent. "Frank, they've got ways to tie you up in such a morass of red tape that it would take a life time to unravel. And the beauty of it is you'd never be able to find out who's behind it."

"It's almost nine. You want to talk to him?" asked Frank. Murdock looked out again and ran his hands through his hair.

"Well, I guess one more group after us really doesn't matter, does it? Let's go find the IG." Moments later they entered the busy lobby of the Marriott Hotel. "Look for a green handkerchief."

"Why'd you have to pick green?" The color was smeared everywhere—in wall paintings, the carpet and in everyone's clothing. Murdock grinned.

"My luck."

"Haven't seen you smile in a while," observed Frank. Murdock looked at his watch. Nine-ten a.m. Two minutes later a man with a green handkerchief approached the two from behind.

"William Murdock?" asked a tall, well-dressed man carrying a beige attaché case. His salt and pepper hair was thick and well over his collar. Murdock turned quickly. The signal was given.

"And you are?"

"Tim Sylar, Treasury IG. Nice to meet you." Sylar stretched his hand to Murdock. Murdock hesitated, but shook his hand.

"This is Frank Laccetti."

"No one mentioned him," declared Sylar as he looked over at Frank.

"He's with me. He knows everything...just ask him," joked Murdock. Sylar was the hesitant one now.

"He'll help fill in the blanks. Besides, I'm not gonna talk to you if he's not here."

"Is he with the IRS?" Murdock nodded. "All right. Let's go over there." The three walked over to the lounge area which was located some distance from the hustle and bustle of the lobby. They sat at a table up against the glass looking out at the myriad of palms surrounding Pier 66.

"It's been awhile since I've been here. Kind of miss it." Sylar opened his expensive attaché case and pulled out a writing pad along with a dictaphone.

"Why the tape?" asked Frank.

"I'd like to take some notes if that's okay." He looked over at Murdock who gave his approval. "And I'd like those notes to be accurate." Sylar sensed their distrust. "Listen, there's got to be some trust here or we're not gonna get far." Murdock was reticent. "I could've recorded our conversation without you ever knowing it," continued Sylar trying to gain their approval and, hopefully, their trust.

"Suppose you could've...okay," agreed Murdock. The red light on Sylar's recorder glowed.

"I understand that you have information implicating top level government executives of wrongdoing."

"Before we go any further, may we see some identification?" asked Frank. Sylar, without hesitation, pulled out his credential wrapped in black leather. The two studied the official looking badge issued from the Inspector General's Office, Department of the Treasury.

"So much has happened, it's difficult to begin." Murdock passed the ID back to Sylar.

"Just start at the beginning and take your time. I don't want you to skip anything."

Murdock pulled a small note pad from his pocket where he had outlined what had transpired.

"You mind if I make a copy?" asked Sylar.

"Go ahead." Sylar retrieved a small, silver device from his attaché case and started scanning the pages. Instantly, they were reproduced. "Sorry for the interruption. I'm ready."

"I was assisting another RO on..."

"RO?" interrupted Sylar.

"Revenue Officer."

"Okay."

"I helped another RO and found property owned by the taxpayer we were investigating. It had been fraudulently transferred to a Miami corporation called Sea Unlimited. When I tried to make the assessments and investigate the fraud aspects of the case, the file suddenly disappeared and no one can find it."

"What did you do then?"

"I talked to the manager, Richard Davenport, about my concerns. He told me not to spend anymore time on it."

"Was that unusual?"

"Yeah, it was. I also found a Porsche paid for by the taxpayer we were investigating. We had an active investigation where property was illegally transferred to beat the government. By the way, the property had plenty of equity in it to satisfy a good portion of the assessment I wanted to make. Anyway, we were going strong on this investigation when we were ordered to stop. A Fort Lauderdale detective assigned to assist the IRS was told to stop. The detective told me that they had developed enough evidence to convene a grand jury, but no one would do it."

"How did you know a detective was assisting the IRS?"

"I found his name in a newspaper article, so I contacted him."

"What information did you share with him?"

"Not much. He had the facts. He just wanted me to let him know how everything turned out because he knew something wasn't right."

"Have you kept him updated?"

"I haven't talked to him since." Murdock reviewed his file. "My manager..."

"Davenport?"

"Right. He gave me an assignment to the Florida Keys just to get me out of the way for awhile."

"Why do you say that?"

"Because right after my last conversation with him about the case I end up being detailed there. Not a coincidence."

"Was there work to be done there?"

"Yes, but the area is worked out of the South Miami office, not here." Sylar nodded and made a few notes.

"Earlier you mentioned Operation Liberty, tell me about that," requested Sylar.

"I didn't mention Operation Liberty to you." Murdock looked over at Frank who nodded in agreement that the subject hadn't been mentioned.

"Maybe I heard it from Rubenstein after you spoke to him. How does that fit in?" Murdock filled him in.

"What was the drug attorney's name?"

"Phillip Ward. We later learned that Ward..."

"And this is the motivation for all that has happened," interjected Frank.

"...Ward is the fiancé of Alena Muller who used to be his law partner and just happens to be the daughter of the last district director we had here." Sylar stopped writing and looked at Murdock.

"Are you certain?"

"Yes."

"So you believe Operation Liberty was stopped to protect Alena Muller."

"We keep coming up with the same answer," replied Murdock.

"Let's go back a little bit," Sylar said as he flipped back through his notes. "How did you learn about Operation Liberty?"

"I looked at CI's...that's short for criminal investigation...I looked at their files."

"Who authorized it?"

"I had a 'need-to-know' whatever information CI had relative to this case since I was involved in the civil aspects."

"Who actually authorized you to review the files?"

"No one. I knew procedures weren't being followed and that Davenport asked me to stop."

"What reason did he give you for stopping your investigation?"

"That CI had them under investigation, but I knew that wasn't happening."

"You learned later that CI had stopped the investigation, but early on you didn't know, right?" asked Sylar. Murdock didn't respond. "So why did you continue your investigation?"

"Because whenever CI has an investigation on someone being worked by us, they always send a memo through channels outlining the facts and requesting we stay any activity. No memo was sent."

"How do you know?"

"Julia didn't get one."

"And she would have been the one to receive it?"

"Right," replied Murdock. "I had someone check CI's files to see if a request had ever been made and it hadn't. As far as I was concerned, no criminal investigation had started."

"Who checked CI's files on this?" Sylar was poised, ready to jot the name down on his pad.

"I can't tell you."

"Is it that you can't remember who checked the files for you or you would rather not say?"

"I'd rather not say."

Murdock spent the next hour going over every detail with Frank's help. Sylar continued his questioning.

"Basically..." stated Sylar, "...you felt an obligation to go forward with your investigation and get to the bottom of this."

"I knew something wasn't right." Just then the recorder made a beeping sound. Sylar turned the tape over.

"You mentioned that Alena Muller was romantically involved with this drug attorney...Ward. How do you know they're involved?"

"I found out she was a one-time law partner with Ward and DEA told me the rest."

"DEA has been helping you?" Sylar appeared very disturbed.

"They're after one of the persons who attend the monthly drug meetings."

"How much information did you share with the DEA?"

"They have all of it. In turn, they gave me information."

"Earlier you stated...that..." Sylar looked back through his notes again. "...Ward routinely called the ex-director's house...Al Wilson...and calls were made to Ward from his house, right?"

Murdock nodded. "How did you learn that?"

"I summoned the telephone company for the numbers being called from and to the Key Largo house."

"Who authorized the summons?"

"I did. I had a 'need-to-know'."

"Your investigation," stated Sylar. "Is there anything else I should know?"

"The journal may implicate some influential businessmen. The group believes I have it and they'll do anything to get it back. I'm not sure if or how they're connected to Sea Unlimited.

"Who's involved in Sea Unlimited?"

"Ward incorporated it and a convicted money launderer, Warbington, is in on it. I didn't mention this to you earlier when I talked about him, but the government gave him a new ID. He's Thomas Farley now, involved in the same criminal activity, but this time he's protected. Anyway, Warbington's in on it and I don't know what role Al Wilson plays. I'm also not certain how Alena Muller fits in. She may only be there because Ward is. I do know people transferred property to the corporation...maybe as a down payment on the monthly drug disbursement...to get their slice of the action. I'm not sure."

"What happens now?" asked Frank.

"I really don't know what to make of this. You have people after you for something you allegedly never had and a possible case of misconduct by a government official. I think..." Frank interrupted him.

"A possible case of misconduct!" Frank leaned forward in his chair.

"As I was about to say, I think you need more evidence linking the ex-director to this. All we know right now is that an investigation is pending and, based on my experience working on government investigations, that's not unusual. We also know that a drug attorney is calling the ex-director's house..."

"Wilson!" interjected Murdock.

"...and someone from his house is calling the drug attorney!" Frank was beginning to boil.

"Doesn't it matter that the attorney has been identified as a target of an IRS investigation and that investigation was about to go before a federal grand jury when it was suddenly stopped?" asked Murdock.

"Not stopped, temporarily delayed," corrected Sylar.

"For no good reason!" asserted Frank.

"If CI were contacted about why they stopped I guarantee you they'd have some very plausible reasons." Murdock and Frank looked at each other. Sylar continued, "So an attorney has wealthy Hispanic clients and the IRS wants to take a closer look, doesn't mean Ward's guilty yet."

"But based on what we know, no investigation will ever take place," observed Murdock.

"You don't know that," replied Sylar. "I'll bet they'll say they've got some good reasons for the delay though." Sylar placed his pencil down on the pad. "You need more than this to hang 'em."

"What about the people after us?" asked Frank.

"What about them?" asked Sylar in a disinterested tone.

"Never mind." Frank looked away before continuing. Murdock knew he was ready to explode. "Listen, Ward's slimy. He represents drug dealers and this whole delay is to protect some ex-director's daughter. What are you going to do to help us?"

"Has any of his clients ever been indicted for trafficking or possession?" Frank didn't respond. He was livid. "You need more, okay!" Sylar raised his voice, clearly annoyed.

"Oh, I remember this scene from 'The Wizard of Oz'..." Frank began sarcastically. "...it's almost as good as the flying monkey scene." Frank turned to Murdock. Murdock just looked at his partner and raised his eyebrows. "You remember this one, Bill. Dorothy and the others finally make it to the Emerald City," continued Frank. Sylar sat there, amused. "Dorothy turns to Oz," added Frank as he looked over at Sylar emphasizing the word Oz. "...and all Oz does is tell her to bring him the broom from the wicked witch. Now everyone watching knew Oz was just stroking them." Sylar was the one agitated by this time.

"My office will review the information you gave me. If it looks like we can investigate, we will."

"Can you help us with the other guys who are after us?"

"No one can prove that government officials are behind this."

"Guess that's a 'no'," stated Frank.

"It's out of my jurisdiction." Sylar raised his voice. "Where can I reach you?"

"You can't," replied Murdock.

"Still don't trust me," replied Sylar.

"It's just that you seem more interested in whether or not we had authorization or followed procedures rather than the facts of this case. I'm still not sure what your role in this will be."

"As far as my role, I plan to sort through all of this and get back to you. Keep in touch. It was nice meeting both of you and thank you for your time."

The three rose and Murdock shook his hand. Frank refused. Sylar glared. He walked back through the lobby and disappeared into the sea of green.

"What now?" asked Frank. The two walked closer to the window and stretched. "You trust him?"

"Nope," replied Murdock.

"Let's see if Palmetto has any ideas."

"What are we gonna do about money?" asked Frank.

"We'll call Davenport and see if he'll put us on annual leave. He knows what's going on ain't right. Maybe he'll have a change of heart."

"If he's got one," quipped Frank.

The two proceeded to a pay phone not far from the bar and placed a call to their manager.

"Where are you?" asked Davenport in his usual condescending tone.

"Can't tell you, but you can help us," replied Murdock.

"I couldn't help you now even if I wanted to. What are you thinking?"

"Someone tried to kill us. How would you've reacted? People are still after us."

"Turn yourselves in and be done with this. You didn't listen to me and now you want me to help. Well, I can't do it!"

"When the dust settles some executives are gonna take a fall. Don't be one of them," warned Murdock.

"There you go again telling me what's gonna happen. I wish I could help you, but you're in too deep on this one. There is nothing I can do for you."

"Put us on annual leave. We need money." Davenport thought for a few seconds.

"I'll see what I can do."

"I always thought you were an ethical man so do the right thing now before it's too late. Tell the IG what you know."

"The Inspector General? You didn't talk to him, did you?"

"Couldn't trust anyone else."

"You're a fool, Murdock. How could you go outside on this? They're never going to forgive or forget."

"I'm not looking for forgiveness."

"Listen, I'll put you both on annual leave, but don't call me again. I can't get involved in it."

"You already are. Let someone know what happened. It's the only thing that's going to keep your retirement intact and keep you out of jail for obstructing an investigation." Davenport hung up. Murdock turned to Frank.

"What now?" asked Frank.

"We seem to be asking that a lot these days. Let's talk to Palmetto." Murdock placed a call to the Key West office in search of the insects.

"Cricket?" Murdock was surprised.

"Speaking."

"And lucid, too. Didn't expect you to be up so early."

"Been getting up at five a.m. every morning and running two miles."

"Really?" Murdock wondered if this was the same inebriated officer he had left behind.

"Yup. How are you guys?"

"Not well. A lot has happened."

"Want Palmetto?"

"Please." Cricket turned around in the small dark island office and hunted down the king insect.

"Bill, what's up?" asked Palmetto.

"Frank and I talked to the Treasury IG this morning. He said we need more evidence linking Wilson to this mess. Got any ideas?"

"Bill, that's nonsense."

"I know, but I don't think he's going to do anything."

"Suppose we need to show his actual involvement in either the drugs or getting the investigation stopped. Pardon the pun, but we'll 'bug' the jerk." Murdock grinned.

"No judge is gonna approve a wire," replied Murdock.

"Judge? Who said anything 'bout a judge?"

"We couldn't use what you taped."

"No, no, no! You don't understand, you're not going into a courtroom with it. We'll tape Ward, Muller and Papa so you can share it with the IG. It'll be enough to get him moving. We'll getcha something you can use, leave it to us."

"IRS won't appreciate you helping me," cautioned Murdock.

"Like I really care," replied Palmetto.

Murdock explained the details. He felt obligated to tell him since Palmetto was about to make a giant leap into a pile of dung and the dung would not be easy to shake off.

"We'll get whatcha need, don't worry. Those morons are gonna pay for this," replied Palmetto. "I'll call you at the boat."

"Be careful." Murdock explained what Palmetto would be doing.

"Hope they know what they're doing," thought Frank.

Murdock placed another call, "Marlene?"

"Are you okay, Bill?"

"We're fine. What can you tell me?"

"Inspection came by a couple of days ago asking questions. Carmichael assigned a couple of agents to find you and Wilson made a couple of rare appearances, too! You have to go for help."

"I did. This mess will be over soon. Anything else?"

"Yeah, be careful."

"Thanks, Marlene." Murdock walked over to Frank. "Carmichael has a couple of his dogs after us."

"Good, it'll take that bunch a month just to figure out we're not at work anymore." Murdock grinned.

"Let's head back to the boat."

Palmetto placed a call to his long-time Army buddy, OJ Gonzales. The two served in Military Intelligence for fifteen years.

OJ spent an extra five years with a private company funded by the CIA. His job was to eavesdrop on senators and congressmen who frequented certain Middle East countries. No one knew more about electronic surveillance than OJ. While Gonzales' Detective Agency concerned itself with more domestic matters like divorce cases and jealous spouses, OJ hadn't lost his touch for eavesdropping.

"Hello, Gonzales' Detective Agency," answered a secretary with a high pitched voice. The nasal tone was more than he could stand.

"Spider, please."

"I beg your pardon."

"OJ!"

"If you mean Mr. Gonzales, he's not available at this time."

"C'mon sweetie, it's noon time. He's in his office eating sardines and cheatin' at solitaire. Now go get him!"

"Now you just..."

"Go get him!"

"And whom shall I say is calling?"

"Palmetto."

"Figures. Wait one moment." A few seconds of silence passed. "He just came in."

"Jake, you ol' sonofagun! Where are ya?"

"Key West."

"How long has it been?"

"I'm ashamed to say...too long."

"You helping Uncle Sam down there or are they after you?" OJ said laughing.

"I'm working with them and I need your help." OJ knew Palmetto was up to something or something was about to catch up with him.

"Whatcha need?"

"Your web for awhile."

"Who's the fly?"

"A retired IRS director, his daughter and boyfriend drug attorney."

"Sounds like ol' times. I'll meet ya half way."

"Largo?"

"Tug Boat Annie's and you buy," responded OJ.

"You ain't changed a bit. See you in about two and a half hours."

"All right."

The leader of the insects called in annual leave and headed north on A1A out of Key West through the archipelagos to Tug Boat Annie's, a rustic diver/fisherman haven. On the way to the meeting place Palmetto reminisced about his earlier years working with OJ and a few of their episodes. Who they monitored and what they heard was top secret, never to be spoken about again. Both Palmetto and OJ's military files only reflected how long they were in the Service and that they were honorably discharged.

The two had lunch and got caught up on each other's lives. Palmetto received the sophisticated equipment and some instructions on it. Palmetto was familiar with electronics, but there had been radical technological improvements so he listened intently. After having a nice lunch with his old partner they left, not realizing someone across the marina had aimed a powerful 35mm telescopic lens at them and clicked a dozen photographs.

22

Nightfall came early for the three insects as they arrived at the south side of Phillip Ward's condominium. Murdock needed proof for the Treasury IG and Palmetto was determined to find it. He pinned a microphone to his collar so he could stay in constant communication with Beetle and Cricket. The tiny electronic "bugs" OJ Gonzales gave him would be placed in several rooms of the condo so that conversation could be recorded. Since he was the only one who could pick a lock and had knowledge of electronics, he'd have to place the surveillance equipment.

Beetle and Cricket formed a stirrup with their hands so that Palmetto could climb the wall which enclosed the complex.

"Okay, we're ready," whispered Beetle. Palmetto placed his shoe firmly in their hands and made the sign of the cross.

"As soon as I'm over let's check out the transmitter," observed Palmetto.

"All right, on three." Beetle looked over at Cricket.

"One..." they started a gentle up and down rocking motion.

"Two-o-o...two and a half..."

"C'mon!"

"Thre-e-e-e-e!" The two gave a mighty heave pushing Palmetto almost completely over the eight foot barrier. The only thing that saved him from breaking his neck on the other side was the fact that his beer belly caught the top bricks. Palmetto was positioned half on one side with his legs dangling on the other.

"What in the ...."

"Well, pull yourself onto the top," shouted Cricket in a muffled voice.

"I can't. This ol' belly won't let me." Palmetto reached with his left hand attempting to snag the wall. Moments later he grabbed it. Beetle and Cricket applauded.

"You sure you wanna go through with it?" asked Beetle.

"I knew this was gonna be the worst part. Just keep listening." Palmetto let his legs dangle on the other side and inched his way over the wall using his belly as an anchor.

"Just drop...ya gotta do it," asserted Beetle trying to encourage his cowardly leader to release the wall.

"Ah-h-h-h." Palmetto dropped to the ground jarring the equipment. "Can you hear me?" he inquired speaking into the mike.

"Sure we can," replied Cricket yelling over the wall.

"I mean through the earphones!"

"Oh, hold on." The two went back to the car and turned the system on. The green fluorescent equipment lights cast a soft eerie glow. "Go ahead."

"Testing...one, two, three. Can you hear me?"

"Loud and clear," replied Beetle.

"Okay, I'm going in." The two parked the '64 Ford Fairlane station wagon across the street in a vacant lot. The location offered a perfect view of Ward's condo and of the lobby entrance.

The first obstacle for Palmetto was the locked stairway door located on the side of the building. He had to go in this door since it was easier than trying to get past the security officer. Even if he accomplished that, he would need a key to operate the elevator. The lights of the lobby illuminated the area near him.

Palmetto unzipped the brown hard leather case and extracted a long, sleek instrument and began working on the lock. Each time someone entered the glass lobby area Palmetto hugged the wall and tried desperately to suck his belly in.

"Testing, testing...can you hear me?" asked Palmetto.

"Yup. Where are you?" responded Beetle.

"Still working on the stairway door. I'll let ya know when I'm in."

"Okay." Five minutes later Palmetto opened the door.

"I'm in the stairwell. Are the lights still out in the condo?"

"Yeah, they're out." Palmetto proceeded to the twelfth floor, stopping for a rest on the fourth, seventh, and tenth floors.

"I'm on the twelfth. Go ahead and give 'em a call." Cricket dialed Ward's number from the cellular phone.

"It's ringing," observed Cricket. Beetle relayed the message to Palmetto. No one answered.

"You're good to go," added Beetle.

Palmetto looked left, then right. For the moment, no one was around. He entered the long hallway and proceeded to Ward's condo. After sizing up the lock, he pulled out a couple of slender tools. Carefully and delicately he worked the tools inside the lock until he heard the unmistakable click of the tumbler falling into place. Palmetto slowly opened the door and entered the darkness. The brightness of the hallway made the room appear even darker than it was.

"I'm in."

"All right." Palmetto felt his way through the apartment. Lights from the city penetrated the curtains that stretched across the wall. Biscayne Bay and the Causeway filled the window.

"Can't find the phone."

"Try near the sofa." Just then he stepped firmly on a soft cushion that reacted very much like a tiger getting attacked.

"Get off my leg!" shouted Palmetto nearly bursting Beetle's eardrum. The calico cat hung on for dear life. "Off! You fur ball!" Palmetto swung his leg so fervently that he and the cat went flying.

"What's the matter? You okay?" There was silence. "You there?"

"Yeah, yeah...hold on." Palmetto struggled propping his body up on his side and took a deep breath. "I hate cats." Moments later he found the phone and carefully placed the transmitter into the receiver. He then proceeded to the dining room and placed a flat disc on top of the light fixture.

"Ahh!"

"What? Another cat?" inquired Beetle.

"I stepped in her bowl." Palmetto then groped about the condo in search of the master bedroom. The last device was placed in the kitchen underneath a small stand in the corner. "Got it!"

"Good, there's a couple going up. The girl had blonde hair...could be them."

"I'm finished. On my way out." Palmetto quickly left the apartment and headed for the stairwell.

"My hat!"

"What about it?"

"I left it in there," he whispered.

"Forget it."

"Where's the couple?"

"Still waiting for the elevator."

"I'm going back in." Palmetto started picking at the lock.

"They're going up."

"Okay."

"You done?" asked Beetle.

"No." He was picking frantically now.

"You in?"

"No!"

"You gotta go."

"A second more." Just then the lock clicked. "I'm in."

"Don't do it."

"Just a second." Palmetto went toward the sofa where he encountered the tiger. He went down on his knees and felt around until he found the hat.

"Get out!" Palmetto's eyes adjusted to the darkness and he zipped to the door, cracked it slightly just in time to hear the elevator stop. He locked the door and closed it.

"Why me?" pleaded Palmetto.

"Now what?"

"My hat's stuck in the door!" The elevator door opened. Palmetto glanced over his shoulder down the hallway as he tugged on the hat. He could hear laughter as people stepped out of the elevator. One more heave is all he could afford without being caught. His heart raced. Palmetto jerked as hard as he could, finally pulling the hat out so hard he almost completed a full somersault as he fell. He quickly regained his composure, slipped the crumpled hat on and proceeded down the hallway as if nothing had happened. The couple passed him just as he approached the stairwell. Once they passed he slipped into the stairwell.

"On my way down."

"Good, but it wasn't them."

Palmetto exited the complex through the front this time, tipping his hat to the doorman. The trauma sustained to his belly was quite enough for one night.

"All right, move over," barked Palmetto, anxious to sit down and rest. Beetle slowly scooted over from the seat. Cricket was half asleep in the back.

"Where's the headset?" Beetle looked around for a moment.

"Don't know." Palmetto's eyes caught a wire leading to Beetle's derriere.

"Wait a minute, you're sitting on the darn thing!" Beetle rolled his monstrous left cheek to the side.

"You see it?" asked Beetle.

"I got it." Just as Palmetto retrieved the wire a thunderous sound ripped from Beetle's massive cheeks.

"Come on, Beetle!" The two rolled the windows down simultaneously and as fast as they could, sucking in all of the fresh air their lungs could hold.

"You ought to see a doctor."

"I'm carrying some extra weight, but I'm healthy."

"I meant a shrink. Hey, Cricket...you awake back there?" Cricket was lying down in the rear of the wagon resting his head on his crossed arms and staring at the tape machine.

"Yup, I'm ready."

"Let's see if the thing works." Cricket raised a switch and the reels began turning. Palmetto and Cricket put their headsets on.

"Hear anything?" asked Beetle.

"Sh-h-h!" A minute passed in silence.

"Ya got anything?"

"Sh-h-h!" Palmetto was still upset over Beetle's gastrointestinal problems. Beetle tapped Palmetto on the shoulder and got his attention. He then lifted his cheek as a warning.

"Okay, okay, settle down." Palmetto passed the headset to

Beetle.

"Someone's opening the door," murmured Cricket. Palmetto looked through his binoculars. A light was turned on. Phillip had just walked in, the first time in a week.

"The thought just occurred to me that someone else may have an interest in this guy," remarked Beetle. Palmetto turned and looked away in thought.

"IRS, CI," interjected Cricket.

"The Colombians," responded Beetle.

"DEA or the FBI," added Palmetto.

"The ex-director. Anyone of them could be watching his condo right now," expressed Beetle.

"Or us," responded Palmetto. "Guess it's a little late!" Palmetto raised the binoculars.

"I've got something," whispered Cricket. Palmetto quickly placed the headset on.

Ward was organizing the crisp bundles of one hundred dollar bills into a soft leather bag. He was ready for an exchange with the Colombians—clients of the Cartel.

The knock at the door startled him. Ward carried the bag with him and looked through the peephole. It was Alena! He was surprised, but elated to see her.

"What's this?" asked Ward looking at her hand as she extended it to him.

"Your key." He reluctantly accepted it. His elation turned to dismay.

"Come in." Ward gave her a light kiss on her forehead.

"You're on your way out?" she asked. Ward nodded. "I'm here because I've got this terrible feeling that I'm never going to see you again and..." Alena began to cry. Ward held her. "...so, I had to try one more time to get you to stop."

"I've thought about what you said and I swear, this is it. Once tonight's meeting is through we're leaving. I promise."

"I don't want you to go to this one. We can leave right now." She placed her head against his chest and tightly held him. He kissed the top of her head and embraced her firmly in his arms.

"They're waiting for me. I have to go. This meeting is different.

I know everyone there," he replied reassuringly. "I love you and I'm sorry I've caused you so much pain." Neither one spoke.

"I'm going with you," asserted Alena. The large reels of tape in the rear of Palmetto's station wagon were recording every word. There was silence. Ward walked into the living room and turned down the lights. The insects could now see a soft glow emanating from the condo. The balcony doors were opened allowing the skyline of Miami to intrude as the 71 degree, salty night air filled the room. Ward sat closely and stroked her hair.

"You can't."

"Because it's too dangerous, isn't it?" queried Alena.

"No, it's not that. I've worked with this group for a while...I know them and they know me... It's just that they don't like outsiders showing up without plenty of notice."

"Call 'em up and tell them I'm coming." She was forceful.

"Doesn't work that way."

"Why?"

"Security reasons. They do background checks."

"They do background investigations?" asked Alena surprised.

"Look at it this way, the meetings are a lot safer because of it." Ward paused. "It'll be safe. I know these people."

"When will you be back?"

"It's almost ten now." Alena nodded. "I'll be back in time to have breakfast with you if you stay tonight. Alena shook her head. "Don't worry. Everything will be fine." There was silence between them. "I gotta go." Ward gave her a last hug with a brief peck on her forehead. Moments later he climbed into his 450SL Mercedes convertible. The midnight-blue car disappeared into the night.

"You want to follow him?" asked Beetle. Palmetto hesitated.

"Nah, we know he's a drug attorney and besides, we've got enough on him right now to share with the idiot from Washington. She's gonna make some phone calls."

The Mercedes reappeared in the soft glow of the MacArthur Causeway as he crossed Biscayne Bay. Twenty minutes later he turned into a string of white warehouses lining the waterfront. He was early. The deep ominous sounding horns of the ships and tugboats communicating made Ward feel uncomfortable. He parked down from the warehouse.

Ward's condo phone rang.

"Hello," answered Alena sniffling.

"What are you doing there?" asked her father. "Get out!"

"I'm not leaving."

"Listen to me, please!" There was a sense of urgency in his voice.

"No Dad, I can't."

"You have to leave. Some people are stopping by to visit him."

"Who?"

"Agents."

"You sent them...how could you?" There was anger in her voice.

"I didn't send them, but I can't stop them anymore. I've delayed this investigation as long as I can. It's out of my control."

"I never asked you for anything."

"You didn't have to. Everything I do is for you...to protect you."

"You mean to protect your reputation."

"Stop it! And get out of there!"

"When he gets back we'll be leaving." There was an uncomfortable silence. "Dad, what's the matter?" The silence lingered. "Dad?"

"He won't be coming back if he went to the warehouse," he replied in a soft-spoken tone.

"Why?"

"Agents will be there, too."

"How do you know?"

"I know."

"I've got to stop him," she shouted.

"No! Honey, you can't!" Her father was emphatic.

"I have to, Dad. You don't understand..."

"No! You don't understand!" Her father inadvertently revealed the agents' agenda. "Alena, they're not going to make any arrests tonight."

"What are you saying?" There was silence again. "Why won't any arrests be made?" More silence. "What's going to happen?" she yelled.

"Key members of the Cartel will be making a rare appearance

and they're going to get rid of them. There won't be any arrests."

"How could you be a part of this? I've got to warn him somehow." Without another word Alena dropped the receiver and ran out of the apartment.

"Alena! Alena! Please!" he shouted.

The insects looked at each other. Palmetto took his headset off.

"We've got enough to dig Bill out. Let's go," ordered Palmetto.

"We've got to help Alena," asserted Cricket.

"Alena?" replied Palmetto.

"We have to. She's walking right into it. They'll kill her, too," interrupted Beetle.

"We can't. Besides, it's probably too late anyway. He's gotta be there by now. We've done our part by helping Bill...and that, my friends, is all we can do." There was silence. "Stop looking at me like that. We can't start a crusade to save everyone." Palmetto looked back at Cricket, then over at Beetle. Their silence continued. "All right, all right." Palmetto turned the station wagon around when a late model Chevrolet blocked him.

"What the..." Palmetto shifted into reverse. Tires spun. A second vehicle blocked him from behind. A sickness filled his stomach as he anticipated the visitors' next action.

"Who do you think they are?" asked Beetle.

"I'm not sure, police maybe," replied Palmetto.

"They're not happy whoever they are," replied Beetle.

Four men in suits exited their car and approached the insects from each side.

"Let's do something!" yelled Cricket.

"No! I don't think that would be wise." The smallest of the four men walked over to Palmetto.

"We want your tape and any pictures you might have taken," expressed the man in a quiet, peaceful sounding tone.

"Then what?" The sickness in the pit of his belly intensified.

"Then you can leave on one condition...that you forget everything you've seen and heard."

"Can we give you copies of the tape?"

The man smiled and calmly denied Palmetto's request. His unusual politeness alarmed Palmetto. The kind of calmness, he thought, that comes from the sheer confidence of knowing that you are in total control...untouchable.

"All right." Palmetto turned to Cricket. "Give me the tape." Cricket began removing the reel.

"Who are they?" asked Beetle.

"Not sure and I don't think they'll say."

"Here," Palmetto handed the tape over. "This is all we have. We didn't take any pictures." The man accepted the reel.

"Who are you with?"

"Let's just say we have mutual interests. You may go. The four men quietly climbed back into their sedans and disappeared.

"What happens when they learn what we heard?" asked Beetle. Cricket looked over at Palmetto who always had the answer. Palmetto was silent. "We're witnesses to whatever the government is gonna do at the warehouse," continued Beetle. "They're not gonna let us go."

"Who can we tell?" asked Cricket.

"Here's the license plate number." Cricket gave Palmetto a piece of paper. Palmetto called the number in.

"No record...their law enforcement," reported Palmetto.

"But who?" asked Beetle. Palmetto shrugged his shoulders. He was unusually quiet. Moments went by in silence before Palmetto finally spoke.

"I'm beat. There is nothing we can do for Alena. Let's head back...we'll think about this tomorrow."

"All right Scarlet, we'll think about it tomorrow," replied Beetle extremely disappointed.

23

Ward continued to wait for the Colombians. There were strict rules governing these meetings. Never arrive before them, no new faces without the requisite background check and approval and always have the cash ready. Ward checked his watch again. Moments later several customized BMWs and Mercedes passed him, forming a line into the warehouse. The 18 karat, solid gold lettering on the vehicles sparkled even in the darkness.

Ward waited an additional ten minutes before going in. Their rules. This allowed the Colombians time to establish security. Ward started his car and pulled into the warehouse. The automatic door closed behind him. The inside was unusually dark and damp. A single fluorescent light hanging down toward the front of the door revealed three Colombians sitting down. Not his clients, he thought. Two were wearing sunglasses. The third was inhaling a cigar. His hair was black and pulled back into a ponytail. While Ward couldn't see the security the Colombians brought with them, he could feel their presence. Twenty feet before the circle of lights, Ward stopped, waiting for the dark shadows to search him. Ward knew the routine well.

"Come...come." The Colombian smoking the cigar signaled to Ward. During these meetings no one could make a move, not even a sneeze without specific permission. Ward entered the white light. The atmosphere was tense.

"Good evening," greeted Ward.

"Yes, it is. I think it will be a great evening."

"I'm a little curious," stated Ward.

"About what?"

"Why are you here?" The Colombians laughed. The Colombian signaled to another dark shadow. Seconds later a cardboard box was produced and placed at Ward's feet. He looked down into the box.

"Oh no...no!" declared Ward. He turned to the side and felt his entire body go limp.

"Help him," ordered the Colombian. The heads of his clients had been removed by a razor sharp saber. "They're a little pale, wouldn't you say?" They laughed again. "Thank you for joining us but, as you can see, they committed the first deadly sin. Now, bring me the money. Let's see whatchew got." Ward handed the leather bag to a silhouette who gave it to the Colombian. He gently opened the pouch, looked it over as he puffed on his cigar.

"Good. We'll take it cause you can't where you're going." They snickered.

"You know the rules, Mr. Ward." Ward was speechless. His stomach felt as though it was being ripped inside out. Dizziness set in as his consciousness began to slip away. Rosario and Miguel emerged from the darkness and stood beside him.

"Have a seat, Phillip," directed Rosario with a remorseful tone. Miguel signaled. Tonight's executioner, a large, stocky man, stepped into the light. His saber, more like a bolt of lightening along his side, reflected the blinding light.

"Why did you have to do business with clients of the Cartel?" Ward tried to speak, but nothing came out. Blood seeped from the cardboard box forming a puddle of dark, almost black, liquid. The executioner stood behind Ward. Psychologically, he was already dead. Ward went numb.

"You were the son I never had," remarked Rosario, looking down and shaking his head. He reached over and ran his hand through Ward's hair as he spoke. "I don't think I'll survive this either." The decision he had made was excruciatingly painful.

Rosario's eyes teared as he leaned over and kissed the top of Ward's head. "Goodbye, my son."

Just as Rosario gave the sign to the executioner a dump truck crashed through the garage door. Gunfire erupted as Uzi's and shotguns blasted through the darkness. The sound was incredible. The light from the blasts cast the dark forms against the warehouse walls. The nonstop riveting of bullets sent the sleeping seabirds on nearby islands to flight. World War III had begun.

Smoke filled the room and the smell of burning flesh was overwhelming. Several shirts were smoldering from the blasts and several caught fire. Bodies were everywhere. The deafening sound stopped and no one was left standing as the dump truck left as quickly as it arrived. Five minutes later a car pulled up to the warehouse.

"Phillip," cried a woman's voice. "Phillip!" Alena went from body to body. Some bodies were faceless. "Phillip!" She knew he had to be alive. Over her left shoulder she caught a glimpse of movement. Someone was crawling on their belly leaving a dark stain trailing behind them. She hesitated. Maybe Ward got away and he's not even here, she thought. Cautiously, Alena approached the man. She heard him whispering as she slowly knelt down beside him.

"Alena," whispered Ward.

"Oh, Ward...I'm here. Lord, please let him live," she appealed through her tears.

"Alena..." Ward reached up to touch her.

"It's okay, I'm right here," cried Alena as she sat down beside him running her fingers through his hair. "It's okay." She turned Ward over and let his head rest on her lap. Ward was slipping away and there was nothing she could do to help him. A blast from a shotgun had hit him in the stomach. He had lost too much blood.

"Hold on Phillip, please hold on. Only a little while more." As the sound of an ambulance grew stronger, Ward became weaker. He could barely speak.

"Alena," whispered Ward using all of his strength.

"Please don't say anymore."

"Sorry...," Ward coughed up blood.

"Please don't leave me. You can't leave. I'll be so alone without you. Please Phillip." Alena cried.

"Black bag...yours." Ward continued coughing. "Our child... tell..." Ward squeezed her hand. "...love...her...for..." Alena continued crying and placed her cheek next to his head. "...love you." Ward squeezed Alena's hand one last time before letting go. The only man she had ever loved with all of her being was gone. Alena kissed him and cried as she held him close.

Alena's father arrived minutes after the first fire truck pulled up to the warehouse.

"Stand clear," barked the fireman.

"My daughter's in there," he responded using a firm tone.

"We're bringing her out. Here she comes, now." A fireman accompanied her.

Alena, still in shock, went to her father and embraced him.

"He's dead," she whimpered in a soft cry.

"I'm sorry, honey." He continued holding her. "Let's go to my car. I'll find out where they'll take him and I can make the arrangements." She nodded. In a few days, he thought, he'd approach Alena on the possibility of leaving with her to Rhode Island.

24

Within twenty minutes of arriving at the Key's apartment, Cricket downed his second bottle of the finest cheap wine that he could afford. That's when he heard movement on the veranda. The sound, he thought, a chair makes while being pulled across a floor. He reached into the nightstand and retrieved a small caliber pistol. Perhaps the sound came from the next room. His head was light and his stomach uneasy as he stood beside the bed attempting to regain his balance the alcohol had seized. He approached the sliding glass door and he heard the sound again. It was distinct this time and definitely emanating from the balcony. His balcony! Cricket rubbed his eyes which blurred his vision even more. He stopped and then took a few small steps.

"Who's there?" His words barely came out as his voice cracked. He gently cleared his throat and opened his eyes extra wide a few times. The pistol was extended out in front of him and aimed straight toward the sound. Well, as straight as he could hold the gun considering the amount of wine he had consumed.

"Who's there?" Cricket sounded confident this time, but still no response from the uninvited guest or guests. His weak fingers barely cocked the hammer. Cricket hoped that the gun was loaded since it usually wasn't. He couldn't remember when he last saw bullets in the cylinder.

"I've got a gun and I'll use it if I have to. Step into the doorway, now!" Nothing. He took a few more steps, but there was no response. The only sound were gentle waves, softly breaking on the beach as they chased one another to shore. Suddenly, a blur of white appeared. She had returned!

Her black hair reflected the light as it gently blew across her face and shoulders. She was stunning!

"It's you!" Cricket lowered the gun to his side.

"Yes." There was always a certain soothing warmth about her voice.

"What do you want?"

"A warning."

" 'Bout what?" She sat on the edge of the bed and crossed her legs. She was barefoot. Cricket sat down across from her in a chair and stared at her gifted body. "A warning?"

"You and your friends are in danger. You must leave immediately."

"Danger from what?" There was silence. "What danger?"

"Your lives are in danger," she replied.

"When?" continued Cricket still trying to make sense out of this new information.

"Later this morning, but you must leave now." She was emphatic.

"Heck, I don't even know if you're real. I only see you when I've been drinking and ya know...it's after midnight and something tells me my friends are gonna have a tough time believing this one. Don't suppose you'd come with me to tell them?"

"I can't."

"Oh, I'm shocked." Cricket began swaying. "I'll tell you why you can't go with me...because you're an aggravating dream of mine."

"I'm not your imagination and the danger is real."

"What danger?"

"I don't know how it will come, just that it will be here later this morning."

"Palmetto and Beetle are gonna love this. Listen, you can't even tell me your name for crying out loud. Please...go away and leave me alone."

"I know this is difficult for you but you must believe me and leave now. My name is Belina."

"Great! One mystery is solved—she has a name! Well, Belina, what's really difficult is that you expect me to believe you. My friends think you're one of my better hallucinations. Why is it we only get together when I'm drunk, huh? I am sick of all of this. Why don't you..."

Belina interrupted this time. "You never got to know your father because he left when you were the age of five. The last time you were supposed to see him he said he'd pick you up and take you to a baseball game. You sat under the tree in your front yard and waited for him until dark. He never showed up and you never saw him again. Then..."

"Stop! Stop! Why are you doing this to me?" Cricket began crying. "...why are you doing this?" Cricket dropped his head down. He tightened his grip on the pistol. "What right do you have to come into my life and do this to me? I never waited under any tree for my father..."

"You waited there until nightfall when your mother came out and brought you inside."

"Stop it! Please...stop it!" Cricket's hands muffled his voice. His grip on the pistol was locked as he lifted his head up. "I know how to get rid of you." Cricket placed the gun firmly to his temple.

"That is no solution. Put the gun down. I only wanted to convince you that..."

"I'm getting rid of you!" he shouted.

"Please don't do it. You have..." Cricket pulled the trigger before the Lady in White could finish. The gun made a loud clicking sound.

"Guess I forgot to load the damn thing." He lowered the gun.

"How do you know about me?"

"I don't know how I know, only that I know. That is the truth, just as the warning is the truth."

"How am I gonna get them to believe me? Don't think this'll be easy."

"Tell them you received an anonymous phone call."

"You're certain we have to leave right now?"

"Yes, right now."

"All right, I'll give it a try."

"You must get out!" Cricket felt the volcanic activity deep within his stomach beginning to commence.

"Wait here...got a few more questions..." he covered his mouth and ran to the bathroom. His body rebelled once again from his digestion of poison. After what seemed like an eternity, Cricket got up from the porcelain stool, washed his face and walked out into the living room. She was gone. The chain on the door was still locked. Cricket surveyed the veranda, but the darkness consumed everything. He sat on the bed trying to figure out how he should deliver the news to his skeptical companions. He believed the Lady in White. She knew things no one else could have known unless they were there. If she knew about those painful times maybe she knew what was going to happen tonight. But how would he explain this to them so it sounded believable? There was no evidence she was even there. Cricket started doubting her existence again.

Cricket slipped his shoes on and followed the cement walkway to Palmetto's room. He hesitated and then knocked vigorously.

"Palmetto...Palmetto." The pounding continued for another thirty seconds and the door opened.

"What's going on?" mumbled Palmetto as he rubbed his belly. His white sleeveless T-shirt rode high on his stomach.

"We gotta leave, now!"

"Why, ya see some more ghosts. Go back to bed." Palmetto turned.

"Got an anonymous phone call saying that we'd be visited tonight by some very unhappy people." Palmetto's eyes popped open.

"The men at the condo?" asked Palmetto. Cricket nodded. "Get Beetle up. I'll be out in a minute. Pack all of your stuff cause we ain't coming back to this place."

Within ten minutes everyone had thrown their bags into the station wagon.

"Where we going?" asked Beetle. They were driving north.

"Marathon?" suggested Cricket.

"Nah, too far for me right now. We'll stop at Big Pine Key."

"Cricket, you think it's the cops who took our tape?" asked Beetle. Cricket shrugged his shoulders.

"Maybe," replied Palmetto. "We're witnesses to whatever happened and they can't have us running around."

"If they wanted us dead, they would've done it then," asserted Beetle.

"Not if they wanted privacy. Too many people around for 'em," replied Palmetto.

"The anonymous caller—was it male or female?" There was no answer.

"Cricket," said Beetle in a firm voice.

"Can't believe it...is he asleep?" asked Palmetto.

"Passed out."

"Cricket, wake up." Cricket raised his head slightly, his eyes still puffy and closed. Beetle patted his face to wake him.

"Come on Cricket, you can do it. Got a few questions for ya."

"Wha...?" responded Cricket in unintelligible words.

"The anonymous call you got," asked Palmetto.

"Yeah."

"Male or female?" inquired Beetle.

"Does it make a difference?"

"Ah-h," replied Beetle knowing it had to have been a visit from the mysterious Lady in White. Palmetto looked back at Beetle and then Cricket.

"It better not be the Lady in White telling us to pack up and go," responded Palmetto. Beetle placed his hand on Cricket's forehead and raised his face upward.

"Was it the Lady in White?" asked Beetle.

"You're going too fast, slow down," mumbled Cricket. Palmetto slowed down and pulled over. He knew what was coming.

"He was sober when we left him," remarked Palmetto.

"Must've had a stash," replied Beetle.

"I don't feel so well," Cricket hung his head out the rear window of the wagon and blew the remainder of the cheap wine and beef stroganoff out the window.

"Throw him a towel. Guess I was too tired to detect he'd been tanked up again. He got us! He got us again! Beetle, I'm really getting tired of this." Palmetto turned the car around.

"Can't go back," mumbled Cricket.

"Watch me," replied Palmetto. "Anonymous phone call, sure! She probably flew into your room and told you to leave."

"No, Cricket wouldn't have done that. He'd tell us if it had been her, wouldn't cha buddy?" Cricket didn't respond. Beetle looked over at him. "Wouldn't cha, Cricket?" Cricket, eyes crossed, looked at Beetle without saying a word. "Ahh, Cricket, why?" asked Beetle knowing they let their inebriated partner talk them into moving in the middle of the night.

"She was in my room."

"Yeah, yeah, we know," replied Palmetto.

"Was this before or after the wine?"

"No, no. She's real...she's got a name."

"Oh really, let's hear it. We have a right to know who got us out of bed in the middle of the night." The words crescendos.

"Her name is Belina."

"Belina?" The two laughed. "Belina?"

"What's her last name?"

"Just Belina."

"Kinda like Cher, uh?" The two laughed again.

"God, help us get over this one."

There was silence for the next fifteen minutes. Palmetto talked under his breath mentioning the name Belina out loud a few times.

"What's the glow up ahead?" asked Beetle.

In the distance an orange light illuminated the dark Key West sky.

"A fire?" responded Palmetto, uncertain. As they got closer they could tell that it was a fire. A massive one. Flashing blue and red lights blended with the flames. An officer in the middle of the road flashed them down.

"The roads blocked for a while this mess is cleaned up. You'll have to turn around," stated the officer.

"What happened?"

"These efficiency apartments apparently blew up."

"How?"

"Maybe a gas leak, not sure yet. With all of this rubble to go through, it'll take a while." Palmetto turned the car around and pulled over. It was their apartments! They looked at each other without a word, stunned. Palmetto turned to Cricket.

"I don't know what to say..."

"So don't say anything," replied Cricket.

"What now?" asked Beetle.

"They'll think we're dead," surmised Palmetto.

"They'd have to think we went up in the blast, wouldn't they?" asked Beetle.

"I hope," responded Palmetto. "Let's go to my houseboat."

"We'll sleep in Miami tonight."

"Fine with me."

"Me, too."

By five a.m. they were at the hotel, wide awake thinking about the next encounter.

25

Morning had finally arrived and found Joel Meyers rubbing his shiny head as he gazed out over the ocean from his penthouse office. The sunrise was long overdue. The officers and shareholders of Sea Unlimited filed into the commodious room and claimed their seats at the rectangular mahogany table. Five of the most influential and wealthiest men in South Florida, together, at one meeting. The men sensed a certain uneasiness with Meyers.

"Joel, I have a full docket today, what's on your mind?" asked Judge Sherman. Meyers, still gazing out, lifted his index finger pointing towards the cloud-covered sun.

"You concerned it's not coming up today?" The men laughed. The sun began to peer back at Meyers and within seconds the blazing orange sphere covered the area. Only after the sun fully exposed itself did he speak.

"I apologize to each of you for this unexpected meeting. I know you're busy, but something terrible has happened which warrants discussion." Meyers was dressed in a three-piece, navy-blue pinstriped suit.

"Sea Unlimited's future as well as ours is in jeopardy." The men settled down and listened. He continued, "Our contact to the south has been..." Meyers searched for the right word, "...eliminated along with our legal representation. Gentlemen, I don't have to remind you that eighty percent of our revenue this past fiscal year was generated from our southern interests." No names were ever used at these meetings and there was never a reference to drugs. The "south" was their code for the company's South American connection who was Rosario. "Furthermore, some of my financial holdings were subjected to painfully close scrutiny once again. If it wasn't for the Judge, I might be incarcerated today."

The Judge smiled. He had saved Meyers from a conviction by ruling evidence as inadmissible or citing the Feds with entrapment. He also ordered all proceedings sealed so the public only heard about Meyers what the Judge wanted released.

"In my opinion, time has come to dissolve Sea Unlimited. Let's distribute and sell the assets."

"The company has been investigated before, Joel, this isn't anything new for us."

"Times are changing..." continued Meyers. "Company members were killed and there'll be a full scale investigation we don't have any control over. We must sell!"

"We're so far removed from this company it looks as though the corporation runs itself. They'd have an easier time convicting our mothers." The group laughed.

"Joel, aren't you overreacting a bit? The money is thoroughly cleaned before it goes into any account here or in Switzerland."

"We've had nothing to do with those terminations," offered another shareholder.

"I know that. We've taken great care and effort to filter us from anything, but let me assure you, my gut feeling is that our time has come."

"This is easy for you to say, you've made your money."

"And you've made yours! Your millionaires...all of you...many times over aren't you? Well, aren't you?"

"Joel, let's explore our options. I hate to see a good thing end over a gut feeling." The men in the room nodded.

"We can recruit another associate to the south."

"...and we'll deal with our encounters with the government or whomever as they arise," remarked another member. "We own a piece of just about anyone who is anything. Let's not forget who *we* are."

"People close to the corporation have been killed while conducting illicit activities..." Meyers stood and leaned over the table tapping his finger as he spoke. "...there will be an intensive investigation. Sooner or later the facts will point to us and it'll be too late. We'll all go down. Let's move to dissolve and go our separate ways."

"Don't you mean Sea Unlimited?" Meyers was in a trance. "Joel, don't you mean the facts will implicate Sea Unlimited?"

"And who cares, we're not affiliated with the corporation on paper."

"That's right," offered Douglas Warbington. "Ward and I were the only ones close to the company. Ward's dead and I'm a protected witness. Besides, the Feds want what I know, they'll stay clear of us."

"So what are we missing, Joel?"

"Is there something you're not telling us?" Meyers hesitated and sat down. They knew he had a near psychotic temper when obstacles appeared and they were the roadblocks this time.

"They've got our appointment book. Names, locations, times and dates. It all points to us once they figure out what it means."

"How did they get it?" shouted one of the members.

"Lower your voice," barked Meyers. "Ward had it at the last meeting in Largo. An IRS agent confiscated the Porsche and, ostensibly, the book was in the car."

"Have we visited the agent yet?"

"We're trying...he's good. Here's what we know about him." Meyers disbursed Murdock's dossier.

"Impressive!"

"He'll bring us all down," declared the Judge.

"He's disappeared with the book and it'll take some time," said Warbington.

"He's *somewhere* and we oughta be able to locate him!" Interjected the Judge. "I have people who can find 'em."

"We should be able to find him, but he's no ordinary fella."

"I don't like the tone of this meeting," remarked a shareholder. "We've never been involved in this kind of stuff. We've kept our hands clean and I don't want to soil them now."

"Do you want to go to prison for the rest of your life?" asked the Judge. Silence fell upon the meeting. The men looked down at the table.

"All right, I've said my piece. Are there any other views we should consider?" asked Meyers.

"I realize I'm not a voting member," stated Warbington. "It's time to close shop. The IRS can't even find 'em and I doubt you can."

"Watch me," replied the Judge as he pointed his finger at him. "I'll have him and that book within forty-eight hours."

"Then, I'm exercising my option to sell. It's been my pleasure working with each of you." Meyers rose. "This meeting is adjourned." Meyers walked over to the window, lit up a cigar and gazed out. Warbington followed.

"Fools," remarked Meyers.

"What are your plans?" asked Warbington.

"South America. Got a magnificent place overlooking Rio. Life's gonna be sweet down there. No investigators. I'm gonna be a king there. Let me tell you, these Feds looking into my affairs..." Meyers shook his head. "...They're ungrateful. I've given millions to charity, built hospitals, libraries, affordable housing." Violet-colored veins throbbed in his left temple as he spoke.

"The appointment book...isn't it encrypted?" asked Warbington.

"Yes, but given time, it'll be broken. When it is, I'll be long gone while the others are trying to defend themselves before a grand jury. I tried to warn them...fools!"

26

The phone on Palmetto's houseboat rang. Murdock let the recorder screen the call. As soon as he recognized Palmetto's voice he answered.

"What's going on?" He hoped they had some good news for him.

"Got some people after us. We're on our way. We'll be there in about an hour." The three cautiously left the hotel and proceeded to Fort Lauderdale.

"They have anything?" inquired Frank hopping around on his crutch fixing grilled peanut butter and jelly sandwiches.

"I don't know. He said they've got someone after them."

"Maybe it's all the free time we have, but this is the first time I've felt like something could really happen to us."

"I want something to happen. I'm tired of this. Sylar has got to get going on this. It's the only chance we've got," said Murdock.

"He will," encouraged Frank. "It'll happen."

"Without Sylar's investigation, we're going to jail."

"If we live that long," replied Frank flipping his sandwiches.

The insects finally swarmed into the houseboat. They parked their wagon across the river and several boats down. The Third Street Bridge would be crossed on foot as they took a circuitous route to the boat. They boarded without a word. Murdock heard someone on the deck. He pulled his pistol and approached the window. Frank grabbed his revolver, squatted the best he could on one leg and cocked his gun.

"It's Palmetto," announced Murdock. He opened the door and let them in. Guns were at their sides.

"Nice greeting." They shook hands and laid their few pieces of luggage to the side.

"Something to drink?"

"Coffee smells good," replied Cricket still breathing fumes from last night's brew.

"I'll take a beer," replied Beetle. Cricket sat in a corner with his head down.

"What's the matter with him? Has he been a bad boy again?" asked Frank.

"Nah."

"Hung over?"

"The Lady in White visited again." Frank shook his head. "He's pretty shook up over it."

"Her name's Belina," said Cricket with his head still down.

"Oh, she's got a name now," replied Frank.

"You actually met the Lady in White?" asked Murdock.

"Belina," shouted Cricket.

"No, but I'm not doubting her existence anymore," explained Palmetto.

"What happened?"

"To make a long story short, she visited again and warned him to get out of the apartment. Keep in mind, this was about one in the morning. He talked us into leaving and within half an hour, our motel blew up."

"Sounds like our trip to St. Thomas. Any idea why?" inquired Murdock as he poured the freshly brewed coffee.

"We taped Ward and Wilson's conversation with Alena. Ward was going to a warehouse to make his last deal with the Cartel. After he left her father called and said the police would be there," explained Palmetto.

"Alena went crazy because the ol' man told her no one would be taken alive," explained Beetle.

"Just as we decided to try and help her, two car loads of cops, maybe Feds, stopped us and took the tape we made."

"Why do you think they were cops?"

"Their plates came up negative."

"We figured they didn't want any witnesses to what took place at the warehouse," declared Palmetto.

"We're hoping they think we went up in the explosion."

Without another word Murdock picked up a fishing pole and began casting a lure off the bow.

"Is he worried about dinner?" asked Beetle.

"He's thinking this mess through. It relaxes him," replied Frank. The others looked on. "He'll be fine, he just needs a little time alone."

"Alone sounds mighty nice. I've been with these guys what seems like forever." Palmetto turned to his larvae. "When am I gonna get a chance to be alone, huh?" Frank smiled.

Half an hour passed before Murdock returned.

"I'm tired of waiting for something to happen. I feel like a prisoner."

"What do you have in mind?" asked Frank.

"I'm gonna see Davenport."

"You're kiddin?" The others looked at Murdock. His expression answered the question. "I'm going with ya." Frank reached for his crutch.

"No, I gotta go alone."

"Safety in numbers," mused Palmetto as he downed Frank's peanut butter and jelly sandwich.

"Not this time guys. I'm gonna have a little talk with him."

"Think it's really gonna accomplish anything?" asked Frank.

"I'm not sure. I'm telling him what I've got and maybe he'll help us. I don't know, I'm just tired of this." Murdock stood up and placed his 9mm in his jeans and put a light windbreaker on.

"Be careful."

He decided to walk to the office. It was a beautiful day despite what was going on and he thought the three block hike to the federal building would do him some good. He wasn't sure if anyone would be there waiting for him and he really didn't care. He wanted it to come to an end.

When he arrived at the federal building the taxpayer service area was packed with people. It was more like the New York Stock Exchange. As he walked by, a couple of people grabbed his arm wanting questions answered. Murdock pulled his arm back and without a word kept walking toward Davenport's office.

The office area was quiet with very few people around. As he walked through the last work area before reaching Davenport's office, Ernie called to him.

"Bill!" Murdock didn't hear him. He was too concerned with Davenport and company. "Bill!" uttered Ernie a little louder. Murdock turned. "I've got something for you. Been trying to find out where you've been. You okay?" Murdock shrugged his shoulders. "Sit down. No one will know you're here." Murdock sat with Ernie behind a large bright blue partition separating his desk from another officer's desk.

"What've you heard?"

"You're going to be removed. Did you ever think it would get this out of hand?"

"No, and it ain't over yet."

"I've been working on this." Ernie pulled out the black journal he found in the Porsche.

"I didn't know you had it. People are willing to kill for this." Murdock opened the journal and thumbed through a few pages. "What's it mean?"

"It took a while, but I understand the code." Murdock leaned forward. "It names some pretty big business people including Judge Sherman and Joel Meyers. Along with 'em is Rosario and Phillip Ward."

"Is Wilson listed?"

"No."

"What else?"

"Swiss, Panamanian and the Lesser Antilles Island bank account numbers are here." Murdock detected the excitement in Ernie's voice. "The book lists the volume of disbursements made, who received the coke and how much it costs."

"Does it show how much they have in these accounts?"

"It sure does."

"It's enough to bring them all down," observed Murdock.

"Wonder how many of 'em reported the income last year?"

"Great job, Ernie!"

"Bill, there's more." Murdock looked at him. "The very back pages of the book are torn but...look right here." Ernie pointed to a sequence of numbers. "...and this is what took so long to figure out. This part of the code appears to be coordinates for something on the ocean."

"What makes you think that?"

"Well, I'm not absolutely certain because some of the digits are missing, but it looks like triangulation."

"What's that?"

"A location is pinpointed using three coordinates. If these two are landmarks then the third point must be the ocean."

"Rendezvous points?"

"Sure looks like it. The book has times, dates and the only thing missing is location."

"Could you give me your best guess at the locations?"

"Without the other numbers, it's a shot in the dark. I'm not sure why some of the numbers were torn out."

"Is there a page behind the torn pages?"

"Yeah, here." Ernie passed the book to him. Murdock looked for a pencil and sharpened it. He lightly shaded the following pages. Very faintly a symbol appeared.

"Mean anything?"

"Hold on." Ernie checked the guide he developed. "You're a genius." Murdock finished shading while Ernie continued interpreting the symbols and digits. Several minutes later Ernie completed his calculations. "All you need is a map of the ocean and you'll have the drop-off sites."

"I've got the ocean charts we found at Farmer's business." Murdock thought a moment.

"What is it?"

"Remember Willie, with the pit bulls?" Ernie nodded.

"He had ocean charts, too." Murdock paused. "He also did some plumbing work for Farmer. He had a piece of this. I've got some homework to do."

"This is unbelievable!"

Murdock walked over to the glass enclosure. Davenport was stretched back in his chair. When his eyes caught Murdock he quickly sat upright, startled.

"Morning, Richard."

"Well, well, well the fugitive has returned."

"I spoke to the Treasury IG. They're investigating this mess."

"Oh really. Funny you should mention it—I received this draft report from them this morning. Looks like they're recommending your dismissal...immediately."

"You're lying!"

"I knew it would come to this. You gotta do everything your way...won't listen to anyone." Davenport shook his head.

"I'll get a copy of the report, if there is one, through Freedom of Information." The Freedom of Information Act provides an avenue for anyone to secure any information collected on them by the U.S. Government.

"No need to, I've got one for you, too." Without another word Davenport flicked the nine page document to Murdock.

"You've caused me a lot of embarrassment. Hope you're satisfied." Murdock started reading the report. "Did you really think someone would help you against the company?"

Murdock slowly shook his head several times while reading the report. Several sections of the report had been sanitized, but there was enough of the report there to clearly indicate Sylar had investigated Murdock's actions rather than the people he had reported. According to Sylar's report, Murdock violated privacy act laws and security since he did not have the clearance to research secret files of the Criminal Investigation Division. The entire investigation by Sylar focused on Murdock's "illegal activities" and not on the facts that had been presented. Davenport remained silent as Murdock read.

"This is unbelievable," commented Murdock.

"No, it's not," responded Davenport. "You went into secured files of taxpayers under criminal investigation and blatantly disobeyed my directives. What's unbelievable is that you thought it would turn out differently."

"I did the ethical thing. Something you didn't consider."

Davenport uttered profanity. Murdock was a little surprised since Davenport never used it. "An investigation was temporarily delayed..." Murdock cut Davenport off.

"Temporarily delayed? How about permanently closed or massive cover up to protect a money laundering scheme and drug ring for starters."

"It was temporarily delayed to keep an innocent person from getting implicated in a felony."

"Do you really believe Wilson would have let the investigation continue against Ward, his own daughter's fiancé? People were being allowed to do anything they wanted just because an ex-director's daughter used poor judgment. Do you think Joe Taxpayer's daughter would have been protected like that? No, I did the right thing!"

"Well, it sure had a price...your job...your career and your family's welfare," replied Davenport.

"I took an oath when I was hired. The same oath you took, I believe. Whatever happened to you?" asked Murdock. "You've come out clean on this..."

"No, I didn't. They gave me discontinued service...I'm out." Murdock looked up from the report. "I've always been a company man..." continued Davenport. "...not because I didn't have the guts to stand up, but because I liked my job. If I didn't, I would've left a long time ago. Times have changed. People like you come along and try to change the whole friggin place regardless of who gets hurt. Now does that make sense?" Davenport snickered. "Yeah, times have changed...guess I'm glad I'm out. It's not the same anymore."

"I'd do it again," added Murdock.

"I'll bet you would," replied Davenport sarcastically.

"Something has got to change now," asserted Murdock. Davenport laughed.

"The only thing that's gonna change, young man, will be the people sitting at our desks." Davenport laughed again. "...read the report and tell me if you still feel like a hero."

"When's your last day?"

"The end of the month."

"What are you gonna do?" asked Murdock.

"None of your damn business." Davenport stopped rocking in his chair and leaned forward over his desk. "Give me your badge." Murdock reached into his pocket and flung his credentials across the desk. "Now you may leave...Mr. Hero."

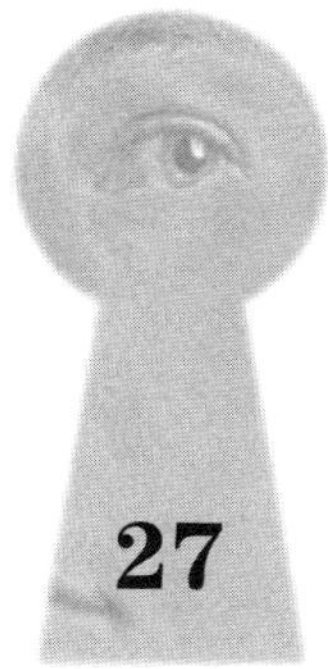

27

Murdock was numb because of his firing, but devastated over the report. The only hope he had was the Treasury IG who had used his own words to recommend his termination. He tried to think what his next move should be. Was it over? If it was, people were still after him. If it wasn't over, who could help him. Murdock walked slowly out of the office. He looked over at Ernie and gave a thumbs up signal. Ernie smiled back.

He kept replaying everything in his mind as he slowly walked back to the boat. How could Sylar turn things around? Why? What purpose could there be for doing this? Question after question plagued him. As he crossed the Third Avenue Bridge, Murdock was oblivious to the men in a white van who had been watching him through binoculars. The van pulled over to the north side of the New River and continued watching him all the way to the houseboat.

Everyone was inside. The group was playing poker when, after seeing Murdock's expression, they stopped playing and the room became unusually quiet.

"So?" asked Frank.

"Not good," replied Murdock. Palmetto pushed his golfer's hat up and off his forehead. Murdock walked over and sat down on the sofa, propping his feet up. "I got fired." The look of disbelief was everywhere. “Sylar recommended my dismissal and the IRS fired me. Can you believe it?”

“Why?”

“I don’t know.”

“How could he with what we gave him?”

“The idiot turned everything I said around. He didn’t investigate the others at all. He said I hindered an active criminal investigation and broke security and disclosure laws.”

“They weren’t doing anything...they tried to quash the investigation,” asserted Frank.

“Here, read it for yourselves.” Murdock tossed the report onto the coffee table to Frank. After reading the document, he passed the papers to Palmetto.

“He was our last chance. Think your brother could generate some interest?”

“Maybe.”

“What’s he do?” asked Beetle.

“He works for the Herald.” Beetle raised his brow.

“Ya know what’s really difficult? See this book?” Murdock pulled out the black journal from his back pocket. “It connects some of the most prominent businessmen in Fort Lauderdale and a federal judge with drug smuggling, money laundering, unreported income and I’m certain a whole slew of other things if someone would investigate...and there is absolutely no one I can trust to give it to.” There was silence in the boat. “I think we’ve even got the drop off points!” Murdock paced.

“The book is worth something to ’em,” recognized Palmetto. “Maybe we can negotiate.” Murdock just looked at him.

“Why negotiate when you’ve got everyone in your pocket?”

The men across the river aimed an amplifier at the houseboat. Every word was coming in loud and clear and being recorded. A man in the rear of the van was assembling an explosive capable of leveling a small building...or a houseboat.

“You’ve got the drop off points and times?” asked Frank.

“I think so. Ernie broke the code. When Palmetto finds his charts we’ll map the coordinates and see if they make any sense.”

“Then what?” asked Frank.

"I don't know."

"What about Rico?" asked Palmetto.

"Yeah, what happened to him?" asked Beetle.

"He finished his business with Nieto...I haven't heard from him and I don't think I will," answered Murdock.

"It's time you talked to your brother at the Herald. They oughta eat this up," asserted Palmetto. No one commented. "I've been in some sticky situations, Bill, but not like this. Call him."

"Nothing will ever top Nam," responded Murdock.

"You're right and we beat that, didn't we?" replied Palmetto.

"How long can we go on like this?" asked Frank. No one answered.

"What's with Cricket?" asked Murdock. He had been sitting on the deck Indian style with his legs crossed for twenty minutes without moving.

"He's meditating. The spirits are strong with him lately," replied Beetle.

"Spirits? As in one-fifty-one proof," laughed Frank. Several minutes passed in silence. "I've been thinking...when this is over I'm going back to New York." The announcement surprised Murdock.

"Where'd that come from?"

"I've been thinking about it for a while. I miss her."

"What about the furniture business?" asked Murdock.

"Maybe I'll be good at it." Palmetto and Beetle sat quietly listening to them moving their heads back and forth as if they were watching a tennis match.

"I'm sorry, but I can't see you being happy selling furniture," said Murdock. Frank looked over the downtown skyline unsure of his decision. "Ah, you'll probably make a fortune at it." A few minutes passed in silence again. "Does she know?"

"She will."

"I'm happy for you," assured Murdock.

"She went through a lot when I got shot and lost my leg. She didn't think I was gonna make it. She just got stressed out from worrying about me. So...I suppose it's time to go home." Murdock gave a reassuring nod.

Cricket continued his meditation.

"Is he okay?" asked Frank a little agitated. Beetle nodded.

"When he feels the need, he does it."

"What's the matter?" asked Murdock.

"I'm not sure. I think Cricket's making me a little edgy," replied Frank.

Beautiful sailboats and yachts traveled east down the winding New River to the Intracoastal.

"Palmetto, you gonna find those maps?" asked Murdock. He was anxious to plot the coordinates.

"I've got 'em." Palmetto left the room and returned within a minute.

Palmetto cleared the dinette of glasses and newspapers. He then unrolled several blue and white charts. The tip of South Florida was revealed. Straight, dark blue lines crossed the map while irregular circles filled in the gaps. Various numbers not in any particular sequence were scattered about the chart. Murdock retrieved the journal while Palmetto gathered his mapping tools, a special ruler and compass, to assist him placing the coordinates and determining the nautical distances.

"You ready?" asked Murdock.

"Bring 'em out." Murdock passed the coordinates. Palmetto began his calibrations. Everyone except Cricket was gathered around the table in silence. Palmetto carefully dotted the chart in pencil and then rechecked the numbers. Minutes passed in silence.

"Gentlemen..." He turned to the group. "...the rendezvous points." Murdock leaned forward and studied them first.

"What do the shaded areas represent?" asked Frank.

"These long areas here are deep trenches." Palmetto pointed to them. "The circles are caves."

"Each coordinate just missed a cave," observed Murdock. The group studied the sites in silence. "You're sure of the locations?" asked Murdock. Palmetto nodded.

"The coordinates may be off a little, but not by much."

"Then it's possible the coordinates are right on the caves?"

"Right."

"Why do you think they used these sites?" asked Palmetto.

"What do they have in common?"

"They're all caves," responded Beetle.

"The largest caves," injected Frank.

"They're all in international waters, too," interjected Murdock.

"Why international waters?" asked Beetle.

"No one patrols it," replied Palmetto.

"I thought these were drop off coordinates for the ocean surface," remarked Beetle. "You think they're storing the coke in the caves?"

"I don't think it's a coincidence that the coordinates happen to be the largest caves in international waters. There's caves a lot closer to the coast than these." Murdock touched the areas.

"What you're saying fits, Bill, but why caves?" asked Palmetto. "Seems like it'd be a hassle trying to get to them."

"It's safer. Think about it," said Frank. "No one patrols the area and there's no record to trace back to someone if it's found."

"So the coke is dropped off at these coordinates and divers secure the stuff in the caves." Murdock began pacing as he spoke.

"Then during the month buyers are found and the exact quantity is removed," continued Frank.

"They meet toward the end of each month at the Largo house to collect the money and disperse the coke," continued Murdock.

"And if they don't have the cash, like Farmer, they transfer their house or whatever other assets they have to Sea Unlimited for their fair share of the coke," explained Palmetto.

"The cash was flown by Ramon Martinez to one of the offshore banks. The money was then wired as a deposit back to Sea Unlimited's bank account as a business transaction," surmised Murdock.

"The clean money was then disbursed and taxed as income on their 1040s," declared Frank.

"And there you have money laundering one-oh-one," stated Murdock. "And I stepped in it when I seized that car. Who would've guessed it had the drugs and journal in it."

"Think there's still coke in the caves?"

"Probably," replied Murdock.

"Okay, we've figured it out...now what?" asked Beetle.

"There's that question again," sneered Frank. There was silence.

"How 'bout this one...what's for dinner? I'm starved!" interrupted Beetle.

"I've been saving these for a special occasion. Guess this is as special as any," exclaimed Palmetto. He reached deep into his freezer and retrieved a half dozen of the largest spiny lobsters any of them had ever seen.

"Where d'ya get 'em?" asked Beetle. His mouth was watering. Anything after Frank's fried peanut butter and jelly sandwiches would've appealed to him.

"Under Anglin Fishing Pier."

"I didn't know you could dive there?"

"You can, just don't get caught."

Frank and Beetle sat down with Cricket while Palmetto and Murdock prepared dinner.

"You okay?" Beetle had never seen Cricket in such a deep meditation. Cricket slowly raised his head.

"I can't explain the feeling," replied Cricket.

"Is it good?" Cricket shook his head.

"No, it's not good."

"What's it feel like?"

"I sense a terrible separation coming."

"Well, look at what we've been through. It's amazing you haven't felt this any sooner," replied Beetle trying to be as optimistic as he could.

"We're all gonna be okay. It's just that we're having such a tough time right now. Stop worrying so much," said Frank trying to reassure them. "This is just another one of those times we'll all look back on and laugh about."

"Suppers on!"

While they ate, the men in the van across the river placed a phone call.

"Judge, we've got 'em."

"What about the book?"

"They've got it and the codes been broken. They know everything."

"How 'bout the caves?"

"Yes."

"I want that book and I don't want them to talk. Do you understand me?" The judge vehemently stated.

"Consider it done."

"Where are they anyway?" asked the judge.

"In a houseboat on the New River, just across from you."

"Good work. You know what to do."

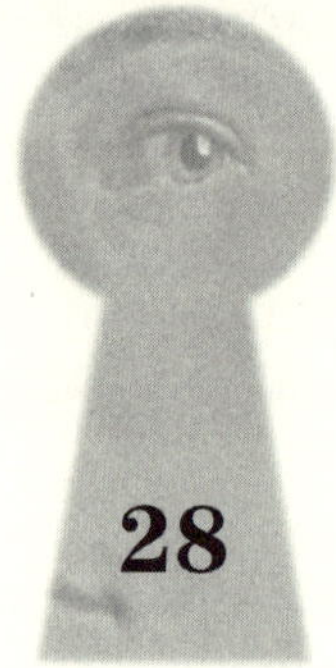

28

Everyone was eating dinner when the phone rang. The boat got quiet. Palmetto stretched from the couch and answered.

"Hello."

"Bill Murdock," responded the soft, monotone voice.

"Who is this?" Palmetto's voice was stern.

"Rico." Palmetto raised the receiver above his head.

"It's Rico." Murdock and Frank looked at each other.

"Didn't think I'd hear from you again."

"Don't say anything more...just listen. There's a white van on the north side of the river..." Murdock looked out the window. "...they've been listening to your conversation, so they know whatever you've discussed on the boat."

"Hold on." Murdock wrote on a sheet of paper, **"White van across the river is listening to what we say. Turn up the radio."** Murdock gave the message to Palmetto first who passed the note around the table.

"The phone's not tapped?"

"No."

"Who are they?"

"Hired by Judge Sherman to retrieve the book and get rid of anyone who knows the contents. They'll hit soon."

"Got any ideas?" whispered Murdock.

"Meet me on the north side of the tunnel. Leave on foot." The tunnel was the New River Tunnel.

"It'll take me about ten minutes."

"Leave after sundown and bring your notes...and the journal. I've got a senator interested in it."

"You sure?"

"He's very appreciative for neutralizing Nieto. He'll investigate.

"Who is he?"

"Senator Earl Daughtrey. He chairs the subcommittee that oversees government operations including the IRS." Senator Daughtrey chaired the powerful and prestigious Subcommittee on Commerce, Consumer and Monetary Affairs of the House Committee on Government Operations. He had a reputation for exposing corruption and getting convictions. During his thirteen-year reign as chairperson his committee investigated and assisted in the indictments of five top level government officials. He was also close friends with the senator who was killed in seventy-four by Nieto. It was through his request that the DEA gave Rico carte blanche to investigate the bombing and track down Nieto. With an unlimited budget and only one case to investigate, it still took Rico, a consummate professional, six years of intense work.

"How soon can we see him?" asked Murdock.

"He's waiting now."

"Where?"

"Washington. I've got a jet ready. Can you leave right after sundown?"

"I'll be there," replied Murdock.

"My guess is that they'll hit right after sunset. Have everyone leave on foot in different directions. They won't know who to pursue."

"What if I just leave quietly?"

"They'll detect the door opening. Regardless, they'll still hit tonight."

"All right, I'll leave after sundown." Murdock continued his whisper.

Rico hung up abruptly. Murdock signaled to the group to huddle. He whispered the plan and everyone nodded. The whispering continued.

"Are you sure Rico doesn't want the journal for himself? With Nieto out of the way, it's all his," commented Palmetto.

"I'm not sure, but who else can I turn to? We can't stay here much longer," he replied.

"Just be careful," added Frank.

They agreed with Frank that he would stay behind since he felt, in light of his physical challenge, he'd be safer at the houseboat. With everyone else running from the boat, they hoped the men in the van would think the book was with one of them and, ergo, have no reason to even go to the houseboat.

"Good luck," whispered Murdock.

"Good luck, Bill," replied Frank as he placed his hand on his shoulder. The group waited in silence as the last of sunlight disappeared. Without another word the squeaky door opened. The van lights turned on and the vehicle's tires barked into high gear.

"They're coming!" exclaimed Frank as he gripped a .38 revolver. Just as the van approached the base of the bridge the red crossing lights activated and a bell started screaming, warning traffic that a boat was approaching. The crossing guard rail lowered quickly. The van's speed accelerated. The men knew they had but a few seconds to cross the bridge.

Murdock, Palmetto, Beetle and Cricket stuck to the plan, running in different directions. Frank looked out and watched the van. The bridge started its ascent as the van continued its acceleration. Frank kept shouting at the bridge to quicken its pace as if he were at the horse track.

"Open! Open! Come on!" Frank continued hoping that the bridge would respond and stretch its long arms skyward. The van negotiated the guard rail and proceeded onto the rising span despite the gap that now existed. Frank gripped his pistol tighter and tighter as he followed the van.

"Good! It can't make it," he mumbled aloud. The van approached the end of the still rising span at full speed. Frank held his breath. The van left the bridge at 73 mph and was airborne. The upward trajectory allowed the vehicle to soar high into the air and clear the gap. The van came down hard, nose first as the impact ripped off half of the bumper.

"I can't believe it!" mumbled Frank in disbelief. Murdock hung on tight to the journal and ocean charts as he ran east toward the tunnel. Beetle had to stop. His size wouldn't allow another step without catching his breath. His sides were aching. Cricket headed southeast down another alley. The overhanging banana trees made him feel more secure as he disappeared in the fronds. Palmetto headed west along the river.

The van zigzagged around the guard rails on the far side and then turned east off of the Third Street Bridge. Bystanders stared in amazement. Frank hobbled over to another window to gain a better perspective, but he lost sight of the van. The vegetation around the river was too thick, too dense, to see through. He caught only glimpses of light as the wind pushed the tree limbs and fronds back and forth.

Suddenly, the squealing tires grew louder and louder. Frank's blood pressure began to rise as he realized the van might be coming to the boat after all. He rechecked the ammunition in the cylinder of the .38. He quickly gazed out searching for the van. He could hear it winding down the snake-shaped road, but he couldn't see it. Maybe the lights were turned off? Frank moved closer to the front of the boat where the tree line ended. Silently and suddenly the van appeared parallel to the boat. Frank squatted as low as he could and extended the gun. Seconds had passed when Frank heard a solid thud on the roof of the houseboat.

Something had been thrown from the van and was now rolling across the top, but what? A fraction of a second later the van barked into high gear and proceeded east down one of the alleys. A feeling of dread overcame Frank. He knew he had to get out fast. The thud was about to explode. He raced to the door and fell hard. Without his prosthesis, balance was almost impossible. He struggled getting up. His leg was weak and the crutch was out of reach. He grasped the door knob, pulled himself up and gained his balance. The door opened just as the deadly canister ignited, instantaneously engulfing the entire boat. Fiberglass and wood shot upward 100 feet. Debris was scattered everywhere. The explosion rocked the ground and the sound was heard for miles. Murdock turned quickly and stood along side a tall picket fence. An orange glow smeared the dusky sky. His stomach tightened. He knew that the explosion meant they guessed wrong. His slow jog quickly turned into a sprint as he raced back to Frank. He reached the end of the alley and saw the thick black smoke spewing out from where the boat had been docked.

Murdock ducked down into nearby hedges as the van approached. He pulled his gun and waited. The vehicle veered to the right and slowed as it entered another alley. Murdock continued, feeling stuck in slow motion, toward the dense smoke in disbelief. The heat from the inferno was unbearable. Murdock fell to his knees as a weakness, he had only experienced in Nam, overwhelmed him. His body and mind were responding to the realization that Frank was dead.

Cricket saw the van approaching and, as he started to jump a fence, his pant leg snagged on the barbed steel. He looked over his shoulder and they were getting closer and closer. He pulled as hard as he could trying to rip the clothes, but nothing happened. He looked over again and saw a bearded man leaning out of the window with what appeared to be sawed-off shotgun. His hands worked lightening fast as he unbuckled his pants to slip them off. Suddenly, he felt a burning sensation on his lower back and his legs went limp. As he dropped over the fence, he couldn't hear anything. The only thing he sensed was an incredibly bright starburst before him. He regained his vision and glanced down at the burning sensation. His intestines were protruding. Cricket went into shock. The bright starburst returned. He looked up and the Lady in White appeared. Cricket smiled.

"Belina," whispered Cricket. He felt no pain.

"It's time to come with me," she replied. Her voice eased the burning sensation.

"Where?"

"On a journey..." she extended her hand and smiled back. "Take my hand."

"But Beetle will worry about me."

"Take my hand..." Tears filled his eyes. "Time is growing short. You must take my hand, now!"

"I'm not ready."

"There is nothing more for you to do here. Don't be afraid, I won't leave you...ever."

Cricket could feel her presence greater than at any other time. Her words were comforting. He felt himself drifting gently toward her as he extended his hand. With one last effort, they touched for the first time.

"Hold me...I'm not scared anymore." Belina looked at him as Cricket fell into a deep sleep and began his journey with his Lady in White.

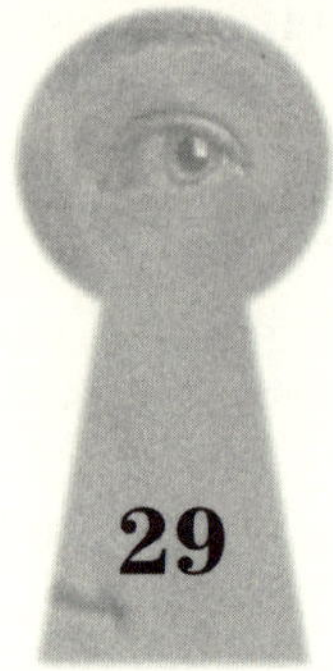

29

The air was filled with the sounds of sirens alternating their pitches. Flames flickering high into the atmosphere crackled. Murdock was only moments away from the rendezvous with Rico. He was out of breath and couldn't believe Frank was dead. Sweat drenched his tired body.

The white van continued stalking down one alley and up another. He carried his gun tightly in his hand. The New River Tunnel was in sight. Out of nowhere, the van suddenly appeared. The men men accelerated the vehicle and it quickly gained ground down the tiny alley. Murdock looked behind him and the van was only two blocks away and bearing down. As he ran harder, the map and journal slipped from his hands. Papers drifted as the alley breeze lifted them in several directions. Murdock looked up again and started collecting the paper. He was exhausted. The van was close, traveling in excess of 75 mph. Murdock dropped his papers, extended his arm and aimed his 9mm. The van kept accelerating. He was too tired and numb to run or even try to get out of the way. A second later he proceeded to unload the fifteen round clip into the windshield knowing that if he could not stop the van, the impact would crush every bone in his body.

He continued firing, but the van kept coming. The eighth bullet found it's way into the driver's throat as the van, only feet away from Murdock, veered off to the right and into the wooden privacy fences that lined the alleys. He fell to his knees and then his hands as he tried desperately to regain his strength. Five more minutes passed before he could stand erect and continue toward the tunnel.

As he approached the end of the alley he spotted Rico who was standing near his car looking over the roof in Murdock's direction. Murdock crossed the street and collapsed into the front seat of the sedan.

"Are you all right?"

Murdock nodded. "There was an explosion and gunfire. They killed Frank," uttered Murdock.

"I'm sorry."

"But I got 'em. I don't know what the other shooting was...I pray nobody else was hurt." Murdock spoke slowly. Rico proceeded to the airport.

"We'll be on our way to Washington where you can bring this to an end." Murdock nodded again, then rested his head against the window, not caring about Rico's motives.

Murdock awoke to turbine jet engines and flashing red and solid blue landing lights of the airport. They entered the airport from the north side and drove into a hangar where a white Lear Jet was fueled and waiting. Rico exited and went to a small office. Murdock watched from the sedan as Rico talked to the pilot and then made a phone call. Rico stuck his head in the car.

"We're ready, Bill." The two boarded the jet as the pilot went through a last series of checks. The aircraft was plush and done in pastel colors. There was a small kitchenette equipped with everything. Two sofas lined each side of the cabin and were covered with pillows in assorted sizes. The carpet was extra plush and there was even a shower.

After taxiing around the runway, the pilot received clearance. Within moments the jet was in flight. The city lights could be seen south to Miami as the jet flew due east over the restless black ocean and then north, quickly drowning the blue lights of the airport.

"Steak or lasagna?" asked Rico.

"I'm not hungry. Thanks."

"If you want to take a hot shower, there's some extra clothes in the cabinet."

The jet was plush, state-of-the-art. It was confiscated from smugglers by the US Customs. Before taking a shower, Murdock went through the closet and picked out a Hawaiian-styled shirt, blue jeans, socks and underwear. The pulsating shower relaxed him but he couldn't get Frank off his mind. His memory recalled a time when Lawrence assisted Frank in preparing the forms for his first seizure. With Lawrence's short, crazed temper and Frank's humor, it didn't take much to get the fireworks going. Lawrence got so mad at him that he hid his crutches. Frank hopped after him with the office watching. Frank was one of a kind. What would he do, Murdock thought, without him. He had lost his best and closest friend since his squad in Nam. Murdock was feeling very alone. After Nam, Murdock didn't get too close to anyone so the relationship with Frank was special. Then he thought about Melissa and who would tell her.

The aroma of steak filled the cabin as Murdock stepped out of the shower. His mouth salivated. Hunger hit him.

"You look like a different person."

"I feel a little better. That steak smells pretty good."

"I'll get you one. Stretch out on the sofa." Murdock propped up some pillows. "I called the Senator. He's anxious to meet you."

"Good, maybe this'll come to an end." A few more minutes and Rico returned with their dinner. They sat across from each other and began eating.

"A French-Vietnamese recipe." There was silence for a couple of minutes.

"You think 'bout Nam much?" asked Murdock.

"Only when I sleep. It's the reason I don't get much."

"Dreams?" inquired Murdock.

"Nightmares. I wake up exhausted." There was more silence. "Nightmares 'bout demons visiting me. They're real but in another dimension. Sleep opens the door to them." Murdock looked at him.

"You getting help?"

"No. I just drown myself in work and try not to sleep too much. Some life, huh?" There was silence again. "They travel in packs. One night I dreamt I shot the little turds. When I woke up my gun was still smoking. I gunned down the aquarium...all fifty-five gallons and four hundred dollars worth of saltwater fish. Put two holes in my favorite paintings...my stereo and TV took a hit. Those lil' guys are expensive." Murdock half grinned. "...but they don't care...they just laugh and come back when I pass out. What about you? Got any demons after you?"

"Flashbacks."

" 'Bout what?"

"The squad I worked with. Just had one a few minutes ago. We were in a gunboat going up the Mekong Delta to our drop-off site. The rain was beating us. It was the last time I'd see these guys alive. Maybe they'll stop once this is over." Rico nodded.

The flight seemed like only minutes when the jet was cleared for landing at Dulles. After touchdown, the aircraft rolled into a nearby hangar. A man in his mid-thirties, clean-shaven, wearing a dark suit, white shirt but no tie, leaned against a black Lincoln.

"Rico?"

"Yes."

"I'm Matthew Cavanaugh, aide to the senator...sometimes. Let me help you." After introductions, the two climbed into the back seat as the aide closed the door for them.

"Nice touch," remarked Murdock. The drive from Dulles to Georgetown where the senator lived took longer than expected. The Lincoln finally pulled up to the townhouse. The air was cool and crisp. Murdock was relaxed. He was finally getting the help he needed, he hoped. The aide rang the doorbell. A grandmotherly-looking woman answered.

"Come in, come in." She spoke with a German accent. The Senator approached the group. His hair was gray, neatly combed and close to his head. Silver reading glasses hung around his neck; his light blue V-neck sweater revealed a runner's physique.

The Senator greeted Rico first with a warm, friendly smile and strong handshake.

"Senator, this is Bill Murdock."

"Bill, I've heard so much about you. Come in.

"Please, join me." They traveled up a tight spiral staircase to a loft that overlooked the living room. The townhouse had an old, but quaint look. Books lined the walls. Law books, journals, novels, and paperbacks. The housekeeper returned with freshly brewed coffee and German pastries. An elaborate looking tape recorder more appropriately suited for a recording studio lined one end of a wall. Murdock studied the system.

"I know these are difficult times, but you have the support of my office behind you."

"Senator, that means a lot to me."

"If it's okay with you, I'll tape the discussion. I'll play back the information to the team."

"Team?" asked Murdock.

"They'll be four investigators assisting me on this. They're top-notch. Two graduated from Harvard Law School at the top of their class. They've got a lot of common sense, too. Another one is from DJ...she's a crackerjack investigator and attorney..." DJ stands for Department of Justice. "...and Matt Cavanaugh here..."The Senator turned to his part-time aide, "...he's been with me off and on for the last four years. He's CIA." Murdock looked over at him.

"Jack of all trades, I guess," remarked Cavanaugh as he gave a reassuring smile.

"That's the team. I've got total confidence in them. Together we've bagged some big ones and we'll do it again." The Senator spoke with passion. This was familiar territory for the team. They were like hound dogs hot on a scent and the Senator was ready to hunt.

"Senator, why do you want to see me? I mean...you have all the information and what you don't have Rico can tell you."

"Bill, it's important for me to hear it from you, personally, before I launch an investigation. The facts must be heard first-hand." The Senator sipped his coffee. "I'm certain there were times when you've questioned whether or not you did the right thing. I want you to know that you did, and that I'm proud of your actions. I'm personally going to see to it you're compensated for all you've lost. I wish there were more like you out there. As a matter of fact, I'm investigating IRS in Louisiana and I could sure use someone like you." He sipped his coffee again. "While I can't undo all you've been through, we're going to put some folks behind bars thanks to your efforts."

"Not just my efforts...there were several others...one lost his life and..." Murdock lowered his head and tried to stop his eyes from watering. "...another person, Julia Black, may have been killed because of what she learned."

"I'm very sorry." The Senator reached out and touched his arm. "We'll get to the bottom of this. I'll do whatever I can for the others who helped you. Would you rather do this tomorrow morning?" Before Murdock could answer, the Senator continued, "...yes, this can wait. We'll talk in the morning."

"Senator, I'm...okay, I'd like to get started."

"Fine." He rose and activated the elaborate machinery. "Start at the beginning and try not to leave anything out. I'll ask questions along the way." Murdock pulled out his papers, the ocean chart and journal.

Murdock began his methodical review of the facts. Three hours later he finished the story. He felt exhilarated as a weight lifted from his shoulders.

"Senator, it's been a long time since I felt this good. This has been such a mess and now with Frank's death, I just feel like justice will be done."

"It will be...I assure you, it will be." The Senator patted Murdock's shoulder. "Is there anything else, Bill?"

"My coworkers believe the Miami Police and DEA are after them for what they heard. What can be done to help them?" Before the Senator could respond, Rico replied.

"I'll get with the DEA tomorrow and take care of it along with what happened to you on the islands."

"You can report to work anytime you're ready," informed the Senator.

"I'm not certain if I'm going back. I need some time off to think about it with my wife."

"Sounds like a good idea. Enjoy yourself. Again...I can't thank you enough for what you've done. Anything you need just call me."

"Thank you Senator for listening."

The Senator passed Rico some keys. "They're to the townhouse two doors down. Help yourself to whatever you need."

"When would you like me to pick you up?" asked Cavanaugh. Rico looked over at Murdock.

"How about we call you?" Cavanaugh nodded. The group shook hands and parted.

As soon as Murdock entered the townhouse, he called his wife to let her know that it was over and he was coming home. She was so happy she cried at the thought of having him back. She knew something had happened.

The jet touched down in Fort Lauderdale at 2:01 p.m. He saw his wife and children waiting by the hangar for him. His heart raced with excitement. As the jet finished its final taxiing, Murdock and Rico embraced.

"Thank you," whispered Murdock.

"Thank you, Bill Murdock. I'll miss you. Now put this behind you and get on with your life. It won't be easy, but you can do it."

"And what about you, Rico?"

"After we wrap this up I'm through."

"Through?"

"Retiring. I'm gonna spend some time with my mother in California. She always wanted to go on a cruise to Alaska, so...I'm taking her!"

"What then?" asked Murdock. Rico hesitated.

"After that...I don't know. Maybe buy a Harley and tour the countryside. Who knows, I might even settle down and have a nice family like yours." Murdock grinned.

The jet came to a final stop and the door opened.

"Goodbye, my friend," said Rico a little sadly. Murdock extended his hand.

"Goodbye." Rico stayed on the jet and watched Murdock's family mob him. He smiled. Murdock's children wouldn't release their hugs and tears filled his and Beth's eyes. He turned to introduce Rico, but, as always...he was gone.

30

Murdock returned to work a month later to a nearly empty office. Walking down the corridor brought back memories. He could almost hear Lawrence arguing with the blue-haired women in the lobby and Hank Goffman whistling zippa de do da. He walked over to the glass cage and found an acting manager. She was nicely dressed, but stern looking.

"Davenport gone?"

"And you are...?" she replied sharply.

"Bill Murdock."

"You're quite a legend." Murdock didn't respond. "He retired. They told me you'd be in this week. What's it like taking a month off?"

"Nice."

"I've got an area I want you to work." She pulled out a stack of cases when Murdock interrupted her.

"Here are my keys, government credit card, receipt book, calculator...I turned my credentials in to Davenport before he left."

"You're resigning?" She was surprised. Murdock nodded.

"There's a few things I want out of my desk." He turned and the memories continued. It was Frank's voice this time. He smiled.

"Well, you gonna turn around and say something." Murdock turned slightly and couldn't believe his eyes.

"My God! I thought you were dead!" He hugged him. The excitement was too much for Frank. He dropped his crutch. Murdock laughed loud. "I thought you died...thank you, God! Wait 'til Beth finds out. Frank, I can't believe it! What happened to you? Why didn't you call me?"

"I've been in the hospital. That night, I barely made it in the water...the currents carried me down. Ya know, with only one leg you just keep turning in circles when you swim." Frank smiled. "Anyway, I suffered a mild concussion, but I'm okay...well, as okay as I've ever been. What are you doing?"

"Resigning."

"Then what?"

"I'm helping an old friend catch lobster and then I'm opening a little restaurant. You want in?"

"I'd like to...I really would...but I promised Melissa I'd be in New York by the end of the month."

"You staying up there?"

"Yeah...I'm staying."

"Why don't you leave now?" asked Murdock.

"They asked me to give an orientation to the new trainees, so I thought I would. I better get back to 'em. Call me tonight...I'd like to hear more about this restaurant."

"Maybe I can convince you to stay?"

"Maybe...who knows...call me."

Before the two parted Frank told Murdock about Cricket's demise and gave him a number to contact Palmetto. Murdock watched Frank in the office for the last time as he left the area. He finished packing his personal belongings and walked to the front door near the room Frank was holding his orientation. The door was open. He stood from a distance and listened.

"...I guarantee you, you'll never be bored here. Too tired, over worked, not enough time, frustrated...but *not* bored. Think of yourselves as shadows of the IRS."

"Shadows?" asked one of the trainees. Murdock remembered their conversation. He picked up his box, shook his head and grinned as he exited the office. The next generation of shadows had arrived.

31

6:00 a.m. As Murdock opened the door to his newly renovated seafood restaurant, a bundle of newspapers arrived for the machines just outside. The Miami Herald headline read:

"IRS, Businessmen linked to Cover Up... Drugs!"

The Fort Lauderdale Sun-Sentinel read:

"Top IRS Officials, Businessmen...Exposed!"

Abbreviations

ASAP - As Soon As Possible
ATF - Alcohol, Tobacco, and Firearms
CIA - Central Intelligence Agency
CID/CI - Criminal Investigation division of IRS
C-4 - Composition Four (plastic explosives)
DA - District Attorney
DEA - Drug Enforcement Agency
DJ - Department of Justice
DMV - Department of Motor Vehicles
EPIC - Enforcement Police of FAA
FAA - Federal Aviation Administration
FBI - Federal Bureau of Investigation
FMP - Florida Marine Patrol
GSA - Government Services Administration
IDRS - Integrated Data Retrieval System (IRS system)
IG - Treasury Inspector General
IRS - Internal Revenue Service
ITP - Illegal Tax Protester
MO - Method of Operation
MOWS - Multiple Occupancy Work Stations
NFTL - Notice of Federal Tax Lien
NLF - National Liberation Front (VietCong Leaders)
NYPD - New York Police Department
OIO - Office of International Operations
One Hundred Percent Penalty -IRS assessment made against responsible corporate officers who fail to deposit employment taxes.
RO - IRS Revenue Officers who conduct civil investigations
RCP - Returns Compliance Project
TDA - Tax Delinquency Accounts
TDI - Tax Delinquency Investigation
VIN - Vehicle Identification Number

Recurring Characters in Alphabetical Order

Alena - Alena Muller; fiancée of Phillip Ward
Beetle - Misfit IRS Revenue Officer Carlos Hernandez
Beth - Murdock's wife
Carmichael - IRS Criminal Investigation manager
Art Cook - IRS Examination manager
Cricket - Misfit IRS Revenue Officer Harry Whittaker
Richard (Dick) Davenport - IRS Collection manager
Senator Earl Daughtrey - Chairman of subcommittee on Commerce, Consumer and Monetary Affairs of Government Operations
Duncan - DEA agent
Mike Durham - Alleged FBI Agent; alter ego of Nieto
Ernie - Ernest Shelton, IRS Revenue Officer
Thomas Farley - President of DUU, Inc.; member of government witness protection program; alter ego of Douglas Warbington
Farmer - John L. Farmer, President of cash register company
Frank - Frank Lacetti, IRS Revenue Officer/Murdock's partner
Hank Goffman - Oldest IRS Revenue Officer
Insects - Misfit IRS Revenue Officers Palmetto, Beetle and Cricket who have been banished to the Florida Keys
Julia - Julia Black; IRS Revenue Officer; possibly murdered
Edward Kmetz - IRS Revenue Officer; former IRS manager
Lady in White - Belina; Cricket's apparition
Lawrence - Lawrence Anderson, IRS Revenue Officer of erratic behavior
Marlene - Carmichael's secretary; Murdock's friend
Melissa - Melissa Lacetti; Frank's demanding wife
MacQuiddy - Corrupt government official
Ramon Martinez - Cartel member
Joel Meyers - Founder of Sea Unlimited; IRS target
Miguel - Cartel's security advisor and executioner
Murdock - William (Bill) Murdock; IRS Revenue Officer

Recurring Characters in Alphabetical Order (continued)

Nieto - Deadly Colombian defector from the Cartel
Palmetto - Jake Democko, Senior IRS Revenue Officer
Pete - Pete Michaels, IRS Revenue Officer
Rico - Special Agent, Drug Enforcement Agency
Carlos Rosario - Drug Lord
Tim Sylar - IG Special Investigator
Phillip Ward - Cartel's legal/financial advisor; Alena's fiancé
Douglas Warbington - Criminal turned government witness
Albert Wilson - Former IRS District Director
Willie - Willie Walker; Pit Bull breeder